Katrina's Sandcastles

New Hope From The Ruins of New Orleans Schools

kaycee eckhardt

Katrina's Sandcastles
New Hope From The Ruins of New Orleans Schools

Kaycee Eckhardt

First printing, November 1, 2014
All text is © Kaycee Eckhardt, 2014
This edition is © Microcosm Publishing, 2014

Microcosm Publishing
2752 N Williams Ave
Portland, OR 97227

In the Real World series

For a catalog, write or visit
MicrocosmPublishing.com

ISBN 978-1-62106-748-1
This is Microcosm #158

Edited by Elly Blue and Joe Biel
Cover by Meggyn Pommerleau, Joe Biel, and Kaycee Eckhardt
Photos graciously provided by The New Teacher Project

Distributed worldwide by Legato Publishers Group, a division of Perseus.

This book was printed on post-consumer paper by union workers in the United States.

To the children of New Orleans,
for teaching me what belief costs,
and why you were always worth it.

And to Johnathan.
Embarking upon a journey without you
would be a pirate's treasure without the ship.

Contents

PART FOUR: THE BUCKET BRIGDE, 173

PART FIVE: CONCLUSIONS, 179

APPENDIX: FINAL TRUTHS FOR NEW TEACHERS, 185

SUGGESTED READING FOR EDUCATORS OF ALL KINDS, 190

WITH ALL MY LOVE AND GRATITUDE, 191

The First Thing

Quite simply, this is the story of my experiences as a teacher in post-Katrina New Orleans: my students, my failures, my triumphs, and the shifts I made to become the successful teacher I wanted to be, while attempting to maintain my sanity, my relationships, and my life. No great work is ever easy. No wrong rights itself in a few short years, no matter what the catalyst and who is working on solving it. But rectifying the damage done to our education system is the greatest work I know.

I was teaching English in an elementary school in Japan when Hurricane Katrina devastated the city of New Orleans. The next year, I returned home to help with the recovery effort in the best way I knew how: by taking a job as a public high school teacher. My year in one of the city's worst public schools was difficult and joyful, harrowing and eye opening.

In 2008, I joined the staff of a school so new it didn't exist yet. Sci Academy is an open enrollment charter school that committed to preparing 100% of its students for college, no matter what their current academics or other obstacles are. A few weeks into our first year, the founding staff realized that the students—we called them scholars—were less prepared than we could have imagined. Our students were struggling with basic literacy and numeracy skills, the vast majority of them were several years behind their grade level.

I was tasked with creating a new, intensive reading curriculum, one that would meet the needs of both the scholars and our commitment to college for each of them. The road we all walked together was paved with challenges, but at the end of the first year, that same class ranked number one in English and number two in math in the school district. Ninety five percent of students in that first class were accepted to four-year colleges by the time they graduated. The reading program I created for Sci Academy's is still in use, helping students improve their reading and prepare for college, no matter where they start.

This is the story of my evolution as a teacher and about the children I encountered along the way. It is also a tale of how education in post-Katrina New Orleans is changing in innovative and exciting ways, and what other urban school systems can learn from our successes and failures.

Chess

The educational landscape in the New Orleans of 2007 looked much like a game of chess, if chess could be played with seventeen people, with everyone moving pieces at once.

In 2005, the statistics on education in New Orleans were appalling.

Only 30% of New Orleans students could pass the state reading test with a minimum score. In some schools, this number was only four percent.

The valedictorian of one of the high schools had straight A's in math but failed the graduation exit exam seven times.

Corruption and scandal regularly rocked the district, which was considered by many reformers to be one of the worst school districts in the country. Those who had money sent their child to private school. Those who didn't could almost guarantee their child an education that was mediocre at best, and at worst appalling. There really wasn't a middle ground.

In the summer of 2005, Hurricane Katrina arrived.

In the aftermath, all district teachers were summarily fired, schools were destroyed, and 60,000 school children were displaced.

Three months after Katrina, the Louisiana Department of Education had taken over the vast majority of the New Orleans Public Schools, calling 100 of the 126 schools in the district "failing." A new district—called the Recovery School District (RSD)—was formed, run by the state.

As the city began to pick up the proverbial pieces, charter schools began to pop up amongst the rubble, in order to serve the needs of the children trickling back into the city.

Charter schools were a preference for the RSD, as well.

These new charter schools would be non-selective; meaning no testing or scores would be required to attend. They would be open enrollment, so parents could select the school and neighborhood in which they wanted their child to attend school. School choice was an option previously unheard of, in a city that still zoned along segregated lines. Charter schools would be publicly funded, just like regular public schools, but could be largely free of local control, asking for autonomy in exchange for academic and performance outcomes. They had the ability to hire and fire staff at will. They could incentivize performance. All they had to do was perform. And those starting them had an extra incentive to do well: competition for scores and students encouraged hard work and growth. Charters had three years to show success and gains—or they could be closed.

Scores went up, but not without problems. Many critics of the "great charter experiment" claimed that charters excluded students with special needs. Parent groups rallied to keep charters out of the historically Black schools, fearing that their legacies would end. Complaints were, and are, regularly filed about what has been construed by some as humiliating and excessive disciplinary policies.

Ultimately, it is important to remember that the transition to charter in the city of New Orleans was a means to an end. Charters were a way to improve schools in a decimated city and, frankly, leveling the playing field for charters to grow may have been the only good that came from Katrina. For New Orleans, the charter movement worked.

In 2011, fifty six percent of eighth graders in New Orleans passed reading exam, a twenty percent improvement from 2005.

But there is no magic potion. Better teaching, the Common Core, stronger leadership, opportunities for growth and development, sustainability models—all of these will help education in this country for the better. But there is no easy answer for a decades-old problem.

We aren't there yet, but it's better. More children in this city are receiving the equitable, high-quality education they deserve. No movement is perfect, but at least there's forward motion, and the momentum is inspiring.

Even if the game of chess is new and uncomfortable and sometimes controversial, it is vastly preferable to the games played before.

That Said

But charter schools, a few handy nonprofits, and some buoyant and surprisingly resilient new talent cannot fully make a solution. Louisiana still ranks in the bottom ten of our 50 states in terms of educational equity, and where there is inequity there is also violence. From 2007 to 2011, a time spanning my first four years as a teacher here, 900 murders occurred in New Orleans alone, mostly due to gun violence.

Reading levels flatlined in 2012, for the first time since Katrina. At the eighth grade level, they appeared to ever so slightly dip. It is this tiny tip that should send all of our hearts palpitating. We have come too far to flatline now.

I believe in the power of excellent teaching, but it is not a magic wand to wave away the ills of our system. To say that it can is to flippantly ignore systemic American problems like poverty, a shrinking and stagnating middle class, and systemic racism. But great teaching is one of the best levers we currently have, and too often we squander it.

Charter schools have worked in New Orleans; Sci Academy has become one of the top school in the state. But the verdict is still out on how far our model can expand, and whether it would be as effective in an environment less thirsty and primed for real change. I like to believe what we have done in New Orleans can be replicated, but sometimes I am not sure it's possible, or if the map we drew would lead to the same places.

Indeed, the system in New Orleans continues to contradict itself and fluctuate. We have exceedingly high suspension and expulsion rates and most schools lack resources for children with the highest needs. The school-to-prison pipeline is still very much a reality here.

Nationally, we fare no better than the New Orleans of yesteryear. We are falling further and further behind other industrialized nations. And the inequity in this data is particularly appalling.

- In 2012, 55% of white fourth graders read below a proficient level. That percentage jumps to 78% for Native Americans, 81% for Hispanic and Latino, and 83% for African American fourth graders. (National Center for Education Statistics, 2013)
- 29 other countries outscored our fifteen year olds on the PISA exam. (The Washington Post, 2013)
- One in five high school students did not graduate in 2013: 1.2 million drop out each year, *one every 26 seconds*. (U.S. Department of Education, 2013)
- For African-American and Hispanic students across the country, dropout rates are close to 40%, compared to the national average of 27% (EPE, 2012)
- Only four percent of African American students and eleven percent of Hispanic students finish high school ready for college in their core subjects (ACT 2011)

There is no panacea. There is no easy fix. And no one in these debates is completely in the right. It's easy to point fingers, to feel bleak. Sometimes, while teaching, it was even tempting to shrug reluctantly and say, "We can't help everyone."

And then I pause and visualize different data. Not bar graphs and statistics and percentages of kids in colleges, or dot chart strings like tangling spider webs tracking reading and math growth over child and age and year: detailed, fragile sinews of progress. I did enough of this in my daily life as an educator.

While this data is so very valuable, it never quantified the reasons I woke up every morning and returned to the all-consuming job of teaching. Data does not, now, push me to do the work on a national level that I do for education reform. What drives me, still, are the faces painted on the inside of my eyelids: all the hundreds of children I encounter, plan for, laugh with, and sometimes held tight, and in these moments my work is like ballast against some insurmountable storm.

Sometimes it wasn't enough. But that's not the point. The storm is not the point. The preparation is everything, the effort to change and sway and hold steady with these children is always, always a reason to try. Beyond the number crunching, the murder rate, the tattered days and frayed nerves, one fact remains:

The children matter.

The children are the reason to believe.

Make no mistake. Every student in this book was a child when I met them, despite their colorful vocabulary, their responsibilities, drug use, choices, abilities, tattoos, children, weaponry, skin color, or where they slept each night.

Each loved with an easy, innocent passion.

Each lied boldly or shiftily with their hands in a proverbial cookie jar.

Each face widened at some point with a smile so radiant it defied every dark corner they had ever encountered.

And even more, each was loved by someone, even if that love came through many filters or unconventional places.

Love, too, is not quantifiable. And love, sometimes, is the greatest proof point of all.

I didn't come to teaching out of a sense of passion, initially, or even a strong belief in equity, or human rights. I came to teaching twice, very simply, because I felt a need to do a job *worth doing*. I followed a long path, from the other side of the ocean, to become a teacher here, and this path proved the power of belief to me forever.

For this path, and for those who traveled it with me, I am forever blessed.

Caterpillar Eyebrows

Majoring in creative writing truly seemed like a good idea when I was nineteen, scribbling lyrics for my punk band into spiral notebooks. Unfortunately, the major required more than adjective-laden, impassioned poetry and a couple unfinished plays.

My school required four semesters of a foreign language. I selected French, assuming it would be the "easiest," and, after a brief perusal at the bookstore, because the textbook was the least expensive.

French 101 was held in a large room with more than 40 students. Most of the class consisted of listening to crackly cassette tapes and call-and-response exercises.

I was utterly unengaged.

Three months later, I failed my first exam.

This failure was a red flag for my scholarship and a week later, I plopped into a chair in my counselor's office with a frustrated sigh. I launched immediately into the litany of reasons why French and I needed to *obtenir un divorce*—I looked that up before my appointment to emphasize my seriousness.

My counselor's name was Mr. Aardvant. He reeked of academia gone rancid. His sallow complexion was yellow under the office fluorescents, and his tie only matched in this anemic light.

At a school as large as Louisiana State University, counselors such as Mr. Aardvant do not have the time to listen long to the bemoaned ravings of a procrastinating sophomore. Though the college brochures claimed, "the counselors' doors are always open," unofficially we were allowed to schedule fifteen minutes of face time a semester—and this fifteen minutes should be all business.

Aardvant eyed me from depleted features, taking in my blue shock of hair with its occasional haphazard dreadlock, my shoeless feet, and my green cape.

I eyed him just as warily as I rambled on. Tattletale blood vessels ran along his red nose. Saggy eyelids and jaw line. Caterpillar eyebrows and wedding ring bound in fat on both sides. A hair curling from the inside of one ear. He was unamused. He scratched at his ear delicately with the eraser of his pencil, sighed, and chuckled.

I paused, waiting to know exactly what it was that he found so funny, still too young and pinhole selfish to see myself through other eyes. Mr. Aardvant met my eyes for a moment, noticed the lip ring I was chewing on, and quickly looked down, saying, "Well, ah, French can be a bit tricky at first, especially if you choose not to study."

An appalled pause, as he placed down the presumption between us and I looked at it skeptically. "You seem like an, ah, artsy type, uh..." he shuffled and pretended to clear his throat, sneaking a glance down at the file in front of him, "Kaycee. Why not a more, ah, picturesque language, like, ah, Japanese, my dear?"

I waited; still chewing over the impertinent presumption that I hadn't studied (I hadn't, really, but still...) I gauged his levity. I knew he was joking when a smirk snuck into the corners of his sallow mouth.

"What... Do you mean I shouldn't? Or I should?"

Aardvant's smirk broadened, and he covered it by tipping his shiny head towards me, shuffling again. "A joke, dear, a joke. I strongly recommend you take yourself to the *Français* study hall, and get yourself some tutoring. *Bien?*"

"Umm. No, not *bien*. What do you mean?"

The way he kept facetiously calling me "Dear" was making my skin feel clammy.

"Well, my dear, if French is *tres difficile,* perhaps a more challenging language might be, perhaps, *invraisemblable?*

Whether this was bait, or an honest if not callous mockery, I have no idea. Aardvant's bushy eyebrows never clarified for me whether he was poking fun at my uncanny appearance, or whether he saw something I did not. My guess is the former.

I do know that my response was as predictable as my nose ring.

"Withdraw me from French, Mr. Aardvant. I'd like to sign up for Japanese next semester." At least, I thought, I'd be rid of French and could postpone difficulty another semester

Mr. Aardvant smirked at me, silently, and filled out the paperwork, shuffled it back into the manila folder and slid it across the desk, already bored.

Fall found me in Japanese 101, with six business majors and a fastidious Japanese woman who refused to speak English to us. It was a five-hour course, and it was *hard*.

Compared to my feisty literature seminars and writing workshops, the pace and rigor of my Japanese classes felt like Advanced Calculus at MIT.

I ended up in tutoring, surrounded by pages and pages of scribbled kanji and note cards. I got a C my first semester: the first C of my academic life. But I *loved* it.

I worked two jobs to pay for college: waiting tables on the night shift from ten at night to seven in the morning at a diner, and as a nude model for the art department. At four AM, the diner witching hour, hung between the drunken late night crowd and the early risers, my manager Fred would quiz me repeatedly from the backs of the flash cards.

Though I translated my studies into a minor in Asian Studies, this minor didn't exactly increase my career-readiness. During my fourth semester of Japanese, Dohi-Sensei handed out a flyer for the JET Programme. "Teach English in Japan!" The bold red letter exclaimed over the outline of the Itsukushima Shrine.

Over beers that night, I pulled it out and shoved it across the sticky table at my best friend Deanna, who held it up to the dim red bar light.

"Wanna move to Japan with me next year?"

Deanna grinned wolfishly. She'd been squatting in Amsterdam while still in her teens, but decorated her wanderlust with a veritable slew of talents and a knack for learning languages— Russian, French, Spanish and, rapidly, Japanese—that would burn me green with jealousy.

A year later, Deanna and I boarded a plane for the Eastern Hemisphere.

Studying Japanese taught me that I loved challenge and rigor.

It also taught me that belief is the first step to anything, even if that belief is stubborn and foolhardy.

Yoshida

I moved to Yoshida, in Shizuoka Prefecture, while Deanna ended up in Nagano. It looked rather close when we saw it on the little map in my Japanese textbook, and I'm ashamed to admit that's about all the research we did. I ended up on the coast, not in the mountains, with Mount Fuji a looming, constant companion.

Deanna ended up in a house so cold in the winter that she kept her shampoo in the refrigerator overnight, to prevent it from freezing in her bathroom. For my better weather, for my springs filled with cherry blossom petal snow, I considered myself randomly fortunate.

Presumably because of my studies, I was hired not just to be an assistant teacher but also to help revitalize an English Program. A teacher named Kai from Hawaii and I were asked to build a language lab, run the summer camp, manage video projects and the English conversation classes, and encourage authentic discussion in classrooms with the Japanese high school students.

Yoshida looks much like a small town in a Miyazaki movie. I rode my bike six kilometers each day along thin, winding, cement-topped roads through rice and tea fields. On summer nights, the frogs in the rice paddies would chant in loud orchestras, only going silent when the swoosh of the wheels of my bike alerted them to my presence. This void of noise would create an eerie pocket of stillness, the amphibian *gero gero* in front and behind, but on either side, a complete stillness filled only with the rushing of the rice stalks.

The cicadas offered no such stillness. Every summer their ceaseless *meeeeeeeeeeee* resounded across Yoshida, causing a racket that would make me raise my voice in the classroom if the windows were open—and, as Japanese schools have no internal heat source or air conditioning, in the summers they usually were. I would lay in my sweltering apartment and listen to their incessant noise; their piteous calling for companionship.

In my relative isolation, their thrumming was often comforting. Their little exoskeletons were everywhere, the broken shell split down the back, releasing the noisy winged monster from its former life. The younger children would take them to the streams and set sail little paper boats filled with them, broken chrysalis pirates. Over all of this, Mount Fuji stared resolutely, a dominating centerpiece to the flat or lightly rolling landscape.

I was cicada-lonely in Japan for the first few months, until I managed to find a rhythm; so different from the one I was accustomed to. I look back with pity for my neighbor, who I never considered at the time. I filled my apartment with loud punk rock and fermented strange concoctions on the front porch. I wore long sleeves to hide my tattoos, because in rural Japan body art is still associated with *yakuza*. I carried a battered dictionary, covered with stickers, to the small grocery store, struggling to determine whether this or that kanji was meat or dairy-related. I stirred up large pots of curried rice and fresh tofu, enough to feed a potluck, and ate it for days.

My little house was steps from the Oigawa River, and each evening I went on long jogs along her still edge. I followed her path all the way to the ocean, taking mental inventory of the day's new vocabulary, whispering the new words to myself like a mage apprentice. At twilight, on the edge of the Pacific, I stared out across the dark horizontal line of sea and sky, stared out towards home.

Dozens of paths twisted and turned, a delta of walking tributaries. Yoshida was a tiny town full of deep squat grey buildings and corner stores, porn kiosks, construction sites, and the endless fields that spilled to the edge of the Oigawa River and the sea. And as Japan does not name their streets, I used chalk and a watch to find my way around, carefully writing an arrow for the direction I went, and the time I did so, and tried to track my way back.

On the weekends, I would bike the ten kilometers to the ocean, blaring music in my headphones and sipping sake from a vending machine, and I would stick my toes deep into the sand and remind myself that I was learning about true distance, defined by the stretch between myself and home, and because of a different culture and language, and even a distance from the myself I had been. Each day I learned a little better to survive in the vacuum of a new place, so very different from what I had known.

My college life had been so full of people: punk shows, road trips, classroom discussions, co-ops, art projects, dumpster diving, bike rides, art cars, Critical Mass, four AM arguments over whiskey and cigarettes, a youth-fueled cacophony that burned through my days. During my first year in Japan, I found the silence, even when filled with scissoring cicadas legs or gulping frog songs, to be disturbing.

The very best part of that first year was teaching.

The school day and year in Japan is very long. Broken into three semesters, school wraps the years round. In addition to their classes, all of my students had mandatory club activities after school. Some played soccer and baseball long into the night; others practiced kendo, judo, ping-pong, or volleyball. They took public transportation or rode their bicycles to school; the parking lot included a two-story garage just for the student's bikes. Uniforms were very strict, the major infraction was wee skirts rolled up around their belts to be more *kawaii* or cute. The entrance was filled with rows of shoe cubbies; students changed into indoor slippers which were color-coded by their grade.

Rebellion amongst the students was an act of fashion, not feeling. The kids who loved the Sex Pistols had backpacks covered in metal studs and punk buttons, but had never listened to their songs, and did not know about the demise of angsty Sid, though they imitated his hair with the assistance of copious amounts of hair gel. When I would play music for them, they would laugh and shake their heads confusedly. When I would ask them about their style, they would shrug and say, "It's, ahhh, fashion, you know Kaycee-sensei, fashion?"

I was annoyed at the co-opting of punk for faddish vogue because it was a politick infraction. Later, when I had more distance from my teenage self, it just made me smile. I wanted these kids in a small Japanese town to embrace a life that I had embraced at their age—not just the accoutrements.

The largest behavior problems in my classes were the students texting on their *keitai* under their desks. When caught they would apologize, very formally and often sincerely, and immediately snap it closed and put it away. My students in Japan didn't have true academic struggles, but I was concerned about their lack of participation, their flashes of startling apathy.

In the hallway, I was treated like a celebrity. Students who were not in my classes would grin goofily, greeting me with a poorly pronounced "Good morning" and awkwardly waving. My own students would lurk around my desk on my off periods. My daily lunch became a source of deep curiosity for them, as I would normally throw my leftovers from dinner into my bento box, rather than making the traditional rice-based Japanese *hirugohan*. As a vegan, I had learned to make large quantities of food when I cooked, and my students would giggle and point at the microwaved pasta and spinach salad in my bento each day.

Responsibility was both expected and ingrained in these children. Japanese students clean their own classrooms and bathrooms; during *osouji jikan* children would hurry up and down the halls with the dust mops and rags, and climb dangerously out onto the roof to wipe the outside of the windows, while wartime work music was piped in through the speakers.

Miho and Yuki, two of my favorite girls, used rubber bands to attach sponges to their slippers and rubbed the room's corners, laughing and chattering about *purikura* and makeup as they did.

Everyone worked incredibly hard, the teachers especially. I constantly complained about the long hours, but I had far fewer responsibilities than the other sensei. The English teachers I worked with put in extremely long weeks.

Besides their responsibilities as teachers, each had a "homeroom," sometimes with upwards of 35 students. They stayed with their homeroom and students for all three years of their high school experience, tracking their grades, meeting with their parents, keeping them accountable to their club activities, and even keeping tabs on their weekend antics.

Yet despite the sacrifice and labor, a sense of joy pervaded both the children and educators. Children loved their homeroom teachers, teachers loved their jobs, and society revered and deeply respected the work being done. There was a sense of both building and belonging, a general feeling that good work was being done to the best of everyone's abilities. Parents were highly accountable to the schools, and constantly communicated with the homeroom teachers. Homeroom teachers were fiercely proud of their hard work and their students, bragging over them much like a parent would.

I spent two years in Yoshida. Teachers at Yoshida High School went out of their way to include me in their activities. We went to karaoke on weekends and embarked upon the duplicitous *nomihodai*, all-you-can-drink *izakaya* bars. Eventually, I made friends, traveled extensively, and studied Japanese. I befriended the old woman who ran the ramen shop near my house, a stop that seemed to exist for construction workers on their way home from larger places. Each week I ate ramen in her shop, chatting with her and these dusty men in their *tabi* toed-shoes, learning an odd mix of slang used by old grandmothers and playfully crass, unmarried men. I took the train to Tokyo to see music on the weekends, and discovered I needed music to be less aggressive than I used to. I went to a *shamisen* concert and felt my heart vibrate with each string.

In time, the cicada and frog songs became less mournful and sounded more familiar: the background buzz of home.

Sugar

The rice paddies and tea fields of Yoshida held me for two years before I moved to Mishima, a larger town further up the coast towards Tokyo. In Mishima, I was hired at a private school to teach children between the ages of four and eight. After two years of grueling but rewarding hours at the high school, working with small children was a delight. Japanese children don't always have a lot of interaction with *gaikokujin,* and on their first day of class they would eye the tall foreign woman with long, straw-colored hair suspiciously as they kicked off their little *Anpanman* shoes at the door. Their anxious, enthusiastic mothers would bow and chatter in the entranceway, waving them goodbye with a "*Ganbatte*, Shiho-chan." Do your best, Shiho!

But no matter how hesitant, most could easily be won over with a rousing rendition of the Days of the Week song, or "Wheels On the Bus," The Creation Zone, phonics *karuta*, or StoryTime. If nothing else, a little homemade Playdough used to form the first letter of their name never failed.

Only one child, Aoka, gave me a glimpse of what challenging behavior might look like.

Aoka would come to class screaming so loudly the neighbors would pop their heads from between their *shoji,* peeking nosily at the child; I am convinced they assumed was being burned alive in some foreign ceremony. Aoka's *okaasan* would attempt to sooth the howling child with unlimited amounts of candy: her purse was a combination of Mary Poppin's bag and Willy Wonka's factory, and I would watch with judgmental trepidation as she poured a tie-dyed sugar crash down Aoka's bawling mouth.

When, in my clinical and often halting Japanese, I would speak to Aoka's mother, she would bow deeply and apologize. With extreme politeness, she would express her deepest sympathies for her naughty child, and implore me to continue her education.

When I asked her to come and observe Aoka's behavior, she immediately agreed, staying in the entrance way and peering around the corner.

Aoka joined the class quietly, going through the motions of the "The Sunday Song" with no hesitation—though she had never done this with me. During Creation Time, she was the first to correctly shape her letter "E," calling to me proudly to look. "Sensei, *mite! Mite!* Look!"

From where did these skills come, if she had never participated in my class? I was livid at this little Elvin creature with her sudden cornucopia of English skills. Her mother was delighted, and felt the matter resolved. When I suggested, as politely as I could, that perhaps too much sugar was causing some of the outbursts, her mother responded oddly.

"*Tai hen. Shou ga nai, ne?*" "It's terrible, but, it can't be helped, don't you agree?"

Despite an occasional glimpse into little Aoka's potential, change came very slowly. Aoka continued kicking, spitting, howling, and generally terrorizing my morning class. Aoka's mother continued to bow deeply and say, "*Shou ga nai, ne?*"

It is a disturbing feeling to loathe the behavior of a four year old, even as I worked to change it.

My job as a teacher was to figure out what Aoka needed to get past her behavior. But I had no idea how to remove Aoka's obstacles, and we continued to struggle together.

Eventually, we came to an unsteady truce. Aoka would come to class, walking two centimeters off the ground because of her blood sugar, shift her eyes at me, and join us for morning circle. As long as she was the one to turn the pages, she enjoyed story time. Her letter shapes were the best in the class.

Aoka, wherever you are, forgive my feelings of frustration. And thank you for teaching me a lesson I would desperately need a few years down the road: behavior rarely has anything to do with the child itself.

There are no bad children.

There are horrid behaviors. There are series of unfortunate factors, both seen and unseen, that lead children to behave the way they do.

But no child is, in essence, bad.

誕生日おめでとう. **Happy Birthday.**

I was in an izakaya celebrating my birthday on August 29th, 2005. Friends and I had met very early and biked the twenty kilometers to the feet of the low mountains surrounding Mishima. From there we hiked up to a forgotten Shinto shrine, intact despite the heavy bombing the area had taken during WW2, where we had lunch and sake. I took photos with my Lomo and sat on the ancient wooden steps. Broad leaves shook with the anticipation of changing their wardrobe for fall, filtering the late summer light.

Earlier that day I had seen my first *tanuki*, a fox-like animal known in Japanese folklore as mischievous shape-shifters with supernatural powers. She had wrinkled her raccoon-like nose at me before diving back into the foliage, which I chose to interpret as a very good birthday omen. I realized again how blessed I was, and allowed myself a small amount of pride in the life I had built. I had been in Japan close to four years, and it was home.

On the way back I stopped by the local camera shop, where Keiko, the owner, wished me happy birthday. I took a bath and met my friends for dinner and drinks at Happie, our local bar.

Happie Izakaya stylized itself as being "American," and had a jukebox, a dartboard, and several rusted tin signs advertising Coca-Cola and farm equipment that the youngish owner had thriftily purchased from eBay. Yoshi, the bartender, was also rather stylized in his flamboyant zoot suits and a cane he didn't need, instead resting it on the end of the bar. He used slang like "groovy" and "far out," but I never had the heart to tell him that the decades he was embracing spanned more than 60 years and were slightly off kilter.

I was sharing a bottle of shochu and brown tea with my friends Taka and Sarah when Yoshi flipped on the news. I'd quit smoking for the most part, in favor of running, but tonight was a special occasion and I lit a cigarette on a bar matchbook, shook it out, and through the first exhale saw my first views of Hurricane Katrina damage.

The shots were grainy and windswept. Streets accustomed to Second Line feet dancing were running with water, the pillars holding up the interstate looking like sodden grey rubber boots. The storm was still raging, and along the bottom of the screen, an alarming bulletin: "Mayor Ray Nagin reports that water is flowing over one of New Orleans' levees."

Because of the twelve-hour time difference, the last time I had seen the news, Ray Nagan was just issuing the mandatory evacuation order. When I'd gone to bed the night before, the levees had not yet broken and the storm was predicted to pass with predictable, manageable damage. I hadn't even been worried enough to reach out to my friends or check in on whether they had evacuated.

The bar became quiet. Everyone was staring at me. I had lived in Louisiana since I was ten, and had moved to New Orleans after college in the year before going to Japan. Even though I hadn't been back in years, I knew the streets of New Orleans well, and every news shot was a familiar place. The Dixie Tavern, punk bar extraordinaire: soggy. Frenchman Street: wadeable. The Lower Ninth Ward: submerged.

帰ります: **Return**

It would be another day before the extent of the devastation was visible and the truly horrific stories began to pour in. Terrifying rapes in the dark stadium seating of the Superdome. Starvation. Dehydration. Theft. Children crying. Families unable to leave the city. Murders and looting. Homes, people, pets, places just... gone.

For the week, I kept track of the news on my computer and tracked down people I loved. I wept when a scrappy little boy, head bobbing at the camera, was interviewed by Brian Williams about the conditions at the Superdome. Wearing a SpongeBob SquarePants t-shirt, he stood in front of a tarp, under which his grandmother huddled.

He exclaimed, "We just need some help out here! It is so pitiful, pitiful, and a shame that they have all these people out here... what are we gonna do? We don't have nowhere to go, nothing to eat... my grandmother is a diabetic, she don't know whether she's gonna live or die...so we just need some help and support."

Suddenly, my insular, simple little life in Japan seemed uninspired; I surprised myself by feeling ashamed. I was able to view most of the U.S. coverage, but I saw another perspective, as well. The Japanese media, in sharp and disturbing contrast to our own, was outraged.

A young female newscaster in a yellow rain slicker kept asking, "Where is this government? Why isn't the U.S. Government helping its people?" The camera would flash and pan, long shots of a battered third world country on our own soil. Elderly people dying for lack of diabetes and asthma medicine. Again and again, the overhead shots of buses, sitting in therapeutic, tiny rows. Unused through the storm and unused after, as the people stranded in New Orleans wrote "HELP" with bleach on the street and stood, waving, waving up at the passing helicopters, which for days after the levees broke waved back with cameras and guns, but no organized assistance.

My shame and anger roiled, as an American, as an expat, as a Louisiana native. I knew I had to go back. Once again, I would become a teacher because I wanted a job worth doing. This time, though, I sought the job to solve a problem not for myself, but for others. My limited skill set meant that I wasn't suited to rebuilding with cement and nails. Perhaps by becoming a teacher in New

Orleans I could be a part of the rehabilitation process. I could use my belief for a purpose, which suddenly became more important than my weekend travels to Kyoto and my kimono and calligraphy classes.

After four years, I was headed home.

PART

2

Broken Windows

Banana Peels

"Sorry," Kaitlin mumbled as we approached her car. "My car smells like banana peels."

She wasn't lying, nor was the reason invisible. Through the back window of her car, I could see several limp, rotting husks thrown on top of a plastic bag, in varying states of decay.

"Oh," she continued nonchalantly, "The window doesn't roll up either, so it's a bit moist in here."

I opened the door and pressed my foot gingerly into the carpet, which made an audible squishing sound. I looked over at Kaitlin, who was throwing her giant bag into the back of her car. Fortunately it was just two of us, because her backseat was a veritable thrift store of wigs, stage make up, sequins, gowns, and fake eyelashes. I learned quickly that to ride with Kaitlin was to submit to a comprehensive, inevitable glittering; we sparkled together, all day.

Kaitlin and I met at my first teacher job fair. Over a hundred first-year teachers convened at a local college to meet principals for a series of speed-dating interviews. Principals sat on one side of the table, and job-seeking teachers stood in long lines that snaked around the room. Each teacher had five minutes to talk to the principal, hand over a resume, and explain why they were more qualified than all the other fresh faces in new suits.

My partner John and I had discussed at length whether wrapping my long blonde dreads would be more or less professional. Would trying to hide the large mass of hair simply draw attention to it? That morning, I had nervously wrapped my dreads precariously into a neutral-toned scarf, tucked in as many of the shorter stands as I could, and stuck my head full of bobby pins to keep it all in place. When I arrived at the fair, ten minutes early, many other job seekers were already waiting.

The members of Teach for America had obviously been coached. A sea of deep blue and black suit jackets confronted me. Each had uncrumpled folders, colorful resume clips, briefcases or tasteful backpacks, unscuffed shoes. They appeared ready to single-handedly rectify the damages done by generations of educational degradation. They were confident, poised. They gathered in little groups, smiling and nodding knowingly. Even their little twinges of rebellion—dozens of little glittering nose piercing dots in their right nostril—seemed righteously appropriate.

Pretending to yawn, I covered my mouth and subtly slid the ring from my own nose and took a place at a long table near the back. The room filled up. No one sat next to me. I relived all of my seventh grade fears, second-guessing my pile of hair and button-up shirt, nibbling my frayed nails and wondering why I wasn't just waiting tables and planning performance art. Wondering why I had ever left Japan.

I sat alone for a few minutes until a flash and scurrying flutter drew my attention and a giant, brilliantly colored bag plunked down on the tabletop. Frida Kahlo's face emblazoned on it. "I'm gonna sit here, OK?" From over the top of the bag, a small face smiled down at me. "I like your hair. I'm Kaitlin."

I learned quickly that Kaitlin has the ability to make most people feel like a better version of themselves. She came to teaching because of a deep passion to make the world better. Her ability to soothe the most frustrated child is one I often envied, and her friendship would become a light in my toughest moments.

I also met my first principal at this fair. Having done very little research on any of the schools, I simply stood in the shortest lines.

Only three sharp-suited TFA youth lined up in front of me for the chance to meet Coach Thomas.

Historic Landmarks In Decay

Coach "Just call me Coach" Thomas, had indeed been a coach.

Before Hurricane Katrina, Coach had coached football and basketball for a historically Black high school on the West Bank of New Orleans: L.B. Landry. He was jovial, infinitely likeable, his belly popping just a bit over the top of his two-button polyester pants. Coach Thomas loved football, the Algiers neighborhood, and the L.B. Landry High School.

"We're gonna bring this school back!" he would exclaim.

L.B. Landry was, and is, the second-oldest Black high school in New Orleans. It was founded in 1938, during segregation, and until 2005 it was the community's center, a source of pride and community gathering and bragging rights. The Landry Marching Band clanged their cymbals and stomped their booted feet in every major Mardi Gras parade. The choir and theater put on several events throughout the year. The Land of the Buccaneers was known to be a "good" school.

Buccaneer fans and alumni lived for football. The football team brought the entire neighborhood to the stands, especially for the annual rivalry game against the nearby O.P. Walker. A neighborhood resident was quoted in the New Orleans paper after the storm saying, "Everybody went to the game, the battle of the bands competition, and the homecoming parade. It was tradition." L.B. Landry marinated in its traditions for generations. Alumni were fiercely proud of graduating from the school and its alumni association was one of the most outspoken in the city.

Unfortunately, over the past few decades the school had been rocked with several corruption scandals, a lack of funding and resources, repairs that went with band-aids or completely ignored, and misspent funds. The structure and grounds fell into disrepair. The students' needs and deficits increased with the level of decay, and the school struggled to keep and hold talented teachers. Both academics and the property were in shambles.

Pipes leaked and ran in the hallways. Stagnant water sat in the drains of the bathrooms. Graffiti festooned the walls of the hallways and classrooms; textbooks had not been updated in more than ten years. Much of the electrical system was inoperable, leaving students and faculty with no air conditioning or heat.

Landry's buildings were in such poor condition that it was declared among New Orleans' worst schools, and deemed "structurally and academically unacceptable" by the state. During Hurricane Katrina, the campus closed its doors to children and the community, becoming a temporary base for the National Guard and FEMA. In the aftermath, L.B. Landry students were sent to neighboring schools O.P. Walker and Karr.

Being forced to attend Walker, their great rival, was a particular affront to neighborhood children who had been raised on the football and pride of the Buccaneer name. Students refused to wear the uniform and fights broke out daily in the hallways. The children of the alumni of L.B. Landry felt homeless and slighted. Where was their legacy? Their marching band? Their blue and white?

In 2006, it was estimated that the building and grounds needed three million in repairs, despite the fact that the building had taken little water during the storm. The superintendent stated, "The building is horrendous. It should be torn down and replaced. The air conditioning doesn't work, the electrical system is shot, and the school barely has windows. The school is behind on two decades of deferred repairs."

The alumni association hung a black wreath on the locked gates of Landry, in protest of its closing. They lobbied the state to have it reopened. A member of the Friends of Landry Alumni Association said, "Landry High School is a monument of great historical and monumental significance. If we lose Landry, we lose a part of our history."

When the school received permission to reopen in a temporary space in 2007, in the back of Henderson Elementary, the parents and alumni association then lobbied for Coach Thomas as the obvious principal. After all, he had been with the school for years, students loved him, and he passionately loved the school. The newly state-run school system was already swamped with a myriad of issues. If Coach wanted to run the school, and the neighborhood wanted its school back, why not let it open? And, surely, passion was enough to get some kids seated and teach them something?

Surely?

I had to believe that. Passion and belief were about all the cards I was carrying, as well.

I liked Coach right away, and he offered me a job almost immediately, barely glancing over my resume before asking how old I was. When I told him, he laughed. "You're 27?" He chuckled, shook his head. "That's good. These 21 year olds don't know what they're getting into."

L.B. Landry would not be rebuilt for several years, if indeed at all. The superintendent promised to consider it, but the West Bank student population was not what it had been before the storm, and the state questioned whether the area truly needed three schools.

Undaunted, Coach Thomas still believed. L.B. Landry would rise again to its former glory. He hummed marching band tunes as we pulled desks into neat rows and washed the dusty backboards—the hallway we had been assigned had been largely unused, except for storage, for years. He was optimistic. We had permission to start with the ninth grade; he had five teachers and the required Special Education coordinator. The children would come. Even without the football team, marching band, textbooks, embroidered blouse uniforms, or even a building, they would come for the old blue and white.

"We're gonna bring it all back."

90 Days

Kaitlin and I had been accepted into the same teacher preparation program, developed by teachNOLA, an initiative of The New Teacher Project. TeachNOLA sent its participants through a whirlwind six weeks of summer training, and placed its "teaching fellows" into classrooms the following fall. As a part of teachNOLA's first uncertified teaching cohort, Kaitlin and I committed to continued education throughout the next two years, taking classes at the University of New Orleans and working towards our teaching certification while also working as full time classroom educators.

We spent our mornings learning about student incentives and tracking data. We had tough conversations about white privilege. We had guest lecturers who presented on "the first days of school," and why teaching the Freytag Pyramid was important for high-needs students. Kaitlin and I did our homework religiously, actively participated in all the conversations, and were the first to volunteer. I filled three composition notebooks with flamboyantly detailed notes. We planned signage and designs for our rooms. Though we had come to teaching for different reasons, we attacked our new mission with the fervor of zealots.

At our first review, our group leader told us to calm down, and not take everything so seriously, lest we burn ourselves out too quickly.

Burn ourselves out? We weren't even in orbit yet! Kaitlin ran on a volatile blend of adrenaline and headstrong blue-heat momentum and idealism. We felt called to the work, and committed to becoming brilliant educators. We joked about retirement paperwork, and found that the visual of a lifetime of teaching was murky but appealing.

Looking back, I should have listened.

Flying Solo

I can't tell you how many hours I spent on my first solo lesson. Though I had been teaching for four years in Japan, this was different.

My lesson plan, for the 90 minutes of my first solo stint, was ten pages long—I scripted every word. My hands shook as the bell rang the warning of the children's imminent arrival, and suddenly I felt a little queasy. I ran down to the bathroom, splashed some water on my face, gave myself a stern get-it-together look, and grabbed the doorknob...to discover that the door had locked behind me.

Ten minutes later, the janitor worked the doorknob off of its hinges.

I want to tell you that I was doubled over in laughter at this point, but I wasn't. I was awash in panic, and my first experience in front of a New Orleans classroom seemed like it would be an utter failure. I wasn't able to laugh it off—the insidious nature of Murphy's Law striking at just the wrong moment.

I discovered this lesson several times as a teacher, and forgot it just as often. Sometimes our situation is so serious, the needs so high, the deficits and demands so incredibly dire, that we forget that sometimes laughter is the best thing—and the only thing.

Had I laughed, immediately told the students what had happened, they would have made endless fun of me. Being the foolish, immature adolescents they were, surely one of them would have fallen from a chair in hysteric mockery, and I would have flushed red—but I would have laughed.

And what better lesson for a child than to know when to laugh at what seems hopeless?

To laugh, and then fiercely carry on...

The lesson was not ultimately a failure. We carried on, strictly. Children learned. But the lesson in that locked door was that nothing will ever go just right. A first hard lesson of teaching is to keep smiling, even when the floor falls out, or the door snicks shut with a click on the best laid plans.

Superdome
Late July.

I was sitting outside, monitoring recess for another teacher, and picking strands of wilted lettuce from the crust of a soggy Boca Burger patty. I had begun summer school bringing microwavable burritos, but those quickly "disappeared" from the fridge, as teachers who'd forgotten their lunch ravaged the spoils of the freezer.

Recess for middle school students translated into two groups of adolescent kids muddled into a big khaki-panted gaggle of a pack. I could almost see the feathers fluffing up into the air.

The girls tended to fan out a bit, gum-popping, eye rolling, elbow gouging, tooth-sucking spittle nastiness and the occasional flash of glass: illicit cell phone use shielded behind a friend's back. The cadence of their voices was a blend of cackle and screech, peppered with flavorful profanity and the occasional, "girl, heeeeellll no!"

The boys clustered into smaller cell-zygotes, necks out, pants hanging low enough for the tails of their hot cotton collared shirts to flap, tossing their heads at this or that girl, only to be fended off by a loud tooth suck and a lighthearted, "Whatchoo lookin at, bitch?" The boys would then laugh and turn their backs, preening slightly at this attention, looking for the opportunity to plume and scuffle.

Reminiscent of penguins huddling together for warmth, occasionally one would get bumped to the outside, where he would mumble, "Hey fuck you, bro," and then swagger off, hitching at his belts. By maintaining a close proximity, and staring right at them, for the most part I could prevent these posturings from breaking into full-blown fights.

Carver sauntered up to me, his shadow blocking the sun and my view of the kids, sucker jauntily sticking from the side of his mouth.

"Miss Eckhardt, where you live at?"

"I live downtown, Carver, on the other side of the French Quarter. In the Bywater."

"You ever seen the Superdome?"

"Yeah, I ride my bike by it sometimes when I'm headed uptown from where I live."

For a long moment, I lean around him and eyeball the cackling gaggles.

The sucker clattered against his teeth as he rolled it to the other side of his mouth, made a little sucking noise to collect the flavored spit—

"It really big as they say?"

"Is what, Carver?"

"I mean, I ain't never seen it. It really that big as it look on TV?"

"Is what so big, Carver?"

Another sun-melted moment. I trickle of sweat ran down my spine under my own cheap cotton collared shirt, and I looked forward with dismay to my next class, when the frigid AC would turn this sweat into a cold walking bath of stickiness, turn my students into a stinky, grumbly pack of unenthusiasm.

Carver was still examining me silently.

Finally, "The Superdome, Miss E."

I blocked my eyes with my hand, still holding the pulpy sandwich.

"Carver, the Superdome isn't more than a few miles from here. How have you never seen it? That's impossible. Don't mess with me."

I grinned up at him, wondering if he was trying to draw my attention from the penguin mating rituals. The question, quite honestly, seemed ludicrous.

Carver didn't grin back. His examination of me quickly turned to a look of loathing, his eyes staring white hot at me.

"I ain't fuckin' with you, Miss E. Just ain't never had no reason to go up there. Shit."

For a brief moment, he was the child he was supposed to be. His eyes widened and softened, hurt. A child that had opened a door for me, just a crack, tried to start a conversation.

And I had told him not to mess with me.

Then the child slid back behind his eyes, and Carver grinned around his sucker, slid it back to the other corner of his mouth.

"Carver, I'm sorry, I..."

"...Nah, Miss E. Fuck it. I was just fuckin' around anyhow. You go on ahead and give me that detention for saying fuck, too."

Grabbing onto his belt loop with a long finger, Carver hitched at his dangling britches, white boxers poofing out over the top, and sauntered into the middle of the penguin pack, leaving me with my sandwich dripping and my white hot cheeks blazing.

The bell rang.

The Perversity of Rubble

Seated in the heart of the Treme 7th Ward, with the three story brick buildings, separated by wide grass spaces and the occasional Live Oak tree, was a familiar landmark. St. Bernard had its beginnings as early as the 1940s for the working class of New Orleans, and over the next two decades expanded to become the second largest housing project in the city. St. Bernard was the center of the community; gardens flourished in the green spaces, Cub Scouts and women's groups met regularly. During desegregation in the 1960s, and the white flight that followed, government interest in maintaining this housing development, and the others within the city, quickly waned and, without assistance, St. Bernard fell into disrepair.

Despite this, the quality of the buildings remained remarkably intact, and while the gardens fell into disrepair and were gutted, the trees and green spaces remained. While not the safest neighborhood, St. Bernard was considered a relatively safe complex for the working class, compared to the more wild-west Magnolia and Desire Projects.

In 2000, nearly 6,500 people resided in the housing development, many of them families. Their children attended Craig Elementary and the historic McDonogh High School, as well as Landry, the very school where I would end up teaching.

St. Bernard did sustain damage and flooding after Hurricane Katrina but, despite this, most of the buildings maintained their structural integrity. Residents returning after the hurricane were dismayed to find a large fence, topped with barbed wire, had been wrapped around the project: it had been slated for demolition.

Others, including B.W. Cooper, Magnolia, and Fischer projects, were destined for the same fate. In their place, cheap split housing was quickly erected, splashed with strange pastel incongruous with the previous look and feel of the neighborhood.

More significantly, these houses are not built to the quality of the buildings being torn down.

In fairness, projects like the Fischer did indeed require demolition. They had long been neglected beyond the reasonable ability to resurrect them. But the St. Bernard was home to thousands and, moreover, could have been repaired. To slate it for demolition was indeed indicative of what policy-makers envisioned for the city... and most especially, who they wanted returning to it after the storm.

Residents and activists formed Survivor's Village. They pitched tents and even inhabited the buildings to protest the demolishment.

Despite their efforts, in 2010-2011, the St. Bernard housing development was "transformed" into "Columbia Parc at the

Bayou District." Columbia Parc, now privately owned, touts a fancy website, a golf course, energy-efficient appliances, and a movie theater.

But Columbia Parc also touts fewer than 500 apartments and only 157 of them are subsidized public-housing, where rent is based on income.

The rest of the units are market-rate, $775 to almost $1,100 a month—far more than the previous tenants could ever afford.

Nicolai Ouroussoff of the *New York Times* described this issue when he stated in his "Unbuilding" Photo Gallery, "There's a more insidious problem with this housing, which is that, although it gives the impression of...what a community is supposed to be, it ends up being very isolated from the city around it...There's another thing that has to be remembered here...The violence of the storm and what it did to [New Orleans] and the violence the city suffered since then, and the mismanagement of it. *The idea that you would actually go in with bulldozers and destroy entire neighborhoods at a moment when the city still hasn't healed from the wounds of the past year is an absolute perversity.*"

Belief

My first grade teacher was named Ms. Bassett. We were all slightly terrified of her. Short and slight, with a thick head of curly hair, she never paid much attention to the myriad trappings of elementary school teacher life. No Halloween broaches, or Christmas sweaters. Only plaid calf-length skirts and turtlenecks made of material that itched if she brushed my arm to reach for the glue. Sensible penny loafers, with no shiny penny to complete them.

Gone was Ms. Van Andel, with her songs about how the letter "B" stood for "bunnies" and how they like to "bounce a basketball." Now, "B" stood for "Ms. Bassett" that "B" was all business.

Robert Holtsoi passed me a sticker once, and we both got into trouble: he for passing, I for not turning him down.

But it was a St. Patrick's Day sticker. One I didn't have yet. It glittered. And it was *puffy.*

Her loathing of festive sticky sparkly things, and, in general, her defiant lack of accoutrement, frightened me.

One day, at the end of the science lesson, she asked all of us to put a plastic bag over our small hands and secure it to our wrists with a rubber band. In minutes, she said, during recess, your hand will be sweating. We all turned our heads towards the window, where, past the fish tanks and plant corpses in Dixie cups, wisps of snow gently fell on the high desert of the Navajo reservation.

Then we glanced at each other shiftily—a full-fledged look could have been construed as conspiracy—and instead stared silent, open-mouthed at her.

Don't you believe me?

She stood akimbo, with a completely unironic smile.

Ok. Just remember not to take it off. Double loop the band if your wrist is too small.

Curious to see if it would work, we all did a double-loop and then lined up for dismissal. I almost snuck some white glue—I liked to smear it all over my palms, wait for it to dry, and then peel it off in one line-printed piece. Then I remembered the baggie—how had I forgotten it so quickly—and put the jar down reluctantly.

In the boot room, many of us pulled mittens over them; those with gloves struggled to wrangle fingered gloves into place while holding the rubber band tight. I had mittens, and was one of the first to run outside into the breath-huffing air, relishing the pink cheek cold. My friend Alison daintily avoided the puddles while I stomped right through.

We immediately attended to our dead bird museum.

While this seems like a rather morbid hobby for seven year olds, it started out innocently enough. We had found a small sparrow, already hard and dead, and had decided to bury it. This was a noble and serious calling, and we earnestly sought an appropriate place. We dug into the sandy high desert soil, placed the bird in the hole... and then couldn't cover her up. It just felt... wrong. We stared at her for a while, then instead built a little cairn of rocks and bits of sagebrush and placed her reverently on top.

Then, every afternoon recess, we would visit. It stayed cold, and she was there when we returned, looking little by little more gaunt and fragile, but still feathered atop her open-air crypt.

Thereafter, we seemed to see them everywhere. A bent wing sticking up behind an air vent grate. A little crooked leg poking from the top of the scant grass along the edges of the buildings. Our school had tall rectangular windows and, presumably, birds often flew into them.

Alison and I gingerly gathered the deceased birds; both fledgling and adult, nestled them into open-air graves, and settled them next to each other in two neat little rows. Because of the abnormally cold winter, the snow and the arid climate, these animals did not deteriorate. We kept them sheltered beneath the low boughs of a pinon tree. We even had a small bird of prey, a kite perhaps, talons curled desperately in the air. We had several sparrows, little common broken-necked things, and blue-chested jays. Today there was snow to brush away or tidying up to do, before we headed to the swings.

But my mittened hand wouldn't grasp the chain tightly.

Oh, the bag! The bag!

I tore it from my sticky hand, which oozed with sweat. I remember being wholly mystified, staring at the condensation-filled bag, puffed up like mist on a window. It was the first time I remember realizing how many questions I did not yet know the answer to.

Belief can do that. It can leave us stunned. It can reassure us that things are the way they should be, even in time of great chaos.

Yet belief is a fragile thing. Like the kite, talons inept and twisted, needing far more than belief and a gust of wind. Indeed, even the wind betrayed it.

Belief cannot exist in a vacuum. It needs science, a Miss Bassett, something to feed and acknowledge it. It cannot exist all on its own.

To teach in New Orleans after Katrina was to believe in the ability to change and improve, or to fail. I never stopped believing. But in my teaching I often attended too much to the kite, beautiful as she was.

How could I forget about my own hand?

Sing

Nineteen students enrolled at L.B. Landry in the fall of 2007. A lucky thirteen showed up. I can only assume that the rest were deterred by the lack of a real building, or the absence of band equipment or a football team. Landry had only gotten approval for its tentative ninth grade opening at the last minute; perhaps families and students simply did not know about our existence.

We were six teachers, including one a year past retirement age and another who was visibly afraid of children. Each time one of our thirteen adolescents would walk near to him, he would begin to stammer uncontrollably. He wore long trench coats, Matrix-style, and had an Ankh tattoo on his hand. When I asked him why he wanted to teach, he said, "Two years of teaching looks good on a resume, and Teach for America rejected me."

In the mornings, our students would have to attend the same morning meeting as the K through eighth graders who were legitimately in their school building. They said the pledge of allegiance, celebrated the successes of the past week, and listened to their principal make announcements and give an "inspiring thought for the day."

The principal was both a stern and jovial leader who brought herself out of retirement with passion for the same ideal Coach Thomas held: the resurrection of her school after the hurricane. She never finished a sentence with a lilt, even if it was a question; each syllable came out clear and booming. The children loved and softly feared her, as did her teachers. She was sharp-tongued and ruthlessly honest. She pushed her teachers very hard, and demanded excellence in everyone, from the janitor to her vice principal, yet she was trusted and well-respected. Her teachers appreciated her honesty and her hands-on approach to governance. Though I was too inexperienced to recognize effective if not heavy-handed leadership, it was here that I first saw it.

Coach Thomas would scoff at these morning gatherings, called them babyish, and after a week declared that we did not have to attend anymore. Instead, we assembled when the bell rang in the math classroom—one of only three rooms we had, at the end of the abandoned hallway.

Coach Thomas gathered us all together each morning. We would begin with a rousing monologue about the L.B. Landry of yore, after which Coach would try to lead us in a singing intonation of the school song. Only he knew the lyrics. As we discovered at our first morning meeting, he didn't, actually, know the tune.

"We have a school called Landry, down in the deep south land..."

We attempted to sing along, bravely and tunelessly, attempting to imitate the Coach's baritone, despite its lack of harmony or confidence. Clarissa stared at the floor, shaking her long braids. Thaddeus made eye contact with me, mouth in a sneer, incredulous. I sang louder, completely off-key, and waved my hand at him in a "come on, let's go" motion. "Ohhhh, Landry..."

After this, we said the pledge. Four of our students didn't know that, either, but for this I was able to print them a copy of it so they could follow along.

The Lucky Thirteen

"The other kids'll be here soon," Coach Thomas assured us.

With only thirteen students, there seemed to be little reason to create individual schedules. All the students just moved languidly from class to class. Additionally, somehow two English teachers had been hired, so I co-taught the Lucky Thirteen with another teacher, an older woman who had students create vocabulary flash cards from the dictionary.

I spent much of my time farmed out to the elementary school as a substitute, as her seniority placed her in a better position to write the lesson plans and develop the instruction. I wrangled first graders with runny noses and no crayons, and got tongue-lashed by pissed off sixth graders in gigantic baggy pants.

"You ain't no fuckin' teacher, you a sub. And what's up with that hair, anyway? Whachoo tryin' to be?"

I ate lunch with our Luckies. We sat in the back of the cafeteria, away from the first to third graders, who were also on the rotation. They picked at the soggy chicken nuggets and rehydrated mashed potatoes, filled with pockets still powdery and dry. They were allowed an extra portion because they were older, but no one went for seconds. After lunch they had "free time."

For fifteen minutes, they stood around under the breezeway, awkwardly. There were not enough of them to form real cliques or flirt. Three boys threw a football and excluded the other four, more gangly males. They halfheartedly picked at each other, occasionally giggled or threw cheesy puffs at each other from crinkly bags and brilliantly orange fingertips. They rallied around their one similarity: a loathing of their current situation.

They invariably complained about being at a "baby school," as if their eighth grade year had not been spent in a school just like the one in which we squatted. Indeed, four of the thirteen had attended Henderson the year before. Two of our girls stood silent and sullen as statues, just out of the sun. Tylan wore little bendable gummy shoes and she kicked them on and off of her toe, stepped on it sideways, and stuck it back on. The two sullenly stood sentry, popping their gum and glaring two ways. To the left, over the expanse of field, lay the jungle gym equipment, towards Landry's decimated structure. To the right, stood the dilapidated Fischer Projects, slated for demolition, rotting and molding in the humid sunshine. Disgusted.

So Obviously…

Landry was open for three weeks in the back of the elementary school before the RSD closed it down. Coach Thomas was devastated, but undaunted.

"Just gonna take a little longer to bring it back. Gonna get a new building, too, probably!"

Despite their complaints, the thirteen ninth graders were surprisingly angry. Perhaps they enjoyed the low student-teacher ratio and all the quiet time, or maybe they simply liked tormenting their skittish trench-coated science teacher. Perhaps they were just annoyed that, after years of post-hurricane transience, their travels were not yet over. There would be no drill team and homecoming for them at Landry. They had been denied their birthright, the years their parents and grandparents spoke of so proudly. They had been denied their birthright, the blue and white.

On Landry's last official day in 2007, I had a four hour block with our kids. I set up a series of workshop areas. Students could read and listen to poetry, look at photos and art books and read articles. We did a series of writing and art projects meant to help them express their feelings about the school closing—or feelings about anything. At Workshop Table Four, I asked them to write me a letter.

"Tell me how you feel about saying goodbye to Landry, and what you are going to do to make this year the best one ever, despite the obstacles so far."

Tylan, one of my two taciturn gum-poppers, whose reading assessment showed her to have reading abilities around the third grade, wrote these words.

> *Dear Miss Eckhardt,*
>
> *I don't know why they lied to me said Landry would be back open. Landry is not open. We stuck here back in the back of this little kid's school. I never would have signed up to come here if I knew it was gonna be like this. Grownups always be lying about something, I guess.*
>
> *I thought I was going to be a cheerleader. I thought we was going to have our real uniforms. I thought I was going to go to a football game and sit in the stands and eat a hotdog. I thought I was gonna be going to a real school.*
>
> *Now I have to go to a school I don't want to go to and I am very mad about that. My mom is really mad too. She went to Landry and she said it was a good school and she is proud to be a Buccaneer and now I have to go to a bad school instead. And I have to go get a different uniform and I don't get to go where I want to go. Well, better than no school at all and this ain't no school.*
>
> *Whatever.*
> *Bye, Miss Eckhardt.*

Tylan, I couldn't have said it better.

The Mighty, Mighty Bulldogs

A week later, I was transferred to Joseph S. Clark High School, home of the Bulldogs and the second-lowest performing school in the district for several years running. I learned of this transfer on Friday afternoon, and was expected to teach my first class, the "ninth grade reading for low-performing students," on Monday morning.

Despite these humble beginnings, I was determined not to fail.

I rode my bike back across the ferry that afternoon, up Canal Street to Claiborne, and turned right and slipped up into the Treme, over to Esplanade, and to my new school. Set back from the street, it looked for all practical purposes to be a small detention center, a grey three-story rectangle surrounded by a tall chain link fence adorned with barbed wire. Announcements on the faded sign out front were for dates in 2005, before the storm.

I met with the principal, who explained why the situation with "ninth grade reading for low-performing students" was so tenuous. Two other teachers had already quit this post. The second teacher to abandon "ninth grade reading for low-performing students" still taught at the school, though had demanded the more civilized English Three. I met him a week later. He had taught the class, he informed me, for three days, "two days too many. Those kids were flipping monsters."

The first teacher, a young woman from Boston, had simply disappeared: after a few weeks, she just stopped coming. It took the school several days to figure out that the adolescents of "ninth grade reading for low-performing students" were unattended in a room for 90 minutes a day. They contacted the RSD, who had a pool of teachers who needed placement, and I was selected at random from this vat.

Too wearily, he gave me the key, and walked me to the bottom of the stairs, before stopping me.

"Whatever you do, just don't quit," he said. "There isn't anyone to replace you."

I climbed the stairs, littered with gum wrappers and balls of notebook paper. The walls declared "9th Ward bound" and "St. Bernard 7th Ward HardHeads." Rudimentary skulls with stick-crossbones. Febrile veined phallic symbols jutting out of stick figures. Guns. Gum stuck to gum stuck to...

I unlocked my classroom door to utter chaos.

A few desks shuttled into a corner in a penguin congregation faced away from the board.

The Smart Board's light bulb was cracked; glass twinkled on the linoleum.

The wooden desks had graffiti, similar to the works of art in the hallway, both drawn and carved into their aged tops.

A few milk crates were strewn around; apparently these had been used as chairs because several of the desks were broken.

Eloquent profanity haikus scribbled on the whiteboard, in permanent marker.

The teacher's desk was pushed against the wall in a full-throttle retreat.

On it were a few textbooks, a stack of battered Shakespeare anthologies, and some grammar photocopies:

Place the semicolon.

Identify the properly placed exclamation points.

Which of these sentences should end in a question?

Shopping List
Wood glue: 4 bottles
Primer: white, 2 gallons
Wall paint: light blue, 2 gallons
Paint rollers: 2
Belief: 10 pounds
Dropcloth: 1
Permanent markers: 10
Duct tape: 6 rolls
Screws and Nails: 3 100 ct boxes
Bravery: 20 bushels
Composition notebooks: 100
Hanging hooks: 12
Colored gel pens: 100
Commitment: 12 tubes
Post-It notes: 6 packs
Degreaser: 3 bottles
Magic Erasers: 3 boxes
Sponges: 6
Bucket: 1
Broom: 1
Pine-Sol: 1 bottle
Hand Sanitizer: 6 bottles
Whiteboard markers: 2 pks, assorted colors
Love: clear the shelves and order more

Red Rover, Red Rover, Send...
Spending the weekend joyously in this classroom, my first very, very own space.

I wanted the room to be completely transformed when my students arrived Monday morning. A new day, spring-fresh and full of promise.

I washed the windows from the threatening rungs of a rickety ladder I found in the stairwell.

I scrubbed graffiti off of the walls and floor with magic erasers and calories.

I cleaned the whiteboards and hung the "Table of Contents" sign to describe where the Agenda for the day would go, and the objective for the day.

Thinking: So much to accomplish, So much to do.

Fixing desks with shiny new screws and less elegant duct tape.

Placing a beta in a large mason jar, fins twirling, and the essential polished apple on my desk.

Suspending Paper lanterns from the high ceilings, and draping Christmas lights around the "Rockstars!" board: a place for exceptional work and "Students of the Week."

Sweeping and mopping linoleum.

Drilling hooks into the wall, an orderly place for bags and oversized purses that would be in the way in the aisles.

Filling in chips and holes with wood glue, paint, prayer.

Touching up the peeling paint, lettering "READ" in light blue stenciled letters haphazardly all over the room.

Lashing the sordid pile of milk crates into a bookshelf, held together with twisties, secured dubiously to the wall with screws.

Placing all the books neatly onto these new shelves, including the paperback collection my partner Johnathan and I had been amassing all summer from thrift stores and garage sales. *Harry Potter, Twilight. Winnie the Pooh. Ramona Quimby. Crank.*

Lettering signs, such as the "Rules and Expectations." Hanging them on the sidewall, bright yellow arrows pointing to them. Hand-painted posters proclaimed, "Own Your Actions" and "Ask WHY."

Daubing sponge paint over the front board, in enormous letters: Reading is Knowledge. Knowledge is Freedom. Reading is *life*.

Johnathan painted me a large, colorful canvas in bright blues and reds: "Be the change you wish to see in the world." Hanging this gift behind my desk, behind my spinning teacher chair, now squeak-free and oiled with WD-40, felt like a pinprick of solace and inspiration.

Placing nametags and desks in a large semicircle in the room.

Standing in my doorway, a permanent memory, scanning for any bit of clutter, any desk a hair out of place.

Smiling proudly, turning the lights off. Awash with the sensation of being ready. Of being *prepared*.

The Rules:
Sit in your assigned seat
Wait your turn to speak
Food or gum is prohibited
Respect the rights of everyone to learn
Do better than your best!

Expectations:
Be respectful.
Be kind.
Work hard.
Own your actions.
Strive for freedom.

Semi-circles

It took me ten minutes to realize that the semicircle was an awful idea.

I had no way to circulate—I was as trapped as my fishbowl in the front of the room. I felt awkwardly pinned, a butterfly still flapping against the collection board.

Tara and Dijon found a way to get across it in five seconds flat, however—they must have been eyeballing each other while I drew the Freytag Pyramid on the board. Suddenly with a screech, Tara flew across the room, snatched a handful of Dejon's hair, and began beating her face into the desk that I had so carefully polished the night before.

This event did not exactly improve my first class, but when it was time for dismissal, I was determined to stand my ground.

"No one is dismissed until I say." I announced. "I am looking for those who are quiet and ready to go."

There was a long moment, when the kids looked back and forth at each other across the room, in bald shock, and I had a single moment of triumph—which crumbled immediately as a tall young man stood and said "Lady, I gotta go."

He pushed by me, my foot slipped, and my head cracked back against the edge of a hook, raising a lump and bringing shocked tears to my eyes. The rest of the kids laughed, shook their heads, and shuffled out.

All that was between eight thirty and ten o'clock. Of the first day.

By five o'clock, I was absolutely dazed. I sat at my desk, noticed the apple had been stolen, and had a long cry.

I want to lie and say, "But I dusted myself off and, undaunted, studied the next day's lesson plans!"

But the bald truth is that I was terrified. More scared than I had ever been. Every teaching nightmare I'd ever had came true. Two fights, personal damage, utter chaos, and, worst of all, almost no successful instruction.

My desire to be a strong educator for these kids had not diminished—I still carried the sense, strongly, that I had to carry on. But the earnest bravery I had waltzed in on had deflated, leaving a flaccid, naked terror and utter sense of failure in its place.

So, I did go over my lesson plans, looked at what student work I had managed to wrangle from fleeing fingers, made adjustments.

I reaffirmed my reasons to be there—these students needed me.

I arranged the desks into tidy rows and redid the seating chart.

And I reminded myself, not for the last time, that passion and love would not be enough—only hard work and a long commitment would earn their respect and trust.

And Some Weeks Passed

My beta fish lasted two weeks.

He came to a toilet flushing demise because a child had pulled him out of the water, taken scissors to his fluttering tail, removed it from him with a snip, and then dropped him, bleeding and writhing, into the still water.

Nauseated horror washed over me when I found him the next day, still flipping weakly with his fins, trying futilely to right himself. His tail floated limply beside him.

And some weeks passed.

Passed with massive failures, enormous tragedies, and also some marginal successes. An extra smile. An extra homework. A full paragraph. A complete sentence. An orderly class entrance. An 89% vocabulary quiz.

And the Boy Was Happy

My classroom was perched at the top of the stairwell on the third floor, and with the electronic warble of the final bell, I had a moment of precarious pride. My students—all seven that had shown up that afternoon despite the 24 of the roster—sat, waiting expectantly. I was so accustomed to at least one of them bolting or bumping past me. They were eyeing me like I had suddenly sprouted book-shaped wings.

Were they actually waiting for me to dismiss them?

I suppressed my exuberance, pointedly set my marker onto the desk in front of me, took a breath, and said, "First row, you are excused. Thank you."

A rumble of consternation and some impatient tooth-sucking. No one was sitting in the first row.

"Oh, yes, hmmm..." I tittered nervously, "all my ladies, you're excused first."

Tamisha, my single female, flounced to her feet, scooped up her bag, and blew a kiss over her broad shoulder. "Later, suckas!"

The remaining gentlemen stood and before they could defy me, quickly, "Gentlemen, have a great weekend! Don't forget your reading..." and they were gone.

I grabbed my purse from my locked desk drawer, using the keys around my neck, and pulled the door shut behind me. All the doors in the school locked automatically "for safety and lockdown purposes." Jason had taught me this lesson my first day. He showed up ten minutes late, sticking his cherubic face into the doorway and said "Hey Miss New Teacher, I got an important question for you." I stepped into the hallway, the door swung behind me, latched into place, and I knew it had locked from the uproar behind me. I turned back to Jason, who was half way down the hall, demonstrating an uncanny ability to be doubled over with laughter and fleeing at the same time.

I spent the next few minutes cajoling a few of the less rowdy students to open the door, which happened once a couple bags of hot cheesy puffs had been passed around.

Point for the home team.

That weekend I bought the lanyard, white letters announcing, "I HEART TEACHING."

Bouncing down the backstairs behind a few straggling students, I was feeling the afterglow of a small victory, They had waited for dismissal.

Point for the visitor.

Other signs suggested that I was covering some ground.

Students were really enjoying the language lab, listening to books and following along, and even leaving the room discussing who had gotten farther with their vocabulary work. Less gum was being chewed. More than half sat in the seats I assigned them; the ones who didn't did it less out of rebellion than the fact that rosters changed so often that it was impossible to keep up with a seating chart. I was making several mistakes a day, but each day the mistakes were at least new, not on repeat. The more mischievous of my students were running out of their usual antics and actually beginning to settle in.

The biggest surprise of the past three weeks was my dubious implementation of storytime, stolen from my days of teaching young Japanese children. In the second week I decided to offer to read to the class for five minutes at the end of each 90-minute period. My first period met this suggestion with a cicada chorus of toothsucking, an awful sound of disrespectful spittle sliding through molars.

Suppressing my fear of a book-burning riot, I ignored them and pulled my rickety teacher stool up to face them, and said, "We'll start with one of my favorite books. *The Giving Tree.*"

This announcement was met with several groans and a hollered "That's a baby book! Come on, man! Go on 'head with that shit" by a feisty Tyrell.

Tyrell, despite my limp protests, ignored his assigned seat in row three and sat front and center, by choice. This seat was perfect for the heckling he did whenever I made a misstep, which was often.

Tremors of agreement and rumbled profanity. I opened the book and scanned the room with what I hoped was a viciously stern glare. Reluctantly, the fifteen children grew sullenly silent. I waited a moment more, drawing my face back quickly from fierce into a smile.

I began by holding the book out to the faces, still scoffing, still reluctantly quiet, and yet... expectant. "Once there was a tree," I turned the page rapidly, "and she loved a little boy."

While the boy played king of the forest a few pages later, I dared to glance away from the book. All fifteen of them were staring at the book. Robyn chewed her lower lip, looking as if I were revealing a deep and mysterious secret. Tyrell rested his chin on his chapped hand. Even Jason was uncharacteristically silent, gazing past me.

And so the tree gives, becoming fruitless, limbless, and finally, trunkless. The dismissal ball rang over the final lines "And the tree was happy."

No one moved.

Outside, in the hallway came the usual sounds of yelling and stomping, the symphony of a chaotic transition from one room to another. My doorknob was tried, clicking back and forth. I sat, on my stool, and made eye contact with each child. They stared back at me, soft and limp.

Robyn looked at me, moist-eyed. "So the tree dies for that greedy boy?" she asked.

"Yup. And that's some kinda bullshit," intoned Jamal.

A third voice: "Come on, man, didn't you get it? At least the tree understood what love was."

"Even if he was some kinda chump, giving him all that."

"What you reading next, Miss E?"

Jason started to rise.

"Hold up, son! Miss E ain't even dismiss you yet!" Jamal said as he threw Jason threatening glance, then looked at me. "Go 'head, Miss E."

Flustered, I walked to the door and dismissed all of them at once. Robyn came last. "Miss E, you crying for that old tree too? I felt bad for it."

(Yes, Robyn, I guess I was.)

Then she was gone, sidebag banging against her leg, khakis too tight and one pant leg folded up crooked against her grey sock.

And the teacher was happy.

Descent

This almost stereotypically beautiful moment came back to me as I walked through the metal detector, which beeped crankily at me, and pushed through the large metal doors of the front entrance. Gaggles of children stood laughing, clutching notebooks to their buttoned chests or fanning themselves with them, knocking into each other as they walked cell phones in hand. In the afternoons, I liked to walk the bus line, wave to students through the window, make a bit more contact.

The day was warm and still very humid. The busses pulled away, I grinned up at Jamal in the window, who was waving, As the last bus pulled away, I turned to tease a group of students about why they hadn't started walking home yet, when

I heard the shots, staccato boom
firecracker loaded up with bass.

The gunshot at such close range
a walloping resonant thunderclap
in the hollow of my ribcage.
The feeling of slipping while standing,
seasons shifting, shifting children,
uniformed crimson falling to the ground,
little avalanches. The principal
yelling without sound, sound swallowed
in another thunderclap
somehow thinner, then
a squalling of dismayed tires.

And one crimson leaf, alone,
crookedly falling,
at the end
of the block.
And then everyone, little leaves, tall men,
all were running. Sound returned with a vacuum whoosh,
the volume way too loud, boots stomping down the pavement,
children bustling into side streets, they knew better,
one runs from the thunderclap, not towards it,
survivors shimmer into the cypress siding
and camouflage well.
The principal reached him first, scooped his crumpled body up,
crackling starch widening moist sidewalk cement scarlet
aftermath.
Stunned and unhelpful, I pulled the scarf from my ponytail
helpless object helpless gesture, I touched his flaming fluttering
face

Then men, coach men, big men, came and lifted him,
carrying him back towards the school. My scarf fluttered away.

Later, the police would ask me,
"Was he your student?"

And I would say,
shamefully, horribly, honestly,
"He's on my roster.
I've never seen him before."

Sick Day. (This happened five times.)
I wake up and immediately feel the twist in my gut, an unwilling surge of fear and bile. I wait, trying to deep-breathe it down, but end up rushing on slippered feet down the hallway. I don't bother to turn on the light, and kneel onto the rug and purge into porcelain, heaving undigested clumps of spinach and spaghetti squash into the dark water.

The vomiting is not new. I do this every morning. My throat is burned raw on the inside, against my neck, all day it scratches. I vomit because I wake up every morning and think about the pressure of the day, all the things that could go wrong, all the battles and challenges, and I cannot control my urge to enter empty-stomached into the fray. Usually I feel better after this awful porcelain sacrifice, but as I lean back on my heels and reach behind me for a towel, a truth comes to me.

I rinse my mouth out at the kitchen sink from a Mardi Gras cup, before I tiptoe back down the hallway and grab my phone from the nightstand, breathe air in, dial the principal's number. I stand in the unlit hallway, fingers and toes crossed with the hope that the principal's voicemail picks up.

The chance of finding a substitute is slim; the chance of actual work getting done is virtually nonexistent. Tomorrow morning balls of paper, the unavoidable spicy cheesy puffs and Chee Wees will litter the floor. Certain desks will appear as if a flock of jays had been there all day, shelling sunflower seeds and cackling madly. New graffiti will have blossomed in desks and, if I am unlucky, on the whiteboards. Tomorrow will start with exceptional unpleasantness; I will pay in degreaser and Lysol for my truancy.

But for now I can climb back into bed, pull the covers over my head, and burrow deeply into the sheets.

Robyn
Robyn was fierce for her fifteen years, but somehow delicate for her sturdy frame. Her large hands moved surprisingly gracefully when she spoke. They seemed to weave patterns in the air, tracers dancing behind her long neon acrylic nails.

She had trouble holding still, always picking at the knots along the strings of her bookbag or pulling at the ends of her braids. Robyn was one of the first to realize that, unlike the previous two teachers, I was not going to scare so easily and she began popping in after the final bell and walking to the busses with me.

She also loathed the lunchroom, an admittedly unsafe place where boys hit each other with belts and girls adjusted the razors in their synthetic hairdos. She would rush from her class, grab her lunch on its styrofoam tray, and clamber up the back stairs to my room.

Robyn had a habit of telling the most brutal of stories in the most nonchalant of ways during our lunchtimes together.

"Miss E, you wasn't here for the hurricane, right? You know how hot it was?"

The world that Robyn described in the days following August 29, 2005 were nothing like the sterile media coverage. Her stories were about family members, neighbors, and photos lost. Robyn was born and raised in the Treme neighborhood, on North Villere, near the interstate, only a five minute walk from our school. Her family home was a four-room shotgun-style house, one room flowing into the next. It flooded, and she, her brother, and her grandmother had waited a day. "We was expecting someone to come through and help us. So we just sat on our front porch with our feet up on milk crates. We was out of water, so we drank hot Coke and waited."

They kept waiting until the Coke ran out. By then, Robyn's grandmother was in need of her diabetes medication. When they heard from some neighbors that supplies and medicine were being distributed at the Superdome, Robyn and her brother loaded her grandmother into a shopping cart and wheeled the two miles, in the blistering heat, to the Central Business District, with a damp hope for help.

This image, above others, resonates with me, perhaps because Robyn carried a picture of her frail little grandmother in her wallet. A light-skinned woman in a loose-fitting cotton dress and tennis shoes, dentures missing behind pursed lips, clutching her purse, as if the corner store might still be open. As they plodded slowly through the heavy, stagnant air and fermenting streets, she complained constantly of feeling ill and muttered to herself. This muttering, more than anything else she saw, frightened Robyn the most.

Robyn had padded the cart with pillows and blankets to cushion her grandmother somewhat from the bumping. Robyn's brother, two years older, had pushed the cart to the edge of the porch so she could step into it without navigating the stairs. The pillows were damp and tepid and starting to mildew, and the blankets were too hot, and the post-storm sun bore down on the little parade. They went down Claiborne Avenue, thinking it would be safest to stay out of the thin streets. They passed a car burning and several other people pushing carts, theirs filled with looted paraphernalia.

"But mostly they was pushing food and water around, Miss E. I didn't see so much stealing as people trying to find stuff to eat and drink." They passed a store, the windows broken, the window a maw of glass teeth. Robyn clambered in, but all the water was already gone. Instead, she ate a pickle-in-a-bag, and the salty vinegar burned her mouth and chapped her lips in the sun like fire.

The Superdome had no supplies, no water, no shelter, no safety. Hundreds, thousands of people were already there, splayed out along the ramps and sidewalks, huddled in the minimal shade along the edge of the building, hassling and snapping at each other. Robyn and her family found a shaded place next to a pillar, and began to wait.

That waiting became agony as grandmother's muttering became incoherent chatter, sometimes bossy yelling, sometimes long moans that were underscored only by the reality of dozens of others, moaning. When the blistering day faded to a slithering, sticky twilight, Robyn's brother lost his patience and strode off to get help. She implored him to stay, but he promised to return with supplies, and medicine, and left.

Robyn huddled by the cart, clutching her grandmother's hand, using the pillar as a shelter when groups of men would come by. Rumors of rape inside the building frightened her, and even when people offered her a Capri Sun, she turned it down, fearing foul play.

Robyn's grandmother passed away late the next morning, broiling in the cart. Robyn stayed for a few more hours, then covered up her grandmother in the stinking blankets, taking her purse from the wrinkled hands, and wandered off to find her brother.

She was twelve years old.

Robyn ended up three states away from her brother for months, first in a shelter, then in a church turned halfway house for Katrina survivors. No one ever asked her why she, a mere child, was traveling by herself, and she, a mere child, had no idea where to begin to inquire.

She told me these things over her apple, the only piece of the school lunch she ever bothered to eat, relating the story devoid of adjective or passion. For her, it was just a story. Everyone in her neighborhood had one like it. No one was special or singular in their struggles following Katrina. Everyone who stayed suffered, and suffering grew in direct proportion to the level of poverty.

Robyn shrugged, mouth full of mealy red fruit. "If you were poor, Black, and stranded in New Orleans after Hurricane Katrina, this is just the way it was for awhile."

Robyn couldn't write very well. She struggled to read aloud, made unconventional spelling mistakes, wrote in all capital letters, and could not punctuate. While this could have been due to minor undiagnosed dyslexia, I suspected a poor elementary education was more likely. She was bright, she caught on quickly; she was attention-starved.

She wanted desperately for me to take down her story about her grandmother and Katrina. So our lunch periods began differently, the first minutes quickly eating, and the rest as "Writing Time," her talking and me transcribing into her notebook. When we had finished, I offered to type it for her, but she said she would rather have it written out. I suspected she planned to claim the writing was her own, which was fine with me. The ink and penmanship wouldn't be hers, but the powerful words were.

Robyn had just turned sixteen when she slunk into my room at lunch and said, "Miss Eckhardt, you gonna be real mad at me."

She was pregnant.

We discussed her options briefly, but she'd already made her mind up. The baby was a tribute to her grandmother, and my logistical questions washed over her like frivolous summer rain.

"Miss Eckhardt," she said, "You're cool and all, but we gonna see this differently."

The next day, she didn't show up for our lunch meeting, and I ate at my desk alone, forcing the food down over my choking sobs.

The week after, Robyn simply stopped coming to school, disappearing back into the Treme with the slightest round curve against her khakis.

I am glad and proud that she was finally able to put down her story, and this was cathartic for her. Someday this story will be meaningful to her child, as well.

Our overwhelmed guidance department promised to track her down, but never did.

Our social worker asked that I not send her any more referrals: she was already at maximum capacity.

Though I drove by several times, I never quite had the courage to brave that story-familiar porch, paint peeling along the sill.

I never saw her again.

The Rock of Love

This, the one reality TV show we ever watched, came as a shocking gift through the stolen cable in our first apartment in the Bywater neighborhood. By Thursday night, Kaitlin, my boyfriend, and I were more than ready to see the week's insanity tied up in chains and dropped, cement-footed, into the Mississippi. We would gather in my kitchen, with its wilted plants on the smudged windowsill, and cook themed meals. We ate Kaitlin's crisp spanakopita with box wine, hummus smeared on John's homemade tortillas, vegan brownies that glued our grinning mouths into smiles. Tidbits of delicious normalcy. Meanwhile, on the screen, Bret re-tied his bandannas and peacock-postured, flexed his surprising muscles, and each week culled his flock of sparrows down to a manageable size as we rooted and bet on our favorites.

A *Rock of Love*, slightly past midweek. A ridiculous routine, a look-forward-to, a time to slosh wine over glasses, snort with laughter, and bolster ourselves with ourselves for the strains of Friday... and the weekend of planning. And Monday. Monday again...

When our favorite sparrow won Bret's heart, our eyes glittered with excited and dismayed tears I am so ashamed to admit to, I will only do so here.

Faculty Room

There are three sofas, 50-odd cardboard boxes filled with brand new textbooks too expensive to distribute for use, a filthy microwave, two wheezing refrigerators and, when many of the teachers were present together, conversations so poisonous that carbon monoxide would be preferable. In this room, the spectres of administration, rules, obstacles, and children were hung like verbal pinatas, and bashed, bashed, bashed. Complaints about students so vicious, so angst-dripping, so familiar, it was all too tempting to take a swing. I brought cold lunches and ate them, lukewarm, from my desk drawer, preferring a possible bacteria attack to facing this frigid venom.

Stilettos

A teacher on my floor was having an affair with one of the particularly muscular members of the football team.

She wore stiletto heels and whipping braids, click-clacking her way down the hallway each day. I wanted to hate her, but I found myself afraid of her. I was intimidated by her flashing eyes and predatory nails, her radiator-hot sexuality that glowed from beneath the hem of her short skirts. The football star hung out in the back of her room, chawing on a toothpick. He skipped his classes and watched her radiate all day.

He was nineteen. He would pass his classes because otherwise he couldn't play football, and his presence was essential to the team.

But this didn't make it OK. None of this was OK.

Jamal

Jamal had an annoyingly adorable nickname from a popular TV show, and refused to answer to any other name. Charming and hyper-intelligent, he watched me silently and attentively, rarely speaking in class, unless it was to disagree with me.

Once he wrote in his journal to me, "Miss Eckhardt, I know you think school is important, but you don't know how little what you're teaching actually means to me. I'm not trying to be rude, but what's a story about Frederick Douglass gonna do for me? A bunch of paper doesn't stop a bullet."

"Jamal," I wrote back, "it can. Not in the way you mean, but it can."

He won an essay contest and met the mayor, and his mother gave me my first giant parent hug.

Charles

Charles was overage, ankle-braceleted, and abrasive. He was the first audacious young man to push by me on the first day of school, and he broke my rules constantly. He spit sunflower seeds on the floor, put his feet up on desks, pulled wires out of the headphones, wrote "7th ward" on *everything*... But he always came to class.

Once, Charles got into a fight in the bathroom. He must have lost, because when he arrived, his split eyebrow was spilling blood down his chin. I wrangled the rest of the students into pretending to write in their journals, and I patched his eye with some tissue, the ever-ready duct tape, and hand sanitizer.

He said nothing, submitting to the pseudo-doctoring with reluctant patience, and then began to write in his journal. He wrote all class, refused to even open his book, did not even look up for storytime: an excerpt from the book *Life After God*.

But he was present, and his presence mattered, each day. Each day I tried to make eye contact with him, at least just once, meaningfully. Each day I tried to push him a little farther, ask a little, more, let him know I expected him, someday, to join us.

Some days worked and some days didn't. The days that did, Charles submitted small scraps of work in his shaky handwriting. On the days that didn't, pushing him with eyes or words would rapidly lead to an outburst, books thrown with the speed of his *fuck you*s and a dramatic slamming exit.

But even if he stayed only a few minutes, he always limped into class on time.

This small victory with him each day was one of the reasons he ended up finally moving to the next grade.

Tara the Weave-Puller

Tara, who fought in my classroom the first day, became one of my biggest allies. She would sit front and center and if anyone disturbed the class she would turn around and scream, "Y'all all need to shut the fuck up. Miss E tryin' to get us up out of here." She would threaten to fight people over any interruption, and couldn't understand why I wouldn't want her to have my back.

After reading *Sold* by Patricia McCormick, she decided she wanted to go to Nepal and save all the children.

Tara is in college now, studying to be a nurse practitioner.

Jason's Windows

Jason had an alligator smile, too hungry and too full of teeth. When he grinned, he looked like he was imagining what my forearm would taste like. I failed at a lot of things my first year; building a relationship with Jason was a monumental disaster.

Wednesday. Rain threatened from drooping skies. We were in the middle of a lesson, when Jason stood up and stretched, dramatically. He said, loudly, "Goodbye" to me with a huge smirk, and walked out the door. I wanted to go after him, but seventeen students were still seated, and every split second I spent watching Jason leave would heighten the level of drama, and distract us from learning, perhaps permanently. So I ignored him, pointedly making eye contact with Tara.

My classroom overlooked the back courtyard of the school, with ten-foot windows split into framed squares of glass. Hefting a rock large enough, and hurtling it through the air with the right trajectory to crack or break these panes would be no easy feat.

Jason, however, was a closet overachiever; he decided that smashing those windows would be his new hobby.

Thereafter my class was incessantly interrupted by the whistling ping of a pebble rocketing against the glass. In the drafty, high-ceilinged room, the sound ricocheted like a trapped bird. When I opened the window to yell down at him, a chunk of cement was likely to come past me, rather than the glass, from around the corner, just out of sight. If I called security, I brought Jason all the attention he wanted, as he took great joy in running from the hefty security guard, who could not take more than a few steps without yanking at his ill-fitting pants. When I reached out to the administration for help, I was asked to "catch him in the act"—which I did, but with no actual proof beyond my own eyes, the situation continued.

I knew I needed to call home, about his truancy, about the rocks, and I put it off longer than I should have. The number was for his grandmother. After three days, I called the number the school had for him, and got voicemail four times before an exhausted voice finally answered. The "hello..." was a statement, not a question. A sigh.

When I explained who I was, and why I was calling the voice said, "What do you want me to do about it?" Not gruffly—really wanting to know. What did I expect her to do about her rock-tossing grandson? She said, "He only lives here half the time, I can't tell that boy nothin."

I asked the tired voice to speak to him, to ask him to stop, and tried to explain the severity of it. I asked her to tell him to come to class, to sit in his seat, to pay attention so he can pass my class.

The voice laughed. "You know Jason been in that same grade for three years now? Maybe he's just bored. He can read fine—just can't sit still long enough to do it." She was right—the reading assessment placed Jason at grade level. He didn't need the intervention my class provided—he just needed to do the work.

"Maybe you need to teach him something he don't already know and he'd come to class."

A great point, I said. Please ask him to come to class and I'll prepare something for him that he has never seen before.

But I didn't. I was busy and struggling with the students who did actually show up for class. I barely had time to borrow the ladder and fix the chips and cracks in the glass with colored cellophane and packing tape. The room began to take on the hues of a church, sunlight filtering through the faux stained glass.

Once, I watched another teacher chase him down the hallway. "Jason, get back here! Get to class!" Jason and his Cheshire grin zipped down the hallway, reveling in the one-on-one attention. Guiltily, I was pleased that another teacher had reached an exasperation point with Jason—his special torments were not just for me.

Jason had no appropriate way to seek adult notice. His antics were barely concealed cries for help.

I wanted to help. Truly, I wanted to do so much more than I was doing. But I was pulling far too many threads. His kept slipping through my fingers.

He slipped through all of ours; Jason is in prison for armed robbery.

I hope he does not dream at night about broken windows, and the unfulfilled promises they make.

Bicycle

One of my great pleasures about my morning and evening routines was commuting on my bicycle. It reminded me of Japan. The distance was about the same, but rather than rice fields, I passed rows of houses in varying stages of abandonment or reconstruction. Weary oaks replaced the cherry blossom trees, their branches and arms battle-scarred and still stripped raw from the hurricane's damage.

On rainy days Johnathan would drive me, but most often my morning started with kissing him goodbye, clunking the bike down the stairs, kicking the big shutter doors closed behind me, and slipping onto the dawn-drenched streets.

Riding a bicycle through the streets of New Orleans is always a great joy; it's exactly the right speed with which to see the city. Slowly enough to take in voices and colors and smells, fast enough to cover a lot of territory in a few hours.

The early morning ride along the edge of the French Quarter and down historic Esplanade into the Treme neighborhood filled me with a deeply emotional civic pride. Sometimes I would take different routes, dodging discarded Styrofoam daiquiri cups and plastic beer cups, or down quiet streets where few cars, or people, had yet returned from their forced evacuation.

In the morning, after my stomach had settled, my recommitment to another day was almost palpable. Anticipation in these moments would hum naively, gullibly through me. I was making a difference. I was the change I wanted to see.

After long days, a twenty-minute bike ride home was long enough to shed some of the toxins of the day, and time to let the triumphs emerge on the surface of my mind. The ride allowed a space for me to reflect, my legs on pedal-autopilot, my mind drifting over the high and lowlights: Robyn's fantastic use of evidence, Tyrone speaking up in respectful disagreement, annotation work improving all around.

I also, very simply, loved my swift little red bike.

I double-locked it to the pillars in the front yard of the school, near the entrance to the office, both body and wheels. It was sheltered beneath the breezeway and away from school and student traffic.

But after a long day, an absolutely awful Friday, in late February, I walked around the corner of the school to find my bike had been paid an egregious visit.

I first noticed the spokes, glinting oddly in the sun. Instead of being attached to the rim, they stuck out like tangled weeds in every direction but toward the center of the bike, morbid cactus spines. The back rim had been bent in half, the tire flapping limply, torn nearly in two. I found a crank arm and pedal in the grass several feet away, completely and violently detached. The whole frame had been beaten repeatedly; chunks of raw metal gleamed between the red paint.

The chain wheel had been pried away, bent out, its teeth snarling in uncomfortable angles. It would have taken a heavy lever to do that. Crowbar? Pipe? What would such an object be doing on a high school campus?

And why had it been done?

I walked over and picked up the pedal. How could this have happened? In full sight of the street? During school hours? Within hearing distance of so many adults, and students?

It was an invasive thing, a brutal and personal and profoundly terrible thing. To me, it felt like a violation of a friend. I had the incongruous thought, "I should have been here to protect her."

I called Johnathan. I tried not to cry. If the assailants (the children?) were watching, I couldn't let them see this impact. The battered remains were still lashed to the pillar. I unlocked both locks, stuffed them in my messenger bag, and lifted the front wheel over my shoulder.

Johnathan met me at the corner. He was tightlipped, rage fuming from his silence, easily taking the bike from me and slamming it too roughly into the back. I winced—as if further damage could be done. Then he met my eyes and pulled me in for a hug. "Goddammit," he said. "You work so hard for these kids. Why would they do this?"

Why, indeed.

A poster hung on my wall, imploring the students to "Always ask *why*!"

I wanted my students to be curious, to look beyond the words on the page, to ask for reasons from the author and from the world. But my hard truth, that warm crisp spring, one that I would not share with my students, was this:

Sometimes there is no why.

Sometimes, there's no point in asking.

That Monday, John had to wake up and drive me to school. I arrived early enough to borrow the ladder, once again. I hung the bent rim, carefully avoiding the cactus spokes of my deceased bike, from the ceiling of my classroom. Below it, on a ribbon, a hand-lettered sign, with hearts and cursive-writing: "I love you anyway."

Both spun lazily, especially with the windows open, an odd and awkward mobile.

Robyn was the first to notice it. "Miss E, that's, like, symbolic!"

Ananda

Ananda was eighteen when she joined my class in the spring, Apparently, her English teacher had determined that she couldn't read much farther than a third grade level, and the solution was to send her to my class, in the hopes of a permanent bandaid, while giving her credit for the English Three class. If she passed, she would finally be promoted to her senior year. There she would have to again face the terrors of the state exams required to graduate, but at least she would finally be in what she felt was her "right grade."

Ananda was able to do the work for me, slowly, with repeated explanations and rereadings. She actually read quite well, though with no awareness of phonics or how to break words into pieces.

I asked her why she'd failed English Three in the fall, and she told me frankly, "My momma died." Crazily, she grinned. "But it's cool. She was real sick. Wudn't nothing nobody could do."

Ananda particularly loved storytime. She was even fond of the Shel Silverstein poems, which I very wrongly thought would be a success after *The Giving Tree*.

Of this epic failure, I wrote in my journal: "Be pleasantly surprised, expect much, and never underestimate."

At the end of the year I proudly gave her a B, and a hug. Her round face exploded into a smirk and she trounced out, report card in hand. She had struggled, but had persevered. She had three gold records on the wall—old 45s I spray painted with gold glitter and gave as awards for achievement and grit. She took a picture with me, holding one out, proudly.

In her other classes, too, Ananda made headway, and finished the spring semester with B's and C's: more than what she needed to pass.

I mentioned how proud I was to the guidance counselor. "Yes indeed," he sighed, pulling at his polyester collar. "Too bad about her absences."

"Come again?"

"Ananda missed more than twenty days of school in the first semester alone. We can't promote her."

"But, she got the B she needed to move on! Her B balances out her failure in the fall, right?"

Another nasal sigh. "Miss Eckhardt, if we promoted students on grades alone, what would be the backstop? Why would they bother to come to school? Wouldn't teachers simply give the grades they wanted kids to have, and promote them so they wouldn't have to see them again the next year?"

"But that isn't what happened in this case. Ananda deserves the promotion. She worked hard for it."

"Deserves is a strong word, isn't it, Kaycee? She worked 50% of the school year. So you're saying 50% is 'good enough?' I thought you'd have higher expectations that that."

He strode off down the hallway, plaid shirt stretched over his broad shoulders.

A Man is Speaking

He begins in a usual tirade,
the one I have been advised to keep silent through
keep still and patient and I usually do
wait out the seething poison of these rants

about the lazy, violent children, the parents who don't care
about the lack of resources, the expense of football equipment
about the audacity of first year teachers

requesting funds for books—the insult!—and today,
a subtle sea change, I cannot bear another second and I mumble,
"I only asked for a class set of *Fahrenheit 451*..."

"I'm the boss, and a man.
When a man is speaking, you'd do better to be quiet. Just
Be quiet when a man is speaking."

I thought the phrase "my face burned" was a cliché until that moment.
My face didn't burn. It roared engulfed itself fumed spit and I stood
Quietly, religiously combustible
and silently scorched from the room.

Journal Entries

I had planned to keep a journal of my first year of teaching in New Orleans. This was rapidly distilled to a single sentence each day—one I mulled over as I rode my bike home each day.

I scribbled the single line into a notebook on my bedside table, a snippet of advice to my future self.

After I was locked out of my classroom, I wrote, "Carry your keys."

A brief but deeply disturbing spitball festival sparked the cliché adage, "Never turn your back."

I had moments of great terror and great beauty that first year. I suppose, though, that it is human nature to remember the worst of it most clearly.

My wallet was stolen—twice. When I bought a lockbox for it, the entire lockbox also disappeared.

I wrote in my journal, "Nothing is sacred."

After my bike was destroyed, I wrote in my journal, "Crowbars have many purposes, and so do wheels." Then, in a rare addition of a second sentence, I jotted, "Sometimes it's better not to ask why."

I scraped gum off the walls and floor of my classroom with a paint scraper, and swept up chewed sunflower seeds that made me gag.

I wrote in my journal, "Seeds aren't always useful."

My poor little fish and his snipped fins gave rise to "If it is precious, protect it."

And when I was told by my principal in a meeting not to interrupt, I scribbled, heavily tracing the words in black ink, "Pick your battles, fight for kids."

I worked hard, and my students did make gains, but not hoped-for dramatic gains.

I wrote in my journal, "I thought I would be good at this."

After the second gun, I stared at the blank page in my journal for almost an hour.

I had no words, in my journal, for that.

"Everything that keeps me together is falling apart..." — Modest Mouse

Each morning, my students would clunk and clamber into the room, grab their journals from the bin, flop onto their desks (usually the ones I assigned) and then write for five minutes on a quote, saying, or song lyric that either I, or they, had chosen.

The morning that my feelings about teaching turned from desperation to despair, I chose one of my favorite Modest Mouse songs. "And that's how the word began. And that's how the world will end..."

This particular morning was bright; sunlight glittered through the glass windows and the fake-stained glass Jason has forced me to make with cellophane, but which added a subtle beauty to the room. We were three minutes into the song and the thirteen children, of the 27 on my roster, had relatively settled in, when Steven strode in, eyes flashing, eyes on me.

By this point in the year, most in the room kept writing, but I felt a few eyes shift away from their personal words and onto the scene unfolding in front of the room.

"Hey, Steven, it's been a few weeks. I'm glad you're here. Your tardy is noted. Please grab your journal and–"

Snipped off.

"Miss Eckhardt, why'd you fail me?" Loudly.

I put one hand up, a feeble gesture, an attempt at relating a calm. "Steven... "

"Huh?" He stepped towards me, crowding me, his posture ruffled and threatening, his rigid body towering over me, staring me down. He took another step, his Nike toe close to my Converse, so close I could feel him breathing, a whoosh of breath.

"S., you haven't been to class in weeks." Softly, the shame, ever-present ache of wanting to save and failing, was seeping into my voice. But I did not step back, or move my toe.

His fury poured from his skin: he defined fuming. He held his progress report in one fist, crumpled, his knuckles clutched white. His eyes narrowed.

"S., we can talk about this later. Right now I'd like you to..."

"No, no, that's some bullshit, Fuck that. You failed me. But, hey, that's OK." Humorless laugh. "You're gonna regret that when I shoot you flat in your ugly fucking face."

And he was gone, yanking the door so that it banged back against the wall.

Three days later, Steven was caught trying to smuggle a handgun onto campus. It was in a backpack that he attempted to fling over the fence.

It was fully loaded.

Clark's State Test Scores

Second lowest in the district. Only the alternative school's scores were lower.

I overheard in the teacher's lounge, "What did we expect?"

Exactly what Clark expected. Nothing.

Teacher Evaluation

I received three evaluations over the course of my first year, observations by the coaches and principals meant to support my progress and ultimately determine whether I was hired for a second year. I don't even remember them happening. I received virtually the same comments each time. We had no conversation, or follow-up about these little progress reports, and the scribbled notes in the "comments" box meant little to me.

Points of Excellence:

- Evaluation 1: Use of materials effective, lesson plans printed and clear, students working
- Evaluation 2: Agenda and objective clearly posted, classroom management improving, lesson plans strong
- Evaluation 3: Agenda and lessons clearly posted, students appear engaged and focused

Ways to Improve:

- Evaluation 1: No use of Promethean SmartBoard visible. You are required to use this daily.
- Evaluation 2: Continued lack of Promethean SmartBoard use. You are required to use some form of technology daily.
- Evaluation 3: Continued lack of Promethean SmartBoard use. You are required to use this daily. If lack of use continues, disciplinary action will be taken.

Over the year, I sent more than a dozen different supply requests for a new SmartBoard bulb. I never received one.

Rush Hour

The teacher down the hall poked her head in the door and asked if I'd be using the TV, on its rolling stand, for the next few days.

I might, I replied. We were watching a documentary, to supplement our readings about Rwanda.

She laughed. "You're still trying to *teach,* this late in the year?"

I said, too snottily, "We have six weeks left of school."

Her smile faded. "You can lay off. State testing's over—nothing more to be done, now. It's not our culture to teach after state testing. I need the TV to show *Rush Hour II.* Let me know when you're done with it."

It was about this time I began to think that, perhaps, this whole "teaching thing" was not for me.

Try Again

Deciding to return to teaching for another year began in the most unlikely of places—a small, darkly lit bar in the heart of the French Quarter, where I met with Marc for the first time.

Spring had burst up New Orleans like ripe fruit. I rode my freshly scarred and rebuilt red bike through the humid sensuous streets, damp with rain. Tourists kissed under iron-wrought overhangs, sloshing Hand Grenade drinks over each other's shoulders. It was April.

Despite the hardship of the year, I was still glittering with the last remnants of idealism. And I held it closely to me—I believed so much more than I was able to accomplish. And terrifyingly, my idealism was rapidly being replaced with something that alarmed me—a feeling of bitterness, and of dismay. I was in a high stakes position and feeling constantly like a failure. Sure, I had won teacher of the week—twice!—it wasn't hard to do when the teacher down the hall was in a relationship with the captain of the football team—but it wasn't enough.

It felt insurmountable.

Emboldened by two glasses of wine, I told Marc exactly what I thought—that every kid can learn. I told him that ineffective teaching was unacceptable. I told him I believed that every kid is capable, and wants to learn, and the system I was immersed in prevented well-intentioned people from truly making an impact.

And I told him I loved teaching, but couldn't continue in the situation I was in. I told him I was working hard and doing my best, but not to expect much when he came to see my class.

"Everything is wrong except the kids," I recall saying. "They deserve so much more."

Earlier that week, Marc had contacted me with a quick email reading, "I hear you might be job hunting. Can we meet to talk?" I had originally met Marc when he taught a workshop for the teachNOLA Institute, and, as any first year teacher would be, was more than impressed. His workshop on the first days of school was the epitome of what I wanted my classroom to look like.

In my first syllabus, I called my students "scholars" and bought a homework stamp and hand sanitizer, just as he recommended. Orderly entrance and dismissal strategies had come directly from his recommendation.

Marc came to see my classroom the next week. I met him five minutes before class started. He walked in and said, "Oh, it's really beautiful in here," and I blushed with pride.

Marc, like me, did not look at the broken windows—he looked at the cellophane, dipped in morning sun. He looked at the poetry wall, at the bright poster board posters the students had created as collages with their first proofread and rewritten paragraphs. He asked without interrogating. He made me feel like I wanted to feel—like I was working hard, and that I had a lot of work to do.

He stayed for the class, notebook poised and ready to take notes. I was sick with nerves for the first two minutes, and then largely forgot about him, consumed in the routines and maintenance of the delicate drama.

The class ran as smoothly as it usually did. The seventeen students in attendance rotated between their different groups. We identified the central idea in our text, conducted fluency practice, and had silent reading time. They largely ignored the visitor in the room, busy with annotations and discussion.

At one point, Jada sucked her teeth at another student for taking too much time while considering an answer. As she began to roll her eyes, I said sharply, "Jada, that was rude. Unacceptable." She paused, considered an outburst—she was rather adept at them—and instead shrugged.

I worried, at the time, that I had spoken too sharply, that he would think I was rude or cruel to speak to children that way.

But when we met later, Marc told me that was what he loved the most.

"You told a child she was rude, and it was still a brief and efficient interaction. You aren't afraid to call things what they are, and she knew you still loved her despite the correction.

"There is enough love and safety in your room for you to be able to make these corrections. You have built a room that doesn't backlash against correction because it's clear, the amount of mutual respect."

The worst part?

Lamar sleeping, two other children doing zero work. This, on my part, is unacceptable.

Marc saw in me a fierce commitment, and an unquenchable desire to learn, to do this work better for children, a potential for great teaching with practice and time. He hired me to join the founding staff of a new charter school he was forming called Sci Academy.

The First Year

I began that first year as a public school teacher ready to single-handedly close the achievement gap with a book, high expectations, and a smile.

By midyear, I was managing my reactions, not crying every night, and only occasionally throwing up because of shot nerves. Johnathan and my family watched me, helpless, as I struggled through the weeks, taking one day off, and then working a twelve-hour day on Sunday to hold the strings together.

The daily struggle to maintain safety in a classroom was a challenge; making what teachNOLA called "significant gains" seemed impossible.

But I gained ground, each day. An extra piece of homework submitted, an extra chair filled. An extra member of the book club each week. An extra wave from a bus window. Each day, small increments.

What I loved most were the kids, and their moments of great strength. I even loved their chaos, in such stark contrast to my sharp-edged existence, their smiling deliberations over hard texts, their dedication.

I did reach many of them; they trusted me, and were relatively open with me about their deficiencies. But I knew that I wasn't meeting all of their needs, and this sense of failure made me depressed and discouraged.

I struggled this year because the rules were always changing. The children I worked so hard for were swallowed up in the roar of poverty, inconsistency, illiteracy, high-stakes testing, failure, truancy, and teachers, like me, meant well but were ill-equipped to do anything except love them, work hard, and hope that the love would be enough to push through another day.

Work, belief, and love: I could give these infinitely.

But I couldn't grow without tending and I needed the sun.

PART

3

The Future is Now

YEAR ONE: WE ARE NEVER DONE. WE ARE NEVER FINISHED.

The Promise

To recruit students for Sci Academy, Marc literally went door to door.

I can imagine some of the questions he was asked:

Q: So, you're a new school?
A: Yes. Brand new, just starting with 100 freshmen, but in four years we will grow into a full four-year high school.

Q: "Where will you be located?"
A: Behind what used to be Livingston Elementary, in New Orleans East.

Q: Wasn't Livingston flooded during Katrina?
A: Yes, but we'll be on a piece of property behind it.

This would cause major confusion for years to come. Google Maps directed visitors to this abandoned, decimated structure, and the modular trailers we were housed in were not visible from the street. The less informed would be startled by this dismay of a building, not knowing a drive around it would reveal our cluster of trailers, half hidden behind the weeds growing in the deserted football field with its one broken-leg goalpost, half standing.

Q: "Do you have a staff?"
A: "Not a full one, I'm hiring now."
Q: How do you get in?
A: The school is open enrollment, free tuition, college prep. Anyone can come to our school, regardless of where they have been before, or what kind of education or background they have. Any scholar can learn, and with us, *your child will go to college.*

To a population that had largely been written off, this assurance seemed like fool's gold.

The academic quality of most schools in New Orleans had been atrocious for many years before the storm, except for the rare sprinkling of selective-enrollment schools, or private schools whose tuition, in most cases, was double the family income of the average New Orleanian. The assumption for the impoverished population of the city was that it would continue to fill the minimum wage jobs needed in a city dependent on hospitality: janitors; dishwashers; short-order cooks.

The low expectations in areas of poverty and vicious inequity bred a lack of anticipation, an unwilling acceptance. Without recourse, the lowest socioeconomic levels of New Orleans continued to stagnate.

Marc sat in the living rooms of each and every child who signed up for Sci Academy's inaugural year and promised that every one of their children would be ready to go to a four-year college, would be successful.

100 families took a chance on us. They signed their ninth grader up to attend a school that had no building, no staff, and no curriculum. They signed up based on a promise.

The vision of Sci Academy is to prepare all scholars for college success, equipped with the passion and tools to begin innovative and world-changing pursuits.

We believed this vision. But, as we quickly found out, belief was not enough.

Green Grows

I was, by far, the greenest member on the staff.

Marc later said that he recognized in me a desire to get better at teaching. Even more, I had a need to feel like hard work produced results in kids and improvement in myself. I could promise him deep and unwavering commitment and love, if he could guide me to the outcomes for myself and for kids that I had been seeking.

Outcomes without chaos and violence.

Safety to try and fail and make progress with guidance, and to seek feedback.

Just like our students, I needed structure, and direction, and a place I could improve.

Marc's philosophy was to measure talent in desire and commitment rather than ability; he valued passion over experience. He sought out those willing to work hard, take feedback, change when needed, and train with him unquestioningly. This training was not a time for critical thinking, but a time for learning at light speed, a time to prepare to do what few had done: start and maintain a school in one of the most decimated school districts and neighborhoods in the country.

Moreover, he intended to do this with *high school* students. Our belief that ninth grade was not too late to prepare any child for college was a tall order—but that belief would be both the boat and the wind in the sails in the days ahead.

If it took walking in straight lines and memorizing words in order, I was already on the way.

School Values

A values-based school is larger than itself. It has training wheels, bumper bars, guiding lights, litmus test strips for decisions. Unlike the reactive, emotion-driven environment I had come from, having a set of values—knowing, teaching, living, and speaking with them—created a code. It was a way to interact, to aspire to, to encourage the best in each other.

Achievement: We focus on results and do whatever it takes to accomplish our goals.

Respect: We treat every person and every thing the way we want to be treated.

Responsibility: We look to ourselves to do what needs to be done.

Perseverance: We never give up.

Teamwork: Helping a member of our team is helping ourselves. When one rises, we all rise.

Enthusiasm: We remain positive. Our positivity give us strength.

Marc selected these six values during his yearlong training with New Leaders for New Schools. Some—respect, teamwork—resonated with me because of my experiences during my first year. The lack of respect and teamwork at my former school left me curious and desirous for these values. Others—perseverance, enthusiasm—I felt more comfortable with, at least within myself.

Each one felt like a levee. For a year, I had erected sandcastles on an uncertain shore, battled tyrant waves, tended my hastily erected structures from the constant storm. At Clark, I felt constantly isolated, alone on an unfamiliar coastline. With these values, with this team, I felt stronger, more equipped to defend the darkening coastline.

The repetition of the word "we" was my favorite part.

No more I.

We.

Freedom

The seventh value, crossed out at some point in Marc's school planning brainstorm. Freedom isn't an inherent value. It's a reward for hard work. Freedom comes when achievement has happened. It comes with respect and personal responsibility for our actions. It comes with perseverance towards a goal, never in a vacuum, always with joy.

I wasn't in the mood for freedom. I'd had way too much freedom at my previous school, without enough achievement.

So put the black line through freedom. Douse me in some enthusiasm and send me back to my team. Clear instructions suited me just fine.

Deliberate

There are no random actions or wasted words in Marc.

Every action is deliberate. He plays chess confidently with the future and the children's stakes are high.

He has made promises—to his teachers, to funders and the board, and most importantly to the children who bump or rattle or bop or stomp off the bus each morning, shake his hand as he meets their eyes and asks them "Why are you here?" and they say "To learn."

Marc's singular commitment and vision was, and is, palpable.

To stand near him is to stand next to a lightening rod of kinetic action. When he is still, it is for effect: intentional and dramatic pause. He is three weeks ahead, anticipation in motion, his focus of the scholars and their future formulating the answer to every question.

He is the architect of an intended destiny, and I rapidly became the zealot of his construction crew, scanning the horizon for the next motion, a constant contrived push towards closing the achievement gap.

Value Village

Celebration of value-aligned successes is an integral part of the Sci Academy team. On the first day, Marc assigned us to a person to watch. We had to be ready at lunch to describe what value we had seen in that person. We gathered in a circle in the narrow hallway. Marc asked us to smile and snap with both hands, joyfully. Then we would take turns calling out each other, pointing to the value we had exhibited, and how.

"The explanation is the most important part," he explained. "Connect it to the definition of the value, make it meaningful."

Shoutout-giver: I've got a shoutout for Jacob!

Everyone: Jacob!

Shoutout-giver: For the value of teamwork. Jacob took a moment to push my thinking when we were talking today, and we both learned from the conversation. He understands that when one rises, we all rise.

We went around in a circle and shouted out our assignments. My fingers began to cramp from all the snapping, and others began to pause, wiggle their fingers, and then snap again. We all showed enthusiasm and perseverance during that first Value Village.

Later, we dropped the snapping, replacing it with vigorous slapping of hand on the thighs. We added a chant at the end, and a final shouting of the name.

In print, the whole process sounds at best trite, and at worst ridiculous, but when a group of people are working hard together, taking a moment to notice the best parts of each other is invigorating and reaffirming.

Value Village reminded us of who we were. A rhythmic reaffirmation, beat out lightly upon khakis. We are values-aligned. We support and love each other. We have an intense and lofty vision, and each day we act in ways that move us towards it. We are a team. We believe in ourselves and our work. And we do it with sincere love of each other and our accomplishments.

Home Visit

Each new Sci Academy scholar received a home visit from Marc and one of us, his fledgling teachers. We knocked on many doors that summer, calling ahead first, scheduling and rescheduling, sweat tracing down our collars in the July inferno.

I was nervous on my first visit. I wanted to impress the family and also to learn to do a home visit on my own. In the end, we would spend at least an hour with each family, discussing the family handbook and explaining all the rules.

Parents would sit down with their potential scholar, many of them looking far too young to be entering high school, others looking wizened, far too old.

Quintrell, toothpick poking from the side of his mouth, shifting it back and forth in response to surprise information. "I hear y'all don't got a football team. No sports at all. Your school gonna be any fun?"

Sebrina, slouched back into the couch cushions, pillow clutched to her chest, staring out of the window at the hazy skyline. Every time we asked her if she understood, her quiet nod was meant to please, but was not indicative that true comprehension was taking place. To everything: "OK...Yes, ma'am."

Malik, sucking his teeth at every rule and saying, "Naw, naw, I can't do that," and looking at his tightlipped mother pleadingly. In response his mother would raise an eyebrow and shake her head sassily. "This is a *good* school. You going to a *good* school."

Ann, hand draped over her prominent belly, shyly peeking out from beneath her bangs and lashes, fluttering. "What happens when I have my baby?"

Tyler and his sister Keira were both entering the ninth grade, though one was a year older than the other. They looked nothing alike but had so many of the same mannerisms, both staring down at their tapping feet or scratching a skittish itch at the nape of their neck.

"So, we can get a detention just for talking in class?"

"Three field trips a year? That's what's up!"

"Two hours of homework? A night? You serious?"

Most memorable was Darius, filled with questions and a body blinking with kinetic energy.

Darius had been Kaitlin's student from the previous year. Kaitlin had leaned on him hard to sign up with Sci Academy, explaining that it would be safe. Darius was a pile of spindly arms and legs, knobby knees, pointed elbows, and a birthmark crossed his forehead like a deserted island. He had been mercilessly bullied at his former school, and Kaitlin had kept him in her room at lunch and protectively walked him to the bus each evening. Despite these precautions, Darius was terrified and wanted to go to a school free of harassment and ridicule.

He met me at the door for his home visit. I heard him bellow, "They're here!" and the house seemed to quiver with the resounding of his feet rushing down the hall to the front door. He flung it open and stuck out his hand. His face was freshly scrubbed; water was still splashed on his collar. "Miss Kerrigan told me I should shake your hand when you got here. Hi, I'm Darius, come on in."

He grabbed my hand and pumped it vigorously, for more than fifteen seconds before dropping it, embarrassed. Then he ricocheted down the hallway, waving us in, and escorted us to the cramped living room, piled with boxes and a hodgepodge of lamps, tables, and overstuffed furniture. Along one wall, Darius's face was framed several times, a visual timeline: his school photo in eight by ten majesty. In each, he wore a toothy smile. In two, he wore the same shirt.

His aunt came down the hall and placed a hand on his bopping head. "Sit down Darius, these people here to talk to you about your new school." I smiled at her, and she reached for his collar, straightened it, a gesture so tender and fussy I glanced away, moved.

Darius, leaned forward with his elbows on his knees and his hands interlocked, bright eyes locked on mine. I introduced myself.

"Nice to meet you, Miss Eckhardt. This here's my Auntie. Miss Kerrigan said your school was different than other schools, I was gonna learn something."

"He wasn't learning nothing at his other schools," Auntie interjected. "His teacher say y'all doing things different over there at your new school."

I rose to shake her hand, as well. "We're trying, Ms..."

"Taylor. Darius's been with me for awhile now."

"Ms. Taylor, we are trying to build a place where every child, er, *scholar,* can learn and prepare for college. I'm here to walk you through how the school might be different."

I opened with the million dollar difference: that in the course of a lifetime, a person with a college degree would, on average, make $1,000,000 more than someone without a college degree.

Darius's eyes widened, a vigorous neck-jarring head nod proffered when I asked, "Do you want that $1,000,000?

I told Darius about his "2.0," a metaphor for his future self.

"Right now, Darius, you're fourteen—Version "1.4" for yourself. Where do you think you'll be at age twenty?

The answer, with no hesitation: "Playing football, probably for the Saints."

I kept a neutral face; I had heard the "playing professional football" line from most of the boys I visited. The facts that none of them had ever played on a disciplined team, or that Sci did not plan on having a football team, and even if we did have one, these boys had a 0.08% chance of playing professionally, did not dissuade this vision for the future.

"Well, you'll be twenty, and in college, so maybe you'll be playing for LSU." If you're one of the 5.8% of high school students who make the transition to college, I thought. "If you're getting all your homework done, and participating in class, and working hard and persevering, your 2.0 is relaxing, he knows how to study for his exams and to manage his time. He got good grades and knows what success feels like. But if 1.4 isn't handling his business, is fooling around or getting detention, his 2.0 is gonna really struggle. He's not going to know the difference between mitosis and meiosis in his classes; he's not going to be able to break down the word antidisestablishmentarianism to figure out what it means. Everything counts now, Darius—the future is now. Everything you do will either help, or hurt, your 2.0. Understand?"

"That's me, for sure. I mean, the first one." Darius assured me, head whipping north and south.

Ms. Taylor placed a soothing hand on Darius's bouncing shoulder again, and paid close attention to my explanation that, though academics would be harder, Darius would receive a lot of help. Teachers were available by cell phone until ten o'clock every night, even weekends. Though the school day was longer—eight thirty to five—Fridays were half days for students who didn't have detention.

Darius again was very insistent—he never planned to get detention.

"Well, everyone will probably get detention at some point. That doesn't make you a bad student—it just means you have something to learn. Detention is supposed to teach you how to do things differently."

Then, we had a lesson in how—exactly—scholars would sit in classrooms: SPARK.

S—sit or stand up straight.

Following my modeling, Darius scooted forward to the end of the couch, yanked his spine rigid.

P—Place hands on desk or pencil to paper

"Because what are hands doing in class if they aren't on the desk, Darius?"

"Um... fooling around? Checking a cell phone?"

"Exactly."

A—Ask and Answer Questions

R—Respect at all times

Darius didn't balk at this—many of the other children did, respect being more arbitrarily defined at times. We defined respect largely as the Golden Rule, and this made more sense to children whose past experience with the word was inequitable, especially in school.

K—Keep tracking the speaker

"Tracking means you look at the person speaking. If you speak to me, I'm going to look at you, If your Aunt is speaking, I'm going to look at her. It's respectful. It shows her that I'm listening."

This was my favorite part of the home visit, every time. Darius and I sat in perfect SPARK, and I would say, "Track me! Track your Aunt! Track the TV! Track the door!" Heads would turn, earnestly or incredulously, back and forth.

SPARK lesson completed, the home visit entered its final stages.

Dress code. Extremely strict, read all about it in the Family Handbook. Failure to comply means you cannot join your peers in class.

"Darius, you strike me as a rather sharp dresser. You'll have no problem looking sharp in your uniform."

Camellias bloomed in Darius's narrow cheeks, and his birthmark flared a pronounced isle.

Zero tolerance for fighting. When there was a threat of violence, only one option was allowed: walk away and tell the teacher. Some met this expectation in particular with naked awe. Others cocked their head sideways with open skepticism.

Darius said, "That means if someone hits me, I can't hit them back?"

I nodded my assent, and assured him that teachers would be present constantly—there would not be a time when he was alone.

The cell phone policy made Darius fidget a bit.

"I can't see it. I can't hear it. I can't even see a little corner of it poking out of your pocket. If we see it, we're going to have to take it."

STRIKE 1: loss of cell phone for a week

STRIKE 2: loss of cell phone for a month

STRIKE 3: loss of cell phone for the remainder of the year

"He don't have a cell phone," Auntie assured me, and Darius grimaced.

Next, Darius signed to show his commitment to the rules. When I asked him to put a star next to what might be hard for him, Darius selected five sentences, smearing a crooked five-point star in the margin.

I will always work, think, and behave in the best way I know how.

I will raise my hand and ask questions in class if I do not understand something.

I will avoid people, places, and things that I know will not help me have a successful future.

I am responsible for my own behavior, and I will follow the teacher's directions and school rules.

I will come to school each day with a positive attitude, ready to learn.

The last step of the home visit was to take a video, asking each scholar why they wanted to go to Sci Academy. I turned my computer around on my lap and pressed record. Darius stared at his own grinning reflection for several seconds shifting his head back and forth, before starting.

He said, quivering in his seat, "I want to go to Sci Academy because I want to go to a school that's organized, that knows what's going on, and where kids be learning. I want to go to college and play football so I'm gonna work really hard."

Quintrell said he wanted to go to Sci Academy to get a good education, mumbling around the toothpick and refusing to look at the camera, even when prompted. All of his body language closed him like a shutter, and when I turned the camera off, he got up without saying goodbye. As I left, I tried not to believe that, like rumblings before rain, his posture was not a forecast for future behavior problems to come.

Sebrina was fascinated by her own face peering back at her on the screen. When asked why she was choosing to be a scholar, she said simply, "It sounds like a good place."

Malik saw the camera and started in with an efficient tooth-suck, before remembering what we had just talked about: sucking your teeth is like swearing in church, and its disrespectful, which immediately gets you a detention. He paused the spittle mid-run through his back teeth and his face burst into a wide grin. "Sorry bout that. Umm... I wanna go to Sci Academy because I'm tired of the foolishness. My old school was messy, lots of drama, and dirty too. And the food was bad." A pause before mirroring his mother's words back: "I wanna go to a good school."

Ann was excited about services for her child, due in September. She was thankful that the school would send a teacher to tutor her until she could return to classes. She was glad that she was going to be able to be both a ninth grader and a mother.

Tyler scratched his neck again, leaving pink streaks on the skin. He said he used to get in trouble at his old school and wanted a change.

Kiera said she wanted to read books.

Each scholar I met that summer, and all the summers filled with home visits, could move me to tears. Whether mumbling like Jamal or proudly enunciating like Darius, each had a clear idea of who they were, and who they wanted to be. Some were insistent and specific; they no longer wanted to attend schools with dirty bathrooms covered in graffiti. They spoke of rotten milk in the cafeteria. They spoke of teachers who told them to shut up. They spoke of wanting to get away from their neighborhoods.

Most, though, spoke in stock phrases, using vague want statements that meant something unique to each of them, something more meaningful—if only they'd been taught the words.

Some were less shy, and more honest.

"My mom wants me to go here so I'll try."

"No other place was enrolling new students."

"The school I wanted to go to was destroyed in the storm."

"I want something new."

Football

During summer training for teachers, we would watch these videos, memorize faces, be moved by each face in turn. We wanted to be able to greet each one by their first name on their first Monday. We wanted their first impression to be both one of difference, and or welcome.

Marc warned me not to place too much importance on behavior during these visits. Children behave much differently in their home environments. It is impossible to predict behavior when they are provided new territory, a fresh start. But it was hard not to glow over Darius. He seemed like the epitome of the child we wanted to serve, the child bullied and ignored, ready for a second chance.

But Marc was right. I learned this lesson later, when after two months of exemplary behavior, Darius received a detention for gum chewing and talking in class. He exploded, inordinately furious over the humiliation of serving the detention I'd warned him he'd probably get eventually.

Over the next few weeks, Darius received a few more detentions, all for minor infractions accumulating: talking out of turn, slouching in his chair, not tracking. Upon receipt, each time Darius fell apart, and his tantrums spiraled into an incident when he went howling down the hallway yelling profanity.

After he'd calmed down I asked him what had changed from the summer, to now. I reminded him of his commitment. I expressed disappointment, but reminded him that every moment was a chance to change.

"Come on, Darius. You're better than this."

He replied, simply, "All these rules are bullshit."

He gave me a moment to digest his profanity, a hard swallow. I met his stubborn gaze, barely.

"I'm gonna play football. Football players don't walk in line and raise their arms straight."

Darius fell into a detrimental trap many of our students did. Through good behavior, a dash of sweetness, and a smile, Darius had been able to move through his previous years of schooling largely unnoticed. His inability to continue under the radar was hard for him and small exposures were humiliating. He responded poorly to our strict rules because of a combination of not needing them and never having had the chance to bend to any before.

I continue to wonder whether Darius struggled more because he refused to submit to the rules, or because the rules weren't necessary for him.

Applying the same rules to every child has its advantages, but in some cases it backfires. Darius, so willing to please, was confounded by his occasional inability to do so, even when the expectations were so clearly laid for him. In our desire to make the school a safe and achievement-focused place, sometimes scholars like Darius moved out of the spotlight. Because being "good" no longer helped him shine so brightly, Darius devised new ways to draw attention himself.

Meanwhile, scholars like Jamal flourished. They loved the positive adult attention, the equitable guidance, the predictability of one room to another. The rules were a compass with which to navigate the school and, upon following the arrows, they discovered to their great relief that it led to the support and acknowledgement they so craved.

We tried several interventions but Darius's behavior spiraled into daily chaotic choices that left him with a quantity of detention hours he would never be able to serve. After his behavior prevented him from attending the first field trip, he withdrew to a high school with a pathetic academic record, but a strong football team.

They never even let him play.

Blueprint

In week two, our DCI—the Director of Curriculum and Instruction—handed each of us a binder that contained our Scope and Sequence: the blueprint for our classroom instruction.

A Scope and Sequence takes the required standards set forth by the state for each grade level and breaks them into a logical map of instruction for the year. The scope indicates when students should reach a benchmark and when these will be assessed. The sequence, then, is the order in which these benchmarks are logically instructed. Teachers take the Scope and Sequence and develop units of learning and then lessons plans for each day.

In many schools, teachers develop their own Scopes, or the districts do this development for them. Increasingly however, especially in charter schools, DCI's are hired in part to be responsible for the path and progress of the curriculum and assessments for all of the classrooms. The DCI develops benchmark assessments aligned to the Scope and Sequence, so teachers can assess regularly how far along their students are, and what they still need to learn.

This framework is the logical basis of data-driven instruction: carefully planned assessments linked to instruction to give teachers specific data on what scholars do, and do not yet, know. This roadmap to student achievement begins with the Scope. It is the skeleton of the academic instruction in each room and a child's learning.

I was especially excited about getting my Scope and Sequence. I was thrilled to have a chance to really build a class, write a working syllabus, and get our scholars involved in ninth grade literature.

Reagan was teaching the Writing class, which meant I could focus on reading and coordinate writing assignments with her. I envisioned myself engaged in deep discussion about "The Most Dangerous Game" with a rapt audience, my students scribbling notes furiously and bantering over the various themes.

My reverie was interrupted, however, when I opened the binder to find an incomplete map. The Scope was only two pages long and the sequence seemed disjointed. The DCI explained that she wanted us to have freedom to develop our own ideas, and that we are free to make any changes. I had been under the impression that the opposite would be true, and that we would receive a ton of guidance, especially around the benchmarks and assessments.

I was an inexperienced teacher; I had never built anything like this before. The expectations for my classroom became instantly murky, and I had a moment of panic as I flipped back and forth between the two scant pages.

I keep my face even keel and glance at the other teachers. I was relieved and alarmed to note that their reactions were similar: confusion, stoicism, masked dismay. Reagan's brow was deeply furrowed; Logan eyes scanned his nearly empty pages.

Our DCI, an infinitely kind and empathetic woman, sensed our concern and asked us to discuss our reactions and share questions.

Questions were hesitatingly proffered, and the answers deepened our concerns.

The assessments hadn't been created yet.

We had no electronic system for collecting data together.

There were no plans to order textbooks. We should request what was needed and it would, if possible, be purchased.

There was no need to worry. We would work it out as we went along.

Later that afternoon, we were given free time, and we all trudged to our respective rooms. I stayed busy for a few minutes, pushing desks into different positions, picking at some tape on the edge of one of them as I eyed the deficient binder. Finally, I plopped into the chair behind my desk, flipped to the first page of the Scope, and said aloud, "I have no idea where to start." Hopelessness washed over me, and I stayed there, still and frozen with inaction.

I was so eager to be a part of the team, and that was a strange feeling for me—to fail would mean I didn't belong in this place, and that fear ran its undercurrents through every start I wanted to plan.

I wandered down the hall to Reagan's room, where she was sitting with Logan, glaring with bald frustration at her own white binder. We all took a drive, smoked an illicit cigarette, and tried to figure out what the first step should be. Try to rebuild? Ask for more? We felt awkward and a little blindsided. We had promised to set sail on this mission of college for all kids, and we had just discovered that our treasure maps were written in disappearing ink, and it had faded in the scalding August sun.

We parted ways at the top of the hallway, sucking peppermints, and headed back to our three-ring calamities. I stopped at the restroom, splashed water on my face, and stared myself down for a moment in the spotty mirror.

Back in my room, I grabbed a big box of crayon markers, permanent markers, and an old pair of rusty scissors abandoned in the bottom of my clunky aluminum desk. I covered a large section of the floor with sticky chart paper. I yanked the two pages out of their rings without bothering to click them open, and proceeded to cut them into strips. Seating myself on the floor in the middle of an islet of white, I began to rearrange them until I understood them, until their requirements felt consistent and logical to me. I taped them to the chart paper surrounding me, and then, careful not to leave too many footprints, hung each piece in order along the walls. I walked the sequence with a pack of sticky notes, jotting down any idea I had for what I could teach, when.

Over the next few days, I proceeded to use my room as a giant easel for my school year. Others stuck their heads in, looked around at the notes, arrows, markered graffiti and scribbles that surrounded me on all sides, and quickly left. After Marc's sessions were over at five o'clock, I stayed late, hammering away at the yearlong map, developing pages and pages of unit plans.

It took awhile to make it work—to translate the scribbles and Post-Its and ideas into something coherent, but in the end I developed a blueprint that I felt good about.

I realized that despite the fantastic team I had joined, I needed to return to my own methods of working, and that my process would be both different from others and it would take longer, because I'd never done it before.

I spent two weeks creating a new Scope and Sequence, and the units to support it. Each genre-based unit was broken down into understandings and questions, with a performance task and rubric created for each one, aligning to specific objectives and placed in a calendar. It was a meticulous effort that took many hours of my life. That time was in addition to an already packed workload of preparing my room, attending Marc's seminars, planning the first two weeks of orientation, and all the details that go into starting a school year.

But I was very proud of what I'd accomplished, both because I'd spent so much time on it, and because I felt like, for a first effort, it was very strong. Both Marc and the DCI gave it a big thumbs up—it returned from their scrutiny with a simple comment: "Looks good! Can't wait to see it in action!"

I glowed under this less than precise praise. The feeling of being nervous but... *prepared*.... came over me.

I should have been wary. The last time I felt this, the Sunday before my first day at Clark, I'd been woefully, tragically mistaken.

On My Door
I Promise You...

I believed in you before I even met you. I believe in you today. I will never stop believing.
I am already proud of who you will become. Thank you for the chance to be a part of it.

I love you more than you imagine. You are very, very important to me. You are the reason I am here.
I will give my time to you, even if I have none.
I will be honest with you, even when that honesty is hard.
I will treat your ideas, concerns, questions, and opinions with the utmost respect. You deserve it.

I will provide you with innumerable skills, strategies, guidance, and knowledge, and passions.
I will work tirelessly to ensure your academic and enduring success.

You will know what it means to love reading. Reading is life.
I will help you reveal the world in between the pages of every book.
Reading will bring you knowledge, and that knowledge will be your freedom.

Everything counts, has meaning and purpose.
I will be deliberate and thoughtful in the decisions I make about your education.
I leave nothing to chance, because that is disrespectful to your intelligence.

I will never give up or tire of helping you chase your dreams.
If your dream changes, we will change, too.
I will have higher expectations of you than you think possible. I will watch you SOAR.

I will not fly for you. I will teach you to fly.

Darkroom

The night before the first day of school, Marc asked all of us to drive out to school for a six o'clock meeting. The founding staff of Sci Academy sat in Reagan's classroom. Marc turned off the lights, and turned on music: "Pomp and Circumstance" filled the room as he read aloud the roster for the scholars arriving the next day. He asked us to picture each of them, the Class of 2012. What would they look like? How would they be impacted? What new knowledge would they have? What would we instill them with, to carry them through the next four years, and the rest of their lives?

We sat together in the dark, envisioning each one of their faces. After all, we had been watching their videos, looking at their pictures, memorizing their names, for the past month. As Marc called each name, I imagined them crossing the stage, embracing me, Reagan, Jacob. I realized that there would be other faces by then, other teachers who would join us next year and the year following. In my head it was still just us, a sturdy little team of believers seeing a dream move through entropy towards fruition.

With the lights out, only the red exit sign in the room shone brightly, and its subtle safelight filter through my eyelids reminded me of the darkroom in college, the smell of stopbath and fixer mingling was somehow fragrant. Like paper processing in a photo lab, with each name read, I imagined myself sliding their faces into the tray, and shifting the liquid smoothly over it. I sat in the plastic desk chair in a room cool but still moist, window condensating against the AC, and I watched both the children they were and the adults they would become emerge in the red-tinted light. Develop, stop, fix. Each face was both transparent and permanent, appearing before me, dreams no longer deferred.

Develop. Faces flush through the burned-in contrast. I thought of the ways they would need to grow and change over the next four years, the experience they would need to have if they were going to navigate the world beyond our trailer walls. What would they ask of me? Could I give it to them? What were all of the moments we had not yet anticipated?

Stop. When would our love and hard work not be enough for them? Where were the places we would start again? And more terrifying, what if we got the strip wrong? What if these scholars *were* the test strips?

After we had left the home visit with Ann's family, Francis, our extraordinary social worker and I met on the curb. Marc said, emphatically, "We cannot fail this family."

But it wasn't just Ann. We could not fail any of them.

Fix. How to establish a path for children, away from poverty, violence, and a history of inequitable and often disrespectful education? When is the right moment to step away, hang the print, allow the photograph to move forward in time of its own accord?

And to what extent does this work reflect back to our own efforts? For how much would we applaud each other, and over what moments would we cringe?

The night before that first day of school was very different from the one I'd experienced just a year before.

We had beauty that evening, and strength, and a closeness I'd rarely experienced. We shared a belief and a passion for making a welldeserved, necessary, and overdue shift in the way children were educated in our city. A time to close the shutters, work hard, and weather all storms. A time to flip on the safelight, roll up our sleeves, and do our work.

On my way out, I stuck my head in my classroom door, where "Reading Is Life!" bolted in bright colors from the wall. Over my desk was the painting Johnathan had done for me.

"Be the change you wish to see in the world."

I wanted, needed so desperately to be.

Catch Excellence

The scholars who arrived on the first morning of Sci Academy had no idea what to expect, but we'd been planning it for weeks. In fact, our final week before school began was spent largely rehearsing for that first day, anticipating every contingency. We had assigned demerits to imaginary children, redirecting them back into straighter lines. We had planned nonverbal gestures and a codeword to indicate a need for assistance or support, and called it a "Smac." We practiced whispering it to each other, as we pretended to escort children into the hallway for a one-on-one talk about their behavior.

We walked through the entire day, again and again, a rehearsal for an impromptu play.

We trusted that, though no one had attempted this level of structure for ninth graders, with the level of detail and specificity of a timed detonation, our little team would pull it off.

We had learned that everything mattered, and we planned, in every and all moments, to *chase perfection*.

First Day

Whatever my advisees expected, what they'd gleaned from their home visit or from their imaginings of what their first day of school would be like, it surely could not compare to the weighted silence, held in place largely by the peer pressure of everyone else remaining silent, blended with the warmth of loving teachers who gave them clear directions at every turn. A relief, in knowing exactly what is expected, and the lowtide roll of a culture of compliance that began the second their faces came out from beneath the awning of the sun, eyes squinting.

We met as a team at the end of the day and looked at each other, bewildered, and stunned. It had worked. And while many things would be harder than that first day, none had come with the seething roar of anticipation, followed with something akin to relief, and triumph.

We would never again spend so much time—a week!—on the planning of a single day as we did, and do, for the first. When the curtain rises, the culture must roil and roll out to meet the scholars, and we are the keepers of that temperature, at just the right degree.

The first day was over.

We spent the next four hours preparing for the next one.

Day Two, Three, Four...

Came and went with tremulous effort.

Troubling behaviors bubbled to the surface, but overall the level of compliance, and even joy, was very high. The vast majority of the scholars responded very well to the structure, and many embraced it, anxious for the praise and attention.

Teachers wrote little notes on Post Its, slipping them onto scholar clipboards.

You were so helpful with passing the papers this morning.
I can see how hard you're persevering today. Keep it up!
Great achievement on last night's homework!

Scholars wore these on their lapels, the only flair we did not ask them to remove. At lunch, they traded and counted them like baseball cards.

Yet some would struggle. We began, on the afternoon of the first day, to tentatively single them out, describe their struggles, and together create an action plan.

Terrence, lanky and sneering, refused to sit up in his chair, rebelliously slouching with his arms crossed and snatching his arm away with a loud, "Don't touch me, man!" if we approached him. He was racking up demerits for his backtalk and incessant gum chewing, and reminded me of some of my Clark students, little spark plugs waiting for the excuse to fire.

Tyler's sister remained sullen but attentive, especially to her advisor Reagan, but Tyler was already, in week two, demonstrating that he would not easily be coerced into good behavior. He watched Terrence carefully, mimicking his antics and even his saucy saunter down the hall. He was shyer than Terrence, but made up for it with stealthier flouts of the rules: pencil-throwing, a constant untucked shirt, the dreaded sunflower seeds.

These students' actions were the pings of rocks on glass. We did our best to teach them, again and again, the ways of being here, at the school, with us. In several one-on-one sessions, we explained the importance of college, how much work we have to do. We reviewed the rewards for good behavior, and emphasized the importance of every moment, and its impact on the future.

What you do today matters to your future.

The "future" was too vague and amorphous of a concept for children who had experienced it only through uncertainty. If their past experiences, their neighborhoods, Katrina, or former schools had taught them anything, it was to be distrustful of anyone who assured them that trust was the best policy.

Each teacher dealt with problems differently. I was stricken with agitation. Every infraction seemed to be the rock that would finally shatter our window; every sucked tooth and eye roll a reason to fear the final unraveling of our little universe. "What if all the other scholars begin to act this way? What happens then?"

Marc talked us all off our various ledges, and if he had his own, he never said. We practiced patience and reviewed the fact that nothing came easily and those who misbehaved the most probably needed something we couldn't yet see—we just had to keep looking.

The responsibility was, ultimately and always, with us.

And so we tried again, etching perseverance and responsibility like ciphers, a cryptogram for the answers to unlocking a future brighter and farther reaching than, "Tyler, please spit out the gum. That's two demerits, and I know you'll make sure not to repeat the mistake."

Discipline

It takes constant diligence, and a lot of choosing not to second-guess the action, and just moving forward, following the decisions of the team and the expectations we began to teach from day one. It is not an easy moment to give a fifteen-year-old a demerit because her shoe stepped outside of a black line, or for whispering to a neighbor in the hallway, or for having pink hearts on their white socks. It is hard to believe, in those moments, that these things matter.

I learned from Marc in summer training how these small things matter. I sat in all of the discussions about "everything counts" and the broken windows theory. But it is another thing entirely to meet the incredulous look of a teenager who just got a demerit for having the wrong-colored hair tie or for not raising their hand quickly enough.

Every night, in the quiet of home, I had to reaffirm to myself that what we were building was important, and that each piece counted. If one scholar chewed gum and wasn't penalized, the next day I'd be stepping in it in the hallway...and I might as well go back to my old school.

The small things matter. Managing small expectations prevents larger issues form occurring.

The details define excellence. Everything counts.

Connotation In The Details

student | stü-d∂nt | noun: a person who is studying at a school or college
2 a person receiving knowledge from experts or specialists

scholar | skä-l∂r |noun: a person who is highly educated or has an aptitude for study
2 a person actively seeking knowledge from experts or specialists

Assumptions

According to new research conducted by Measures of Effective Teaching (MET) Project, classroom control and time on task is the number one indicator of value-added data.

Translated out of teacher talk, this means that the more time students spend learning in a classroom, the better their achievement over time will be.

For children, no matter what their age, learning ways to be on task means learning first, what that means, what it feels like and looks like. It means practice.

The worst thing you can do to a child is to assume that "they know better."

Do they?

Have they been taught, truly taught, the right way to do what you're asking them to do?

Who taught them? Their family? Community? Other teachers? Expecting that a child knows the proper way to behave makes assumptions about their background, and those who have had an influence on them in the past.

Better to approach every child as a blank slate.

Teach first, and then hold them to a new expectation for their actions. They cannot own their actions until we tell them what to own.

Teach first, ensure you've been very clear, teach them what you need from them, explain why you need it.

Teach first, teach everything, then practice to perfection, and also remember they are children, and will need reminders of their new learning.

Assume that we all come from different life experiences. Saying, "Be quiet," to a child who does not experience quiet in the same way I do is pointless. The assumption is that only by teaching exactly what we wanted could we hold them to the behaviors we needed to see, in order to increase time on task, and therefore increase scholar achievement.

This was not a condescending training of children. This was preparing for a marathon whose terrain was rocky and stakes were excessively high. Four years. All scholars. College.

Uniforms

I lobbied for every teacher to have to wear the uniform, exactly as the kids do, every day of the week, all year. We did this for the first two weeks, but why stop there? How powerful would the modeling be if we modeled the correct uniform all year long?

Reagan shuddered. "Thinking about wearing nothing but this uniform every day makes me want to cry." The possibility rightfully terrified her.

Uncompromising, I still pushed—me, formerly of the green cape and bare feet. "Think of the solidarity with the children!" I said. "Think of how powerful the message would be."

We both left the conversation unswayed. I consider this debate now and shudder at my own foolishness.

But I *am,* by nature, a zealot. As assuredly as punk rock grabbed me at age fifteen, or Japanese at age twenty, Sci Academy was my new altar, and I was bound to drag everyone through the same austerities.

This may have been the first wedge between Reagan and myself. I was a fanatic; she was, in these first weeks, still agnostic. We inhabited the same church, but said very different prayers each night, and I was both stubborn and idealistically pragmatic.

In the end, we established a dress code that required teachers to wear ties and to put on the uniform every Friday—that made me feel somewhat vindicated.

Me, I wore the uniform every day all the way through September, before a desire for a change of shoes forced me out of khakis.

Common Language

Dialect, familiar words, turns of phrases and similar sayings sprout from the core of a strong culture. In trying to build one, we started with a set of common catch phrases to emphasize our value system and create a unified way of delivering messages to the children.

I used these phrases constantly in my classroom, a Morse code to communicate their inevitable future.

When a scholar's eyes began to wander from a book or assessment: *Focus. Desire.*

An "I'm done" might elicit: *We're never done; we're never finished*, or *Assign Yourself.*

A foolish moment in class might spark a spatter of laughter, at which I would call out: *Silly to serious!* This even became a chant in my room. I'd say "Silly to," and snap. The scholars would respond, "Serious!" and the room would go back to focused work.

Minor mistakes, sloppy homework: *Show me college! Everything counts!*

Missing work, late work, any attempt at alibi or explanation for less than meeting my expectations: *No shortcuts. No excuses.*

To emphasize responsibility, or a lack thereof: *Handle your business.*

My favorite inspiring words for difficult times: *Without struggle, there is no progress... and no greatness. Chase perfection, catch excellence.*

If a scholar spoke harshly to another, or was overtly critical of an answer or response: *Be nice or neutral and nothing else!*

When needing someone to pay attention, a gentle reminder: *Track the speaker.*

Often, scholars will want to discuss an "emergency" situation, right in the middle of class. To solve it quickly, we would say, *Time and Place*, indicating that the problem would be discussed but at a different one.

For the slacker: *Push beyond the break! Go above and beyond!*

For the sneaky, those struggling with maturity or a need for supervision: *How do you live your life when no one is watching? Do the right thing without being told.*

For a moment of floundering: *Fail forward!*

To inspire in times when other students from "easier" schools might mock them: *Tower above the rest.*

To ask for more from an answer: *Stretch yourself. Dig Deeper.*

Finally, the school's motto as well as a catchall for any moment of struggle, sacrifice, or success: *The future is now.*

Snaps

We taught the scholars to snap, loudly and enthusiastically.

This was their one non-structured participation, and it became a constant interjection. Scholars would snap to agree with answers, let a teacher know they too were thinking the right thoughts when someone else was called on. Scholars snapped when they liked something, when they were excited, when they learned something, or when they wanted to express joy.

On a good day, my classroom sounded like a slam poetry event, with scholars snapping for each other and for themselves and, sometimes, for me. Visitors who observed this quirky behavior found it charming. For me, it was essential—an outlet for joy and enthusiasm within a structure where even the volume of the voice was regulated.

Advisory

Eleven ninth graders entered my care this year—it would soon be ten. Eleven girls, who traveled together through their first lessons, sat together at their lunch tables, became the LSU Advisory—so named because of my alma mater. For the next four years, their academic, behavioral, and social accomplishments and shortcomings would be mine to explain. I was beholden to their families for phone calls and their report cards, as well as detention announcements and behavioral progress reports.

It is not easy, as a high school teacher, to truly be close to all of your scholar's families. Though I had tried the year before at Clark, it simply wasn't possible. It is not nearly as hard to be responsible and close with a small few, and this advisory program reflected the idea that families needed a point person at a school—and scholars needed someone to whom they could be eternally accountable.

My advisees were my charges, my missions, my great responsibility beyond being a teacher. I checked their homework, drove them home, walked them to detention, pouting and crying, I told them when they were amazing, and had made me proud, and I never hesitated to let them know when they disappointed me, and themselves.

They became my family too, these girls I saw each morning, in class, at lunch, throughout the day. When we sat in the darkroom and pictured each face, I saw theirs the most clearly, these girls-soon-women. I beamed my dreams upon them like a spotlight; I held them to the standards I dreamt for them at night. Their constant presence was a gauge of my success and faltering, not just as a teacher, but the mentor and educator I wanted to be.

Rickia, the quiet leader of our group; the most mature, and the greatest peacekeeper. She kept track of upcoming dates, reminded me when birthdays were coming, who likes what kind of cake, and kept me updated on catty drama when it was time to intervene.

Katina, another one of Katlin's former students, whose rebellious nature couldn't overcome her ability to win, and break, adult hearts. Haunted by her desire to remain a child and be respected as a grown-up, she would eventually pickpocket bad decisions until I couldn't see her beneath the pile.

Erica, picked on playfully but constantly for her books, her grades, her lilting voice, would turn out to represent the best of our school's definition: all scholars.

My LSU Ladies were different from other advisories. We were edgy, and cranky, and emotional, but we were fiercely loyal to each other, and more than one verbal fight was started over insults to another member of the Lady Tigers. We weren't filled with team spirit, but we had a sense of ourselves and an accountability to each other.

That being said, the advisories all shared one thing in common. Each member was loved, ferociously and fervently, by their advisor, and The LSU Ladies were no exception. I loved, and love each of them, with a raw strip of feeling that sometimes clouded me. My love for their families, as well, evolved sometimes too intimately.

It was a love I could only be allowed to feel in a school like this one—a school that builds the space for this kind of love to cultivate and take deep root. Though sometimes it was hard to manage, this love gave rise to a new feeling for all of us: pure, unadulterated hope.

A New Broken Window

In these first weeks, I thought a lot about Jason, his tiny face in the corner of my vision, a pebble flying through the air, nicking away at the glass.

I thought of the hairline fractures in my former classroom's window panes, which I had plastered over with colorful cellophane, filtering the thick yellow sunlight. Sometimes windows break, despite our best efforts. That doesn't mean the effort isn't worth it, every time.

I thought of him every time our team discussed Broken Windows theory, which explains that, basically, a community will maintain what is already beautiful and appears to be supervised. But if a window is left broken, the community will assume that no one cares, and no one is responsible—moreover, that another broken window won't make much of a difference. Yet if a window is quickly repaired, it is far less likely to ever be smashed again—and its neighboring panes receive the same deference.

In my neighborhood, I see this constantly where neighbors allow their dogs to defecate all over the church's lawn, adding pile to pile. Walking across the expanse of grass, badly in need of trimming, is taking the soles of your shoes into a messy minefield. But the beautiful garden and verdant lawn down the street is left free of this odoriferous detritus. The church's lawn allows these offerings to go unmaintained; no one cleans them, and one pile leads to five.

Yet the well-maintained garden, with its hibiscus and swamp lily, remains pristine. The large grassy areas walled in by flowers are spacious and well maintained. It looks cared for; *loved*. When I walk my own dogs by, I yank them away from this little Foamflower oasis and obviously others do too.

I had intuited this concept each time I covered the chipped and cracked panes of glass in my window at Clark, and each morning when I swept up stray balls of notebook fringe from the floor. Unraveling is averted if the beginning string is immediately cut, the end tied firmly back in place.

The little things matter, and, I might add, beauty and structure matter, too.

I attempted to prevent my own Broken Windows by mending the cracks.

I thought of Jason and smiled.

He taught me, in our colorful little battle for the windows, what professors and scientists have been studying for years. He taught me to reinforce beauty daily, to focus on details, and to seek the level of order I envisioned each and every day.

Graffiti of a Different Kind

"No way Miss Eckhardt. You ain't coloring on my shoes."

Our uniform policy was absolutely uncompromising. All black or all white shoes. Not a smidgen of color, anywhere. No green stitching or neon shoelaces. No off-colored insignia. No grey or midnight blue. The colors and styles were as clear in boundary as penalty. An uncorrectable uniform meant an inability to attend class.

With his red Nike Swoosh, Dominick was not going to class.

Unless we could color it in? I pulled out my marker.

"No way, Miss Eckhardt. *No Way.*"

I waited patiently.

"Dominick, it's your choice, but it seems silly to me for you to miss out on your education, one step on your path to college, because of a little bit of red on your shoe."

"You right, Miss Eckhardt. So let me slide this time, and I won't ever wear them again."

"Can't do that, Dominick. If I let you through, I have to let others through. Or others who made the right choice and colored their shoes would believe the rules to be unfair or bendable. I can't have that. No shortcuts, no excuses."

He just glared at me, but his eyes seemed to soften, a little.

"You need to handle your business and fail forward on this one. Fix the problem. Or we have to call home and someone bring you a pair of white or black shoes."

Eyes solidified again. "Ain't no one home."

"Come on Dominick. I would hate for you to miss class. It's an unexcused absence—you know you can't make up the work. Let's just get this done."

"So?"

"Dominick." I met his eyes. "You came here because you wanted something different for your life. This feels like it doesn't matter, but it does. We want you and everyone focused on college, not on uniform issues. If you have a uniform issue, I have to fix it. That's my job. I get in trouble with my boss; that's just how it works. Can we solve this problem? Right now? Together?"

Dominick sighed, deeply aching, conflicted, and then placed his foot onto the chair beside him. I was conflicted, too. He wouldn't be able to return these shoes now, but neither would he be able to wear them again—he still would have to replace them for a uniform compliant set. The Nike shoes looked expensive, and I wondered if his family could afford the extravagance for a second pair.

Broken windows were broken windows, and a Red Swoosh was definitely one of the proverbial ping-and-cracks.

Looking away, as if I were about to pull a splinter or peroxide a bleeding wound, he said, "Go 'head. Do what you've gotta do."

Swiftly, before he changed his mind, I colored in the red Nike Swoosh with permanent marker, attempting to stay within the lines. When I said, "All done," he held out his pass to class without meeting my eyes. I reached out to touch his shoulder and he pulled away from me, but on his way out, he mumbled, "See you in class, Miss Eckhardt," and I knew we'd be OK.

Hurricane

Two weeks into school, Gustav crept up the Gulf and made landfall on our coast. We evacuated, and schools were closed for a week.

Kaitlin and her boyfriend Matt came over. I met them on the steps of our Bywater home, handed them two of Johnathan's homemade beers, and said, "We gotta drink 'em before the power goes and they get hot." We spent the next several hours watching our favorite weatherman, Bob Breck, describe the increasingly urgent situation, debating whether to wait it out or head for higher ground.

Kaitlin finally made the best point. "It won't be the hurricane that's bad, probably. Do you want to be here," she gestured to our high ceilinged apartment—"for a week while they figure out how to turn the power back on? I'm not scared of the hurricane. I'm scared of the city sauna that'll come after it."

We compromised, and decided to head for Baton Rouge. I felt extremely uncomfortable going farther than that—who knew when schools might reopen, or when I would be needed back at Sci Academy? What if my advisees needed me? Or if the hurricane turned and we had school two days later?

The next morning, Johnathan and I drove up the contraflow and made it as far as Baton Rouge before the roads closed altogether and we ended up sheltered in a friend's house, Kaitlin, Matthew, and their two cats in tow.

Gustav changed direction and hit Baton Rouge the hardest, and we sat and watched the LSU's arboretum lose its roof. Deanna's house shook and shuddered, and her street flooded. College students sailed pirogues down the street, laughing and waving and throwing ludicrous Mardi Gras beads at the sodden houses and drowning cars.

We drank warm beer and ate Zapp's potato chips on Deanna's porch, fanning with old feminist zines and anarchist pamphlets.

Two days later, I plugged my phone into a car charger, gleaning enough power to talk for an hour. I locked myself in a sweltering back room of Deanna's little cottage, the room she stored her boxes of crafts-not-yet-done, sewing, and rapidly warping vinyl in.

I called the families of each one of my advisees. Most of them picked up. Most had not left the city.

Are you OK? Where are you now?
Yes, school will be open next week.
I know you'll be there.

Do you need anything?
I miss you. I can't wait to see you.

Once I had reached a panic point—the small, claustrophobic room, with no light or air—I emerged. I texted Marc: All of my advisees will be at school on Monday.

On Monday after Gustav

90% of our student body was present at school.

Was it the threat of six hours of detention? Or the sense of belonging, the need for normalcy, that sent them to their bus stops several days before the rest of the city's schools reopened?

Was it because there would be cold air flowing from the vents, in a city where half the houses—tellingly, the poorer areas being amongst these—were without power?

Or was it simply, that they knew they would be welcome, that we'd all called to say we wanted them there?

Practice in ¾ Time

Marc would come in daily during classroom instruction that first year and watch carefully. I'd glance up from my whiteboard and try not to pause in mid-statement; scholars were redirected quickly back to their work until his presence was as insignificant as an extra chair. They became accustomed to his stealthy arrivals and departures. His shoes did not squeak on the floor as he moved intentionally but silently, eyes scanning student work and the day's objectives, the alignment of their bodies in the chair and my pace in the lesson.

I, too, quickly learned to ignore him, unable to predict what he was looking for, or if he was targeting anything in particular. At a moment when scholars were writing or discussing, Marc would walk right up to me, in the middle of the lesson, lean over and whisper into my ear a small adjustment or correction in my teaching practice.

In the beginning, this was incredibly demanding, both the observation and the in-the-moment refinement to my course of action, but I rapidly began to welcome these small interventions.

He never gave me more than I could handle, the instructions were always clear and actionable, and importantly, they were actionable in that moment, a new dance step to immediately practice.

Ask the next question, and then pause three seconds before you call on someone. Give them time to formulate their answer, and anticipate what they might say if they're called on.

I noticed immediately that scholars were more attentive, mentally preparing to be called on rather than feeling off the proverbial hook because it was someone else's turn.

Keep your feet planted, you're shifting back and forth. Cross your arms behind your back to keep from fidgeting.

Fidgeting was distracting, and caused me to look nervous, unprepared. Crossing my arms behind me felt awkward, but it pulled my body posture up, taller and more confident. This more formal body posture slowed me down and helped keep my range of motion under control, and the scholars immediately responded with a twinge more attentiveness.

When you sense trouble or off-task behavior, pause and scan the room. Address the small behaviors first with nonverbal gestures then slowly, deliberately move towards the issue.

Slowly, calmly moving towards trouble with confidence and poise is opposite to our fight or flight, our inherent desire to react or flee from dangerous, or even annoying, situations. Teachers do not have the luxury of giving in to their instincts. We must intervene in issues ranging from note-passing to name-calling to hair-pulling, and we must do it with control and elegance. We are the locus of control in the room, and our every ministration counts.

Use proximity before eye contact—stand near the scholar who is misbehaving, but give her the ability to address the behavior on her own, without having to meet your eyes.

A bad leftover habit from Clark: I would glare at misbehaving children, setting the stage for a confrontation Some scholars responded well to the sharp reprimanding eye—but determining which would respond poorly took practice, and allowing these scholars to correct themselves simply by my presence was a great first step.

Turn your body sideways when you're at the board, and switch sides. Never turn your back fully to the room.

This minor adjustment allowed the periphery of my room to stay within my control, even when I was writing.

When you ask for actions from all the scholars, do it commandingly, but cheerfully. Let them hear that you are confident it's going to happen, and you're already thrilled about the upcoming moment of success.

I made my next request to the class in the same tone I might say, "I'd love extra avocado," rather than "Stop pulling her hair!" The entire mood of the room shifted from domineering to anticipatory, and instantly we were all happier to be together.

When you circulate, don't make the same loop. Rotate randomly, keep proximity to all of them.

This also meant seating arrangements that allowed for facile, unfettered movements across the room that could still appear smooth and coordinated, unrushed.

When you're flustered, don't let it show on your face. Give a small smile—let them know that you're in control and unconcerned, even if there is misbehavior. Assure the rest of the room with your posture that the behavior will be addressed.

This was the first adjustment that I struggled with in real time and, on the way home in the car, I practiced. My face would react, crinkle back in annoyance or frustration or dread. Then, I forced myself to pull my shoulders back, tilt my head up a little, smile, and take a single deep breath.

The next morning, I even practiced with my advisees. I asked them to misbehave, and they were more than happy to do so, while I practiced quietly redirecting them with proximity and a serene upturn of the mouth.

Tyreon said, "Miss Eckhardt, you make me nervous with that smile. I don't know whether you're gonna pat my shoulder or snatch me baldheaded."

Not exactly the feedback I'd been looking for, but it was a start, and later that day things were smoother. As I controlled my body, reactions to the unceasing little crises of the classroom became smoother, less flustered.

Never end your sentences in an upward lilt, even if you're asking a question. Instill your voice with authority.

Naturally, in informal speaking patterns, many of us end every sentence in an upwards tone. Our voice becomes a little lighter and higher. In a classroom, dropping the vocal tone down slightly, and becoming slightly quieter, instills an immediate sense of formal authority. This, more than any other of Marc's redirections, was a game changer. Children respond to, and crave, firm authority. Louder, more high pitched tones make them anxious and agitated. Calm, even keel voices put them at ease. Tone should communicate an unperturbed power, and changing my voice at the end of sentences had an immediate impact on the crackling energy of the room. The authority in my voice soothed the static, and this in and of itself was powerful.

Then Marc would stay to observe the adjustments, which I would make in real time.

Often, he'd speak to me again, having me tweak the move until it was efficient, streamlined.

He'd return the next day and look for the new direction in my practice, look for the new gesture or word or action incorporated seamlessly into my muscle memory. I worked hard to incorporate them. I practiced redirecting scholars while getting ready for school each morning, while the blender ran and the kettle sent white clouds of steam up the tall windows of our kitchen. I rehearsed in the mornings in my room to empty chairs. I marked little X's in black tape on the floor to help myself circulate slowly, smoothly, from one place to the next. On the back wall, next to the clock, I posted little reminders to myself.

"Watch your corners!" "Proximity!" "Wait Time!"

"Breathe. Calm. Smile."

"How's your posture? Where are your hands?"

These observations helped me stay hyper-reflective about my practices, and pay attention to all aspects of my classroom.

My teaching improved rapidly, as did my confidence. I also learned to take feedback at face value. Feedback, when given in love and with mutually good intentions, is the best way to improve. Effective feedback isn't criticism, and it's not intended to hurt. It's intended to make something better.

This daily, intense, intentional feedback benefited me, but more importantly it helped the scholars and the school. My new muscle-memories turned my classroom rapidly from a set of different instruments and musicians into a finely tuned orchestra.

It Always Starts With Us

Working for kids with extraordinary needs means constantly turning your eyes inside to what can be improved. That's the cardinal rule of operating in a school that works with high needs kids. Look to yourself to get done what needs to get done.

Even though our team was strong, and united by a single vision, each day we erected our own sandcastles, sheltered and cultivated what we could. Each scholar is a responsibility, a fragile commitment to a future we dreamed of but could not yet see. Each scholar, the line of a horizon, weather unpredictable. Each day, a careful study of sand and water and gritty hands. Each day, a chance to build stronger, craft the angles, start anew.

Clipboard

One of our first withdrawals was De'Jena. She liked to hit scholars with her clipboard, hard but playfully, on the back of the head. The first scholar she hit reported her immediately, as we'd asked her to do. De'Jena admitted it, and refused to apologize.

The second scholar yelled "What the *fuck?*"

They both served detention that day.

De'Jena served her sentences, dutifully, reading and doing homework.

Her mother picked her up at the door, and I could hear the high pitched screeching from quite a distance, "What the hell you thinking, smacking people? They gonna turn round and beat the hell out you, little girl."

De'Jena was indeed little, with tiny feet in bright white sneakers, and tiny hands and tiny round face that would squint with concentration and delight as she stretched up to administer her now infamous *thwack!* A mix of flirt and favoritism, she only smacked the ones she thought were cute, interesting, or smart.

Play with me, the smack seemed to say. But it hurt, and she *just wouldn't stop.*

At her disciplinary hearing, her mother cried.

We asked her, "De'Jena, do you feel remorse?"

"No," she replied.

"Will you do this again?"

She sighed a sigh so deep and resigned that the air caught in my throat.

"Next time I get the chance, probably." She stated this, not rebelliously, but matter-of-factly, as if the choice had already been made. Her mother withdrew her and placed her in another school, a more chaotic one nearer to her house. I drove by her house a few days later, hoping to catch a glimpse of her, but the shutters were drawn, lights dimmed.

I heard later that she'd taken her Sci Academy clipboard with her and, true to her word, smacked a female classmate on the back of the head, the first chance she got. True to her mother's prediction, her new classmate did, indeed, beat the hell out of her.

We regretted her loss for a long, long time.

Complaint

I was learning to be a calmer, more focused and intentional, person. I was learning to communicate better. I was impacting scholars—though I had little understanding about whether the work was turning into learning gains, as we still hadn't designed any assessments. But the work was undeniably meaningful, and being on a real team was incredibly gratifying.

I felt for the first time that I was not just folding paper boats to set sail upon raging seas. What we were creating was nothing akin to permanence...yet... but something more resembling the shape of shelter and reform.

Enter entropy, settling like sediment in the heart, in the body's joints.

I was working twelve to fourteen hours each day, six days a week. I missed my boyfriend. I missed cooking. I missed my bike, making art and crafts, and writing postcards.

A deep exhaustion resides in making decisions for the first time, knowing full well they may be the wrong ones, and are definitely not set in stone. Like sandcastles, the foundations rippled with changing tides; we adjusted, bailed out our moats, refitted our molds with fresh damp sand, and again tamped the ground, knowing the next day's upheaval could send us reeling.

The emotional toll of this shifting can be grueling. Everyone has emotional reasons to be involved in education, and those emotional connections make conversations and decision-making challenging.

Does backtalk count as two or four demerits? (How high should the towers be?)

Is a cheek resting in a hand breaking *SPARK*? (Is that wall leaning?)

If a cellphone's shape appears in a backpocket, does that count as seeing it? (How many windows should the turret have?)

In the early days, everyone faced the truth of what making good on our promises was really going to take, and that realization was daunting, and scary. It was tempting to resurrect the Bret Michael evenings of yore, to sit around and whine about these trials, to pick apart all the things that were wrong with the school and to assign blame to others for all of the struggles.

I came home one Friday night, poured a glass of wine to the rim of a mason jar, and pried open the dam of complaints I had been walling back for weeks... I railed about the inconsistency of our decision-making, the effort of each moment. I bemoaned my fate as the most inexperienced, feeling like the weakest link and constantly fumbling, my team didn't need me, I was *tired*, kids were misbehaving....

Johnathan listened patiently, for more than an hour. I stopped to take a breath, he said, "Do you feel better now?" The tone in his voice was almost sarcastic, and I bristled. We glowered at each other.

But, in the long silence that followed, I realized that... I didn't feel better. Not at all.

These conversations were toxic for Johnathan and our relationship. They provided no solutions, made my friends worry for me, and made me feel *worse*.

Afterward, when I opened my mouth to complain, I tried to remind myself that complaints are poisonous and detrimental. While this wasn't the first, or last time, I let loose a steam of noxious fuming, I made a concerted effort to be more aware of it. Complaining breeds complaining: if I complained to those around me, I should expect nothing less from others.

The Lottery

It was early November when I finally realized that, while generally attuned to the rules and compliant, our scholars weren't learning what they needed to learn most: to read.

We were receiving tons of practice with behavioral support. Doug Lemov, a managing director of Uncommon Schools, had come to observe and record his practices in action at our little school. With the exception of a few outliers, the scholars of Sci Academy were culturally aligned and very responsive to the rigid discipline system we had put into place. They were polite, compliant, and only spoke when spoken to. They appeared calm and focused in their classes. They raised their arms straight, passed papers efficiently, and this deep into the year, we still had not had a fight during the school day—an anomaly for a New Orleans public school.

We as teachers were growing in our practice. Classrooms were orderly, homework was assigned daily, procedures were in place. Our days passed, each at least twelve hours long, but with tangible progress.

Yet very little was moving with the academics in our classrooms. I woke up on Sunday morning, early, and began working on my lesson plans, submitting them by the three PM deadline with only minutes to spare. I was told the plans looked good, and so I delivered them. As far as my Scope and Sequence, I simply assumed that no news was good news, and I trudged forward, my shiny class sets of *Lord of the Flies* and *Romeo and Juliet* lined like eager soldiers ready for battle.

I taught Elizabeth Bishop's poem, "The Fish," which they thought was very strange, and "The Jabberwocky" to teach context clues and determining the meaning of words in sentences. When it came to assessment, I had them analyze "To a Friend Whose Work Has Come to Triumph" by Anne Sexton.

> *Consider Icarus, pasting those sticky wings on,*
> *testing that strange little tug at his shoulder blade,*
> *and think of that first flawless moment over the lawn*
> *of the labyrinth. Think of the difference it made!*

When their ideas were rambling and inconsistent, I blamed the poem selection, and my own inadequate questions. "What is the theme of this poem? Who refuses to be blessed? Who do you think is 'gone'?" I had suspicions that I should be doing more, but had no idea where to start. Our DCI was always busy, and I felt hesitant to bother her.

I spoke to other teachers as well, and learned they, too, were struggling. Logan had never received his Scope and Sequence, and was teaching "whatever he wanted." He'd stopped turning in lesson plans, and gave long lectures on his world travels and projected maps of countries for scholars to identify. Reagan's students were writing, but she and I had not coordinated our teaching at all, so they weren't writing about what we were reading, which made reading and writing disjointed for them.

Beyond teaching, we were all kept incredibly busy. We arrived at school at school by 7:50, for Value Village and our morning meeting. We had morning posts to guide scholars to and fro, advisory, classes, cafeteria and walkway duty, planning periods that were usually eaten up by meetings with scholars or phone calls to families or demerits entry. Each of us taught a daily elective such as drama or outdoors skills, and then afternoon advisory time with lessons on culture and values, then dismissal at five fifteen. Then detention, which we monitored in shifts, and meetings together afterwards, including disciplinary hearings with parents nearly every day. On Saturdays, we took turns monitoring detention, which usually included rounding up several scholars by car to get them there and taking them home again afterward. Sunday, all day, was taken up with lesson planning, phone calls, and grading.

Marc would often say we were "building the plane while flying," and nothing was closer to the truth. We had no time to examine the individual pieces, we were too busy slapping them together and coercing them into operable status.

October brought me to our short story unit. My scholars and I were struggling through Shirley Jackson's "the Lottery." I knew that our scholars came with a lot of deficiencies in reading. I wasn't fully sure who exactly was at what level. Their grades had given me a general idea. The reading assessment we'd given them at the start of the year returned vague data on all except our most needy.

Despite a lack of concrete data, it wasn't difficult to intuit that the texts I was selecting were several years ahead of them. I compensated for this by reading in groups, reading aloud in class, providing summaries, using visuals and answering as many questions as I could.

When I called on a student, more often than not, they responded, "May I please have some help?" a coin phrase we provided for them if they got stuck, and of course I could help! I would provide hints, or have them turn and talk to their neighbors. They worked dutifully, if not reluctantly. It was hard for them, but most believed in the promise we'd made.

Do what I ask, and you'll go to college.

It was towards the middle of "The Lottery" that I knew something had to change. Without my constant answer feeding and interventions, they weren't retaining the material—worse yet, they couldn't even read it. While they enjoyed the class, with its games and chants, they weren't actually improving.

I was working hard, but we weren't gaining ground.

The sandcastle I erected each day was washed away, leaving a blank slate. I knew this blank slate had potential, but I knew no other way to build.

Punchline

How could I have thought after a year teaching Robyn and others at Clark that my population at Sci Academy would be easily reading *Lord of the Flies* by December? I ordered the books, believing that my "high expectations and hard work" would get the kids where they needed to be.

Looking back on those first few months, I marvel at my own stupidity. I can at least say I had the best of intentions; what did I know about preparing "all scholars" for college? What did I know about the process of truly teaching deficient scholars to read? I approached this job with the understanding that I would meet and exceed all that was expected of me, and I had been doing my absolute best. I needed to believe that they could read everything I had read and loved—but I didn't know how to get them there.

At Sci Academy, we had built a culture of behavioral excellence, but not an academic one. So, I chose to model for them what I had loved about high school—challenging, engaging literature, lively discussions, and lots of "big words." I deeply wanted for them the rigorous, absorbing education that I had received; they deserved it and I could give it to them, but without a map I was truly lost.

How does a child learn to love the written word when it has caused them only frustration? How does one read the word scythe without phonics? How does one visualize a meadow if the closest they have even come to one is an abandoned lot?

This meant going off of the proverbial map, and scrapping weeks of my life and time. Most poignantly, it meant leaving the notion that a high quality education would look and feel like the one my team and I had received. It would mean designing a new kind of education—one that truly met the needs of all scholars. These kids took a chance on us. I needed to take a chance too.

Changes

Marc called us together and announced that our DCI would be leaving us, and that we'd be taking a couple of "development days" to get our academics up to par. Two local veteran educators came in to work with our team. I recognized them as the women who had been doing observations in our school for the previous weeks. They were warm, but firm, and a little intimidating.

We created a long makeshift boardroom table in Jacob's classroom and arrived to a thick packet of materials and an agenda on the board. The second bullet point, in crisp black letters, was "Reading Program." Dread slipped around in my stomach like a water snake. "Reading Program" implied to my sensitive ears that I had been doing something wrong.

They bluntly shared with us the truth we were just coming to grips with: that behavioral compliance cannot lead the academic achievement unless the academics are developed for intentional and rapid progress. Sci is a high school, allowing for scarcely four years to fill every deficiency, plus prepare the scholars for success on their own. Now, we only had three and a half years left.

We sat in silence for a minute. We weren't being blamed—but each of us internalized the words like stones sinking into our chest. Their reality sounded too much like rocks against windows, and tears welled up in my eyes.

Over the next few hours, my name came up a lot—Kaycee will be doing this, Kaycee will be implementing that, follow Kaycee's lead on supporting the implementation of...

None of it had been discussed with me beforehand.

I attempted to look humble and knowledgeable, but inside I was torn, and confused. Looking forward seemed very difficult, when my mind kept turning back. Everything I had done up to this point felt worthless. All the long hours and late nights, time away from home and Johnathan, the work I'd put into lesson plans and assessments each Sunday, not to mention the weeks I'd spent recreating the Scope and Sequence, the units... gone.

I was embarrassed that my class wasn't meeting expectations.

I was furious that no one had spoken to me about my new role before this meeting.

I felt betrayed that no one had intervened beforehand.

I felt excluded, left out of discussions that had obviously been about my classroom, my teaching.

I was nauseous over all the wasted time, both the time of my scholars, and my own.

I had worked so damn hard trying to make my class perfect, and hearing that everything had to be done differently, especially with reading, felt like a personal affront.

It felt like I had utterly failed.

We wrapped up the morning, with introductions to a plan that "Kaycee would be responsible for rolling out." I excused myself from our ad hoc boardroom, and barely made it to the hallway before breaking down.

Ego

It took two loops around the trailer to gather my emotions and take a moment to reflect. What was it that was truly making me so distraught? If this would be good for scholars, why wasn't I enthusiastic? Why was my heart so twisted and embittered against these changes? I knew it was necessary, so why was it so hard to embrace?

The voice still muttered in my head—you're a failure, they should have included you, all your work was pointless. Where was it coming from? Surely not from an acceptance of feedback and a desire to grow.

Assuming that everyone's intentions were good, I had to come to the conclusion that no one meant to hurt my feelings; indeed, no one was even telling me that I had done a poor job. What I had heard that morning wasn't personal. The morning had been about the need to make a lot of changes for the good of the students.

My pride was wounded, and my ego was licking imaginary wounds, but if this were about me, or about failure, surely Marc would have spoken to me about it long before.

I returned to the vision, each word a mantra, and I returned to the reasons I was with Sci Academy.

On the first day of summer training, Marc had asked us to open a fresh composition notebook and answer the question, "Why are you here?"

I had written the following:

The children of New Orleans deserve a clean, focused, loving, place to learn. They deserve to be educated respectfully and appropriately. They deserve to have their needs met. They deserve to be able to prepare for the future of their choosing. They deserve to have the same opportunities as everyone else, and they deserve great teachers and a lot of love.

I am disgusted with the year I spent at Clark. I am disgusted with myself for not doing more, and with the school for not doing what kids needed, because it was "too hard" or "too late."

I made a conscious choice to look at the new curriculum assistance as feedback. After all, I was with the school for a reason. Marc believed in my abilities as a teacher, and in me. No one on the team saw me as a failure. I needed to swallow some pride, believe in myself, and do whatever it would take to effect change. A gasp of air after drowning, I took a breath. I felt like I'd pulled myself up from out of the sea, and lay gasping onto the warm sand. *I felt released.*

I went back into the school, changed and determined, repeating to myself, "Because it is what they deserve."

Thereafter, I used this self-awareness like a lifesaver, red and white striped. I made the choice not to take hard shifts in practice personally, and remembered instead that each day was a chance to make our school and our scholars, better. Making changes would continue to be a common theme; nothing was too sacred to alter if it served the scholars and their path. Learning not to complain, accepting change as normal and necessary—these lessons made me a better teacher, and a better human being.

Tempestuous

I scanned over the data and felt a burning, itch along my skin I would never be able to scratch. Nearly 30% of our ninth grade scholars read below the third grade level.

I took a few minutes to just be angry at all the reasons so many of these children were now in the awful place they were in. Anger at discrimination and segregation, generations of neglect, broken homes, corporate money diverting tax incentives away from public services like education. At disgraceful teacher salaries, at expensive and aloof higher education. At technology and globalization, which funneled money away from our middle class as well as our most needy. Unfairly or not, these children's past teachers, who shuffled them forward, pushed them along, inattentive, unwatchful. Neglectful. Disgraceful. Couldn't there have been one teacher, somewhere along the line, who had noticed? Who could have done *something?*

Then I thought of Kaitlin, in her high needs public school, teaching eighth grade. She had noticed, and all year she had done her best to intervene. She had done something else. She had sent her neediest students to me, with the assurance that *something more would be done.*

Once again, a starting line. There had already been so many in the past two years, and I allowed myself one last little flicker of rage at this continual sea change. Once again, the pull of the sand around my bare feet. The raw material and blistering sun. Once again, work to do.

Winter "Holiday"

Two weeks later, the winter holiday started and I focused my attention on developing the new reading program. I worked with our two consultants, who were prompt and cheerfully critical of my progress, and I made headway fast.

My students needed to read. A lot. Of books. They needed to read at a level they could access to practice fluency. They needed books that were appropriate for their age and to be guided and supported through them. They needed to talk, write, analyze, argue, express, and do it again and again. I redid the class schedule, restructuring the scholars into heterogeneous classes, with homogeneous breakdowns in each. I designed rotating groups and an independent reading class that each teacher would be partially responsible for.

Lord of the Flies would have to collect dust for a while, for most of our scholars. First, they needed to go home and read books they could understand. This meant that Jennifer, reading at a seventh grade level, would not read the same book as Catherine, who was still learning to decode words. In class together we could have meaningful discussions around the same text—but independently, I needed to meet them where they were.

I spent eight days of my winter holiday completely revamping my Scope and Sequence, focus, and procedures. I put stickers on the bindings of all of our books indicating different levels, and organized them by interest and genre.

I reinvisioned the school as a place where every moment was a chance to read.

Being a teacher, I realized, meant new beginnings all the time. The landscape would always shift and change, and there would be no assurance that what I had built would last.

It was a leap of faith, of belief, and of hope to try something new, to feign expertise when my feathers quivered. I was afraid, so afraid, to fail. Yet to pause, or to hesitate, or to forget to innovate because of fear is the only moment that we might fail.

As dusk fell, filtering a bluish light through the window in my classroom, an unhurried quiet fell over the trailer. Soon the halls would fill again with the squeak of tennis shoes on cheap linoleum, of giggling laughter from girls whispering about the boy across the hall, papers shuffling. It would fill again with the smells of bad cologne and the adolescent boystink of basketball practice, socks and hormones and deodorant and detergent. But for these two weeks, alone with my spreadsheets and stickers and emails, I strapped on my wings and thought of their poetry assessment.

Anne Sexton did have it right, after all.

Icarus, indeed.

Archipelago

The end of winter vacation brought changes for all of us, and moments of grave discomfort. Reagan and I had to begin to work more closely together, which we did, tentatively at first and then more systematically. Her classroom transformed as well, and she initiated some of the most inspiring initiatives I have seen. She brought her classes out into the yard to bury "Banned Words" and gave badges to "Grammar Police" who were allowed to give tickets to people for using incorrect grammar. This was wildly successful, and brought joy to an infinitely tedious set of skills.

My room became a balance of intensive reading on Monday and Tuesday, diving deeply into books and stories, asking questions and teaching scholars to discuss the ideas in the book with each other. On Wednesday and Thursday, they entered the "Archipelago" and rotated through different learning stations. Those who needed guided reading got it. Those who needed direct phonics instruction got that too. Those who needed a challenge read nonfiction articles about child labor and inequity, and others worked on context clues and expressing, visually and in writing, their visualizations and inferences.

We learned to meet scholars where they were, and design plans to elevate them.

We collected data, and used it to guide this process. Data doesn't lie.

This also was a time for hard conversations with both scholars and their families. What mother wants to hear that her sixteen year old child reads at a fifth grade level? What family wants to flip through their scholar's homework to find practice with phonics, or a book called *Number the Stars*, obviously meant for a child much younger?

I knew that I would have to massage these reading levels, especially to those who would struggle the most. To provide less than honesty would be both disrespectful and unfair, and I had promised to be honest, even when that honesty is hard.

I wrote out a checklist, of what I needed to say, and spent my planning period pulling scholars from class for a short conversation, glancing once in a while at the checklist for reassurance and strength, as much as a reminder of what to say.

1. (name), I want to talk to you about your reading level. According to the assessments we took, you are several years behind in reading.
2. Your current level is X grade.
3. Before you say anything. I want you to know a few things.
4. *This is not your fault.*
5. You haven't done anything wrong.
6. It would be easy to blame or to point fingers, but we don't have time for that. The future is now, and we have no time to waste.
7. We are going to start, today, getting you caught up. And we can, and will, do it.
8. I promise you that we can do this together. You don't have to be afraid of failure anymore.
9. I promise you, right now, that you will go to college, and that you will be a lifelong reader.
10. This is going to be hard.
11. I am already proud of you, and all the work you have done.
12. We are going to do some hard work together, but I, your other teachers, and your advisor, we will never give, up, never leave your side, never stop fighting for you.

13. No one will work harder than you, but I promise you that *you will not be alone.*

Tears were shed, denials were made, obscenities flung, retests demanded.

Honesty is not always easy. It's just the best place to begin.

Chance

It was during this time that I had a conversation with Trevor. Trevor was soft spoken and polite, with a posture too straight for someone so young. In his home visit, he had informed us that he'd be going into the army right after high school, but hoped to attend college afterwards. His uniform was always neat, pants at his hips, shirt tucked in fastidiously. He used "ma'am" and "sir" with the habit of someone who said it both in public and at home.

When we'd checked out books around Thanksgiving, he'd selected *Lord of the Rings*, hardcover, a mammoth tome from my own collection. I watched him pull that enormous book out of his backpack to "assign himself" if he finished early, but he'd just stare at the page, occasionally turning either forward or back. When the bell rang, he'd deliberately replace the bookmark and put the book back in his backpack.

The bookmark stayed right there, halfway through the book. With a fourth grade reading level, he wasn't able to make a lot of progress.

When we met for our conversation about his reading level, he gave no outward reaction. As intentional about himself as he was, he probably had an awareness of this struggle. He told me one of his past teachers had told him he wasn't ever going to be able to read well, and that's why he was planning on going into the army. He'd been told that he'd had a learning disability, and reading would always be hard.

"Ridiculous," I told him, shoving my rage for this teacher away into a dark place for later. "There's nothing wrong here that a little hard work won't cure."

He looked relieved. Hard work was not something Trevor was afraid of. Hard work, he believed, built the character he would need for the army.

"We start today, and we need to find you a book you'll be able to read and enjoy on your own, OK?"

He nodded solemnly. "Yes, ma'am."

Then, without prompting, he reached into his bag and pulled out *Lord of the Rings*, and slid it across the table to me. We both looked at it, between us.

"How about *Harry Potter*? The whole series is really good." I stood to get it from the shelf, but Trevor stopped me.

"Miss Eckhardt," he informed me, a trifle condescendingly, "*Harry Potter* is for children."

"Hang on," I said. I pulled a Whole Foods bag from the shelf behind my desk and quickly cut a large rectangle from it. I flipped the paper over so that only the brown showed and taped the edges around the cover of *The Sorcerer's Stone*. With a whiteboard marker, I wrote *Lord of the Rings* across the front in big, black letters.

I handed it to him, and he looked at me skeptically.

"Trust me," I asked him. "Give it a chance."

Give me a chance, I thought.

He did.

Two weeks later, Trevor dallied after class.

"Miss Eckhardt, do you have the next *Harry Potter* book?" He handed me the first one back, still wrapped in its cover.

In the cafeteria later, I brought him *The Chamber of Secrets*, wrapped in the *Lord of the Rings* cover—I'd only needed to replace the tape. He read them all, each with the increasingly tattered *Lord of the Rings* cover made out of a recycled Whole Foods bag.

That year, he made the honor roll for the very first time in his life. Two years later, as a junior, Trevor took the AP History practice test and scored a three out of five, one of only a handful eleventh graders in New Orleans open-enrollment public schools in 2011 to score above a two.

Trevor proved that tremendous, astounding growth is possible. Trevor was no different than the other scholars, or even from my students at Clark.

We must believe that this is that is possible for all children.

Reading Is Life

Independent Book Checkout Day was uproarious, chaotic, and fun. I stood in the middle of the room with a clipboard—on it was a printout of everyone's reading level. The scholars went to the back and dug through the shelves and bins of books, looking to match their reading level and interest. They would bring me the book they were interested in, and I would check to see if it was on their level. If it was, they'd write their name, the title, and author on a notecard and give it to me.

If it wasn't appropriate, I'd send them back. Ironically, the advanced readers gave me the most trouble, wanting to read books far below their levels. The struggling readers actually looked relieved and thrilled to have a book that interested them that they would actually be able to understand.

At the end, I'd have a stack of notecards with everyone's book selection on it—an easy way to know who'd checked a book out and if the book was appropriate for them. The scholars relished book day as a chance to talk to peers and wander around the library making recommendations and expressing their opinions.

Within two weeks, every scholar had books in bags. They were reading every day—books that interested and excited them. If they got bored, they could trade in for something new with no penalty.

I learned how to treat my classroom more as an intervention, helping each student access the rigorous texts by slowing down and focusing on what mattered most and being intentional about teaching not just the text, but also how to access it, working slowly from comprehension to analysis of texts worth reading.

Scholars were talking about books, sharing books, and feeling confident in their reading choices.

They were learning to read.

Better still, they were learning to love it.

Sea Change

Over the next few weeks, we saw a shift in our scholars.

They were starting sentences with "The central idea here is that..." and "I had great visualization on the part when..."

In class, they learned to respectfully disagree. "I disagree with Tyler and I agree with Kayla because here in the text it says that..."

We read our first school novel. It was easier than it should have been but I chose to sacrifice rigor, for a little while, for interest and engagement. We read it aloud together, pausing to examine interesting words and questioning the author's choice and tone. It was a simple little novel called *Nightjohn*, about a slave who teaches others to read with grave consequences. The book sparked passionate discussions about inequity—and about why reading was valuable enough to make such sacrifices. It was an easy read—the rigor would come later—but it worked. Many of them told me it was the first book they had ever enjoyed, or even finished.

Winter gave way stubbornly to spring. I had to continue to devise new ways to help our scholars develop reading skills, but the process became a pleasure as I began to see true growth.

We read piles of books. We read them together, independently, and in the school's nine reading groups. True, they weren't all books I had read in high school, but they were books, good books, and the kids loved them.

They cried when Dallas died in *The Outsiders,* and held embittered discussion groups about Ponyboy's different impressions of the Socs. They howled with rage when the gambler in *Bang* robs the hero, and wrote about how his parents change and whether or not Mann's internal wounds had healed. Sitting in homogeneous circles with books that they had chosen, they argued with equal ferocity about *The Lovely Bones, Where the Red Fern Grows,* and *Lord of the Flies.*

Many would repeat Trevor's resistance, turning their nose up at a childish cover. "Yeah, Miss Eckhardt, I know it's on my level but it's a *baby book.*" I would repeat my mantra.

Give it a chance.

All the while, I was giving all of this change a chance, too. All of us were; the risk was very high, with so little time left for these children and so very much for them to learn.

Throw the V

An offhanded banter between the Twins and I inadvertently became an institution.

The Twins were two lanky teenagers who were difficult to tell apart and often changed their meager dresscode-aligned accessories halfway through the day to further confuse their teachers. They wanted to attend LSU and become veterinarians, so even though they weren't in my advisory, on College T-Shirt Friday they claimed LSU.

Both of their reading levels were beyond ninth grade, and they sat in my challenge group on Archipelago rotation days. We'd recently read an article from *Time* on the stem cell controversy filled with formidable vocabulary. The Twins loved figuring out new words, picking the paragraph apart for clues to their meaning, trying out replacement synonyms with a critical curiosity that would prove very useful in college biology class. They kept meticulous vocabulary cards and quizzed their advisory at lunch. Weekly, I would pull new words from our whole-class readings and scholars and I would work through their definitions as we encountered them in the text. The Twins would be the first to memorize the words and try to use them in their writing for Reagan's class.

To reinforce them, I began trying to use them in sentences while teaching and the Twins quickly picked up on this game, trying to use the words in conversation. Others joined us as well, and it quickly became a running joke among many of the scholars. Some of the sentences were more successful than others, but the attempts were... well... *gratifying.*

"Oh, the smell of the cafeteria food is so *pungent.*"

"It stinks so bad, it's almost *tangible!*"

"Even though the smell does not *tantalize* me."

"But I'm *famished* so I'll probably eat it."

"Gross. The milk tastes like *stagnant* water."

"I ain't gonna be *gratified* by this food, for sure."

"If you eat it, you gonna be in *peril.*"

At some point, The Twins began throwing a peace sign at me whenever they used a word. "V for Vocabulary, Miss Eckhardt."

"Throw the V" was born.

It was my turn to monitor Saturday detention that weekend. Weekday detention was a silent, sullen affair, students sitting in rows forcing themselves to read or do homework. On Saturdays, we sometimes asked the scholars if they'd rather help out with "school beautification projects." Scholars helped weed the wilting little garden, put stickers on graded papers, clean desks and chairs, and alphabetize the notecards of currently checked-out books.

This Saturday I brought our new puppy, a pitbull mix named Kuro, to give Johnathan a few hours without the incessant whining and potty breaks. Detention quickly unraveled into puppy playtime and bulletin board making.

Many schools have corkboards, onto which teachers pin graded work and inspirational quotes. Since our school was a large, modular trailer, no such cork existed and we simply stapled and nailed directly onto the plastic walls.

The scholars and I hung gigantic pieces of blue paper down the hallway, using what felt like half a million staples to secure the edges to the wall. We bordered it in colorful squares on which we drew the letter V in thick, black letters. I stenciled "Throw the V!" across the middle, and three scholars colored in the block letters. Then we took all of our vocabulary words, wrote them clearly onto large notecards, and stapled them to the makeshift bulletin board. Finally, we took clear packing tape and affixed the entire construction to the wall.

On Monday morning, I explained the board to the teachers, and everyone grinned at each other—a new game to play with the scholars, a challenge.

Teachers used the words in class, and scholars would race to get their hands up, to be the first to recognize the word. They began to attempt to work the words, sometimes awkwardly, into sentences in their other classes.

"So, um, when you multiply with fractions you have to be very *vigilant* with your work, right?

Throwing the V became a game that everyone played, and still plays, in the hallways of Sci Academy. The Class of 2012, and the Twins, though, will always own it as theirs, laughing when they hear underclassmen using it.

"We've been Throwing the V since ya'll were in sixth grade."

Excel

We retested everyone's reading level in late March, with both a written and oral comprehension test. This was a labor-intensive process, especially the oral exam. Each scholar met with me or one of the other literacy teachers and read a series of passages aloud, then answered questions about the vocabulary and content. Each passage was timed and assessed for both fluency and comprehension. Each session took fifteen minutes, which meant we needed 24 hours total to complete all the tests.

These tests were much different than the ones we'd done in December. Scholars were reading more fluently and with more confidence. It was inspiring, and while entering the data several intense jumps stood out—in just a few months, some scholars had leapt years ahead.

Still, when I dumped the data into a spreadsheet, I was unprepared for what I was looking at. Each scholar's current reading level sat next to their score from December, color coded for ease.

When I averaged the column, I squinted at it, uncomprehending. I reloaded the page and clicked it again.

I rechecked all the data entry from the assessments for mistyped numbers. Then, I carried my laptop down the hall to Jacob, who was better than me at Excel. Surely, I'd done something wrong with the spreadsheet settings.

I stood behind him as he reshuffled, and averaged by columns. We both squinted at the smudgy screen, and then Jacob let out a sound that was half-gasp, half-whoop.

I'd averaged it correctly.

In just three months, their average reading level had taken a 1.5 year jump.

Testing

State testing, for the children of New Orleans, is a fear-wrought trial by fire. In both the fourth and eighth grades, the state exams are high stakes: failure means grade repetition. Few exceptions are made for this promotional standard. Even in the other grades, scores on these test historically determined preferential treatment in the next grade, and whether a child was placed into accelerated or regular classes. Scores are shared as status symbols. The coveted "Basic," outranked only by "Advanced," was worth celebrating.

Families pinned their understanding of their child's learning on these scores, often because of a lack of communication from the school, or because grades from the school just did not paint a true picture of academic progress.

These discrepancies reflected upon classroom instruction, on adequate education and preparation for these tests, rather than on the children themselves.

These scores were more essential to our school. Charter schools promise a high performance on these tests, in exchange for autonomy in how these gains are achieved. Failure to make a strong presentation on test scores could cause a charter to close within three years. High scores assured a school's survival, as well as the potential for private funding and nonprofit support.

Two days before the state tests were to be administered, we had our first full-blown fight in the hallway. Katina, from my advisory, had already been warned repeatedly about her drama with Leanna. We were transitioning in the hallway, when, according to Katina, Leanna rolled her eyes. This was enough to send Katina flying across the hallway, claws bared, where she snatched a handful of Leanna's braids and pulled. Leanna batted back at her face, pushing, then grabbing a handful of Katina's maroon extensions.

There was a ripping sound, and as Jacob pulled Leanna, and I pulled my struggling advisee apart, hair, a detached braid, and chunk of scarlet weave, remained like the evidence of a crime.

I looked back at Jacob, and out over the two shuffling, agitated rows. His brow was furrowed, and not simply because of the girl, still scrapping weakly, in his arms. The last thing we needed was a heightened level of anxiety, and a loss of control. We'd already seen more misbehavior in the past two weeks than we'd seen all year, as the scholars worked out their nervousness and panic over the approaching exams.

I pulled Katina into a room and called her mother, and we sent both girls home.

But we would have no disciplinary hearings over this fight. Not until after the tests. We would even break our own rules to keep scholars focused on doing well—for themselves, and also for us.

The year had been a great experiment and we refused to pin our hopes on only one measure of data, yet, for better or worse, this was an important measure. It would prove publicly whether our risky experiment had been a great success or abject failure.

The scholars were nervous. The teachers attempted to be outwardly confident, but we were terrified.

Death Delivered

A moment of drama of my own: the school gave each advisor funds to provide breakfast for their advisees every morning of the state tests. Frances was making microwave waffles for her little gang, with orange juice. When I suggested this to LSU, they all grimaced.

"Miss Eckhardt, you know we all want McDonald's. That's all we want," said Rickia, smirking.

They all nodded vigorously, except for Erica, who exclaimed, "I'd rather have Burger King." She was immediately shushed, and they looked at me expectantly, and a little deviously. They knew I was a vegan, and I'd spent many hours extolling the hazards of their junk food, fatty, meat-laden diet. It fell on deaf ears.

So Monday morning, day one of testing, found me drenched in that foul but unmistakable stench of Mickie D's, ordering breakfast sandwiches and hashbrowns. I'd purchased real orange juice and chopped strawberries and pineapple for them the night before, in what I knew would be a futile effort to inject some level of sustenance into their morning.

The heavy paper bag was immediately soaked through with grease, and I held it out in front of me like the carcass it was. Foolishly, I set it on the back seat behind me, rolling the window down to prevent myself from gagging. When I arrived at school, the seat was damp with condensation and greasy oil.

When I distributed the "food" to my girls, they devoured it hungrily. Rickia smiled at me over her dead pig squished between two sopping pieces of white starchy carbs. "I don't eat fruit like that." She pointed at my untouched plastic storage container. She, like many of my scholars, would only eat canned fruit, and the occasional apple. "It's sour. And you forgot the jelly, Miss Eckhardt. Where am I going to get my fruit for the day?" My ladies laughed, I rolled my eyes dramatically, and ate the fruit with a plastic fork that smelled like decay.

Once finished with their food, they began the tests. A hush fell across the building as they sat every day for a week, attentive, their faces fluctuating between forlorn and stony-faced. At the end of the week, we took a three-day weekend and then went back to work. We would wait nearly two months for the results.

Because You Go To Sci Academy...

At the end of May we gathered our scholars into the team room, the floor still taped to show the neatly defined rows. We'd drawn up a script for the scholars, who know their scores had come back and were hyper and jittery. We turned the lights off and stood before them—all their teachers and administrators, the adults who had worked with them all year. One by one, we said our lines.

"Because you go to Sci Academy, you spent 160 minutes more in a classroom than students at other high schools.... you have taken 136 tests.... you have completed 574 Algebra problems."

"Because you go to Sci Academy, you have completed 5,250 minutes of reading." Snaps at this—they had, indeed, read *a lot*.

"Because you go to Sci Academy, you have said 'work hard' in the credo 370 times." We went down the row, reciting trail after trail, some humorous, some that made the scholars groan with remembrance.

And finally,

"Because you go to Sci Academy, you have some of the top scores in the district."

Dead silence, for a split second before Ciarra jumped from her chair. "What? Woooo!" A war whoop, a triumphant howl. The scholars leaped from their chairs, hugged each other, stood, and then sat, and then stood again. We called them back and they sat down, quivering.

We proceeded to list, specifically, all the schools whose score came in behind ours, names they knew, undiluted bragging rights.

With each announcement, our cheap oblong trailer shook with noise. One scholar jumped so hard her foot literally went through the floor—our janitor covered the hole later with a piece of plywood. We had reason to scream, shout, cry, howl, dance, and embrace. We'd attempted the improbable, and it had worked.

In Math, Sci Academy was number two in the district.

In English, we were number one.

Only the three highly selective schools had higher scores, and selective was never what "all scholars" was about.

Reading Is Knowledge, Knowledge Is Freedom

A final round of reading assessments was done in the last weeks of school. I blinked again at the data. Again, I made Jacob recheck it. Since we had reworked the curriculum in December, our scholars had grown an average of three and a half years in reading. Some had grown more than six.

We rejoiced.

Process

I am not embarrassed to admit I cried openly, during all of this.

I cried because I was so proud of each and every one of our scholars.

They rose to the challenge of the new curriculum, they went even farther than I pushed them, they proved to the whole city that *every* student can achieve.

They had risen to the challenge of literacy. Some of them had to come to terms with the fact that they were on a second or third grade reading level. I can't imagine how horrified, ashamed, and discouraged they must have felt, and how angry they were with those who were supposed to have taught them. Yet they persevered, and made the decision to improve their lives and intelligence. They *read*.

Our scholars had placed their trust in us. They had embraced our school culture in ways I never would have imagined, and through this they had become more confident, more respectful, and more enthusiastic about their academic progress. Every demerit led them to this, and everything we did culturally as a staff brought their focus to more important things.

It is not always easy to believe that little things matter, and some mornings it was hard to force enthusiasm into the Credo, hard to demand SPARK, incredibly hard to keep snapping and smiling. Our culture though, each little piece of it, puts our scholars on the road to college, and seeing this evolve over the year was magical.

These were the same children I had taught the year before, from the same neighborhoods, families, backgrounds, and with the same needs.

The difference was what we did for them, and with them, to make a lasting change. This is a lifetime chance, and a lifetime change for them, and one that only belief and hard work could have brought to them, and to all of us.

So much growth felt deeply personal, as well. I had proved to myself that there is no such thing as wasted time when it is spent on work worth doing. I proved that starting over could be worthwhile, even if it had to be done at high cost, and more than once.

The process by which we achieve greatness is a long one, and it is not always a well-lit road. Sacrifices are made, plans fail, egos are bruised, but by staying true to the path, following the dream and trying new things is always worth it.

Cause to Celebrate

Reagan and I were jointly awarded Charter School Teachers of the Year in 2009. After so much celebrating, it felt like an afterthought. A little speech, a little plaque, and lunch with coworkers who, over the past year, had become my closest friends. It grew in significance only because it was prestigious for our school. The award was a special one, but was not won in a vacuum, and I knew this most deeply of all.

Still, the significance of all this growth and achievement was not lost on me.

Only a year before, I had been struggling in a failing school, dodging pebbles and battling the impossible odds armed with a few fervent hopes and a brave smile. In just a year, I had become a teacher worth acknowledging, a teacher worthy of my scholars and their valuable time. I was not a great teacher yet, but I was making astounding progress, and I deserved to be proud.

I, like my scholars, had been willing to take great risks, in exchange for the promise of improvement. I had stayed late, rehearsing new practices to an empty classroom. I had taken hard feedback and implemented it without question, believing that the work would pay off. I had been willing to be vulnerable, to accept my mediocrity, and had been humble enough to change. I, like Trevor and Rickia, had faced hard truths and made the decision to change, rather than stagnate in denial.

Perseverance is a value I held dear this year. Good work is hard work, but with it, great change can come at astounding rates.

Terrence's Final Essay

Terrence submitted his final essay a few days later than he should have. I was relieved that he'd completed it. I told him I'd "take a few points off," but that I'd still grade it.

"Cool. OK. See you." He turned and shuffled out, pants sagging around his thin waist.

Attached to the front of his essay was a folded piece of paper, held precariously by a paperclip.

When I came to Sci Academy, I hated reading. I liked playing video games a lot more, because of all the pictures and the action. Then we began to have Island Days on Wednesday and Thursday, and you taught me to see the pictures in my mind when I read. Then reading became like a video game, if I read the interesting books. Even the boring ones, like that story we read about the husband and wife who bought each other gifts they couldn't use, even when I didn't like the story, I could picture the characters and that made it better. Anyway, I still like playing video games. But I think I like reading just a little bit more. Have a good summer, and see you next year.

Terrence.

A Thought For Other Sacrifices

Giving up what I loved doing in other areas of my life was part of what had to be done in order to make the first year of Sci Academy work. I don't regret giving these things up, because the job was rewarding and the scholars and my team are worth that, and more.

But the moments of temper tantrum frustration, when I wanted to scream, "I can't give anymore!" were very real, and had to be faced, and shared, and released. The first year of Sci Academy was all-consuming. A school, if it's an effective one, takes a priority over personal life, virtually all of the time. In anyone's beginning years as a teacher, in a new school or otherwise, that's just the way it is.

Johnathan moved with me to New Orleans because of my position with teachNOLA. He cared for my ramshackle emotions as well as my physical being during my first insane year. He cooked lunch and dinner and kept our house straight while running his own time-consuming business. He made the bank deposits, went to the post office, did most of the shopping, separated the recycling and took out the trash, and cared for our slobbering, grinning pitbull.

He was often lonely; he missed me and was not afraid to tell me so. We had several raucous arguments about how I was never home, and when I was, I was distracted and selfish. I would always counter that there was nothing I could do about it, he was being demanding, and that he should give me a break, I was already stressed enough. I needed him to be patient and to give me time to figure out how to do things more efficiently, and to remember that even though I wasn't home much, I was far happier than I had been, and was learning, and was actually seeing achievement in kids. I felt fulfilled by my work, even if it exhausted me.

We found no easy solutions, and the argument was never resolved. I renewed commitments to being home more, to setting aside work to invest time in our relationship. I did my best to shine my light on him, as well as on my scholars and my team. But, like pouring sand into a bottomless bucket, I felt constantly rushed to give, either to Johnathan or to my scholars or to the school.

At some point, I forgot to pour light onto myself as well, and this lack of self-care left me feeling bone dry and wilted. Inside I felt a whispered thinness, one that would not be healed by ignoring it.

Know Your Emotions, Own Your Actions

A few days before the annual retreat, Marc asked me to be the Freshman Culture Dean, a position I eagerly accepted. It meant that he trusted me to take on more responsibility and valued me as a permanent member of the team. Once we arrived in Breaux Bridge, I discovered that every returning teacher was being placed in a leadership role. The school was doubling and distributed leadership would be the only way to make that work.

Marc had clear ideas about what leadership would mean for all of us if we were going to recreate, and sustain, the year that we'd had. Our discussions centered around the idea that being a leader was nothing like being a teacher. Leading adults was not leading children; they had different needs and expectations. They needed different guidance. They weren't new, either to the classroom, or to the work of educational reform.

Now I realize that being a leader is exactly like being a teacher. It requires exacting preparation and a deep awareness of the individual's needs. It takes a willingness to allow failure and natural consequences, and an infinite amount of patience.

Leading adults. Teaching scholars. Teaching adults. Leading scholars. We would have to do it all simultaneously.

Teaching is a work of heart, not just sinew. It would be important to know those we would lead intimately, and also to know ourselves. So, we learned about emotional intelligence.

Simply put, Emotional Intelligence (EI) is the ability to manage relationships effectively, first through self awareness and management, and then social awareness and relationship management. EI is the ability to understand the emotions that flow like circuits through ourselves and all our interactions, in order to better understand how to meet emotional needs for the good of the school's mission: college completion for all scholars.

The first two—self awareness and self management—explore how we understand and manage ourselves. The second two—social awareness and relationship management—address how we relate to others.

Having strong EI is not the same as being emotional.

I was by far the most emotional, on the surface, of the team. Tears would spring to my eyes during a rousing iteration of the credo, or when scholars snapped for a strong answer. I would cry when delivering good news and bad, when a scholar got detention or failed to get detention. Emotion for me came with the territory— I'd been a spontaneous crier since the days of my bird farm.

We took an assessment of our level of EI, and my scores came in low around self-awareness, which surprised me. I learned that exhibiting emotions is not the same as recognizing their effect is on others; I was driven by emotion, but this didn't mean I had an awareness of the impact these outpourings had on others. One is often self-serving in the guise of empathy, I learned.

We were asked to take a hard look ourselves and what might be our leadership styles. Our own perception is often different from what others know to be true, and with awareness comes a greater ability to lead and be led with trust and optimism. Fortunately, developing emotional intelligence is possible, even though these skills are not innate.

We discussed ways to support each other in our growth. I committed to being more introspective about my feelings and being more confident and solution-oriented. Being humble would no longer serve me in the way it did, and I became more decisive in my actions and spoke with more clarity. This new awareness helped me communicate with my team more effectively, as well. I considered my own feelings when approaching a conversation first, rather than running on fluid emotion. I became more thoughtful, and the practice of mindfulness made me a better teacher, and teammate.

Power and Influence

We studied types of power, developed by John French and Bertram Raven in the early 1960s. Power not as a bludgeoning tool but as the ability to act for the good of the scholars. Power comes in many forms, and leaders use power in different ways to accomplish goals.

1. COERCIVE POWER: The most like a blunt tool, coercive power accomplishes goals through the threat of punishment. We were cautioned to consider this one for emergencies only, as it can easily corrode a relationship. Fear of demotion or consequences may get something accomplished, but rarely does it build confidence or expertise.

2. REWARD POWER: Reward power is conveyed by recognition, praise, and incentives. A leader influences others by praising what should be continued. Value Village shoutouts, letters of recognition, bonuses, and personal compliments are all forms of reward power.

3. LEGITIMATE POWER: Legitimate Power is when you use your position of authority to justify making a unilateral decision, preferably after hearing everyone's input. We were up to this point unaccustomed to much use of legitimate power, as our team spent so much time talking to consensus. We expected to have to use this more in the next year. Our staff would double, and decisions would sometimes need to be made quickly.

4. EXPERT POWER: Knowledge and expertise can influence others to act or take advice. Often when someone is an expert in one area, others believe them to have expertise in other things as well. When Marc brought in consultants to assist me with the reading program, I followed their instructions explicitly—they were the "experts." But before this, when I assumed that our academics were fine, because I assumed he had as much expertise in curriculum as he did with culture and behavior. In truth, he didn't have much expertise at all in this area, but the Expert Power he held over us made us feel secure in his knowledge of all things.

5. REFERENT POWER: The most powerful type of influence, Referent Power is the ability to influence others even in absence. Others will want to act in a way that would please a leader, even if she is not around. Marc held huge referent power over all of us. Even if he was not at the school, in moments of crisis we would ask ourselves, "what would Marc tell us to do?" We would act in a way calculated to not disappoint him. His influence kept us all striving to meet the high expectations he set for the scholars and our team.

We considered the different ways we held power over each other. Megan held expert power over us, as her wealth and breadth of knowledge about special needs was immense. Frances, as our social worker, also held expert power, as it was she who would guide us through the emotional needs of our most challenging behaviors. Reagan had a lot of reward power over me. In much of what I did, I sought her praise and approval.

I learned that I held referent power over members of my team. What I had considered zealotry for our culture and cause, they considered a lighthouse, a beacon upon which they too could focus.

The stringent, unyielding commitment I brought to the decisions we made about the school helped many of them to uphold them as well.

Jacob, in particular, expressed that in moments of doubt or difficulty enforcing the roles, he would say to himself, "Kaycee would do things the Sci Academy way, and I need to do so, as well."

I was deeply honored by his words.

In David McClelland's 1961 book, *The Achieving Society,* he described different motivations that all humans have for taking action: achievement, affiliation, and power. One of these is dominant within each person, depending on background and experiences.

Reagan was highly motivated by power. The desire to enact change, win arguments, and make an impact on her world drove her to be wildly successful, even against high stakes.

I was learning to love being on a team. But I was also motivated by power. I was prompted to act because I wanted to see a change for scholars, for New Orleans, for education. I loved my team, but it was the desire for *lasting change* that drove me to keep going every day.

There is often hardheadedness with the power motivation, perhaps another reason Reagan and I struggled to make compromises to each other in the beginning. We each had a clear vision of the world as we wanted it, and it is hard to make concessions on deeply personal dreams.

We would learn to do this better, but it would take years of practice.

We carefully avoided the word "manipulation" in these discussions, though at later retreats newer team members would express a lot of unease knowing these lessons had been given and then practiced upon them. Kaitlin joined our team in year two and spoke up, "I feel like our conversations have not always been straightforward and honest, and that's hard for me to take," she said, making eye contact with me.

I felt like I had betrayed her, even as I considered the several times that year I had convinced her to act based on my expert power and her power motivation. I had, for example, needed her to improve her organization of files we shared. Rather than simply asking her to change, I suggested to her that by improving her organizational skills, she could have a swifter impact on the scholars. This nagging sense of possible betrayal gnawed at me, and weeks later I even looked up "manipulate" in the dictionary, seeking a subtlety that would help me negotiate these practice.

manipulate | m*uh*-**nip**-*yuh*-leyt | verb: to control or influence (a person or situation) cleverly, unfairly, or unscrupulously

In this word, unscrupulously, I found some solace. Using power and motivation in order to make changes needed for scholar achievement could never be considered unscrupulous.

But I also could see Kaitlin's point. Used in other ways, this knowledge could have both a negative and lasting impact.

I still have very ambivalent feelings about this knowledge and the use of power and motivation on teammates. It seems a necessary tool when guiding someone as a leader, but also feels manipulative to ask myself, "What kind of power do I hold over Kaitlin? How can I influence her to act in the way I need her to act?" Worse, when it's done inauthentically, it is both obvious and trite. Worse yet, I can see how these kinds of theories are used *unscrupulously* all the time.

With the knowledge and practice of power comes the responsibility of always doing it with good intentions and love.

Ocean

A reminder pops up on my phone and computer every morning at six AM. It says, simply, "ocean."

I placed it there years ago and, even though I am not teaching right now, the message comforts me. My first year at Sci Academy, everything felt like an emergency, and in some ways it was. So few of us stood between structure and the chaos of one more poorly-run school. So many children had so many needs. New ideas had to be imagined on the spot.

Every decision, every action felt significant, not only because we were making them for the first time but because they impacted everyone else on the team. I lived in a constant state of panic. Am I doing this right? What if I fail? What if this kid doesn't do what I asked? What if he does? What if I can't teach reading? What if I let someone down?

What if I can't do this at all?

Clinging to some semblance of a routine was my way of coping with these fears, but there cannot be a sense of normalcy in the first year of building a school. The roles and systems must change, many times, before they make sense and are structured correctly. These changes, almost always last-minute, almost always urgent, caused me to panic. Any change in the schedule, any alternation in the routine we were trying to develop, was a case for alarm for me. I feared, greatly, each change. Small alterations brought tears to my eyes. I snapped at people and increased everyone's sense of alarm and fear because I could not control my own.

A retreat is a time for coming clean, starting again, rekindling affections, hashing out hard feelings, and reuniting as a team. At this retreat, we were given the opportunity to share a plus and a delta about each other person. After learning about Emotional Intelligence, these confessions were far more poignant.

These conversations were also intense. It is an easy thing to say to someone, "Here is my plus for you. Without your unfailing optimism, many moments would have been much harder. You see the good in every child, all the time, and this has inspired me to love harder in tough moments."

What is harder is to say, as I said to one teammate, "My delta is that I feel like you judge me, harshly, and that nothing I do is ever good enough. I feel like I am constantly trying to please you, that you're often annoyed with me, and I don't know why. I need you to communicate with me when I am being successful in your eyes, because I look up to you and living in a state of disapproval is so hard for me."

It is a heart exposure of the deepest kind. The plus and delta activity is to say, "I love you, so many things about you, but there are things that need to change if we are going to stay together." Yes, this does indeed sound less like a work relationship and more like one between lovers, but starting a school with such a small team becomes a sort of love affair. It is not a job, but a resonant devotion. It is sacrificing everything to be what the team needs, even and especially when the worst times come. It is a matter of both business and heart.

It is the raw emotion-drenched business of giving birth and early parenting. It is also modeling the very best kind of relationships for the students we served.

My pluses for others came so easy that year. Even after a year with this team, I was starstruck and humbled to be included with them.

Rachel, you have talents I am so envious of, and your ability to handle the business side of this school is incredible.

Frances, your infinite love for children is awe-inspiring. You never lose your temper, or get impatient.

Reagan, your classroom sings, children feel so safe with you and do incredible work for you. You always take things one step farther with them, and I draw on you for inspiration when I am struggling.

The plusses I received were both surprising and passionate.

Kaycee, you are the heart of this school. You are its gem.

You embody and believe and do everything we have said we were going to do.

Whenever I question what is the right decision by our standards here I ask myself what you would do.

Your sheer passion and love for kids shows in everything you do.

Your unwavering faith in the vision of the school shines like a light for all of us.

You illuminate what we believe like a beacon. We all look to you for strength when our belief wavers.

The deltas were difficult to hear.

I felt chastised and embarrassed, largely because I should have seen it coming.

I was told, by every member of the team, that I had to get my emotions under control, that my panic attacks and tears, panicked looks and sharp remarks, were incredibly damaging.

Megan told me that she had begun to hesitate to come to me for help or assistance, because she was afraid of my strong emotional reactions.

Frances told me that there were times when she had needed me, but had decided not to bother me because she knew it would send me into a tailspin.

Jacob told me that, many times, he had found himself avoiding me, because my negativity might wear off on him.

My first instinct was to apologize. I was horrified to think that my team chose not to come to me, because of my actions. I held back; apologies will not do what a commitment to change could. Instead I promised each of them that I would control myself better. I was, in these moments, dismayed that I had been so oblivious, and that my actions had isolated me from the team.

I was ashamed, but also empowered to change. The power of this type of honesty is poignant. By opening and being opened, both strengths and flaws laid bare, each team member could support the others in their desire to grow.

My commitment started with the ocean.

A long twilight lit stretch of beach, cumulous huddled on the horizon. A surging, yet strangely silent sea. Deep resounding waves battering the shore and, following them, a dark and brilliant calm. I imagined myself at the edge of this ocean, toes pressed firmly into the sand, eyelashes encrusted with salt, unwilling to move.

I stared across the surging depths and watched the wave come, felt it course over me and then, dreamlike, vanish into the stillness on the other side. If I shut my eyes I can return there, taste the salt on chapped lips, the dampness of my clothes. The waves come, and go, and return. I cannot prevent this—this is the world I have chosen, the moment I have selected to stand and not be moved.

I asked my team to help me, that if they saw me begin to panic, or freeze, or refuse to change, to simply say the word "ocean" to me. A reminder to return, for just a moment, to my sea, to let the wave come and go, to await the stillness on the other side.

My team helped me become a stronger person, not just a better teacher. I cannot forget. I do not see them very often now, but each morning, I wake up to "ocean" on my phone, and I remember to be calmer. I remember that in every moment there can be a stillness, and embracing the stillness helps me help others. It will pass.

Oyster Hearts

This retreat was a time of learning and bonding for all of us. Two members of our team would not be returning for another year with us, and we felt their absence even as we bonded together.

The little set of cabins we had rented sat along the edge of a bayou. The air was hot and still. We'd held our plus/delta discussions, a means of identifying what is going well and what needs to be changed, on the back porches of these wooden cottages, or sitting side by side on hand-sewn quilts. That evening after dinner, we brought a cooler of beer and whiskey onto Megan's back porch, and toasted the year behind us, and the year ahead.

And then we talked, late into the night, sharing stories far too personal for a simple work trip. The retreat was about learning to be leaders, but it was about learning to be a better team as well. Each of us opened our hearts like oyster shells, and revealed sheltered secrets or hurts. These stories were our ways of tying ourselves to each other, confessions creating methodical, sinuous bonds.

"You're right. I've been lying."

"I attended his funeral and only there found out that he'd been seeing another woman and that this was the woman everyone knew about. She sat next to his mother and held her hand, and I sat in the back of the church, appalled and sobbing."

"I wake up every morning to remember again that he's dead, but for a split second, before I remember, I feel wonderful. And then I remember, and I don't."

"Here's your ring back. I just don't love you."

"It took me longer than it should have to realize how much I was hurting her."

"After the imprisonment, I couldn't look her in the eye."

"I can't make him stop."

"I want to be deserving, I am afraid that I will never be."

"Isn't it strange that each one of us has lost someone deeply important to them?"

In the morning, we saw each other through blurry eyes, differently. We'd already been side by side in our battles for children. We'd been colleagues, collaborators, and friends. We would leave Breaux Bridge touched by one another, changed because of a fragile trust.

Reagan and I attempted a truce, eggshell brittle and smooth. We found new avenues through which to explore and communicate. We decided to start again.

At the end of the retreat, we drove down to the edge of Bayou Tec, standing together on the mushy ground, slapping at mosquitos. We knew the next year would not be any easier, and each of us had taken on even more responsibility. We would have new team members. Our school would double. We needed each other, and our belief, more than ever.

Cut the Strings

At the end of the first year, we went on a series of observations of the "good schools" in the area. These consisted of private schools and the highly selective charter schools. The handful of schools that remained with the Orleans Parish School Board (OPSB) after Katrina were not failing largely because they were selective-enrollment schools. Students take tests to attend them. These schools returned to the OPSB following Katrina, and continue to be run by them.

We visited Ben Franklin, one of the top 100 schools in the nation, a public charter school set at the edge of the University of New Orleans. We observed the classrooms. Students were slumped in their chairs, lackadaisically taking notes in neat outlines as the teacher meandered through the biology lesson. Students in the art class were drawing the Golden Spiral, playfully bickering over measurements and use of color.

No one was monitoring the hall, no adults were speaking intensely to students about their futures. The kids seemed to be meandering towards their future in a safe, unhassled way. They mostly ignored us, bouncing along in their illuminated, privileged little bubbles of jean shorts and loafers.

They had free time! Imagine—free time!—built into their schedules. And they used it wisely! Small groups of students sat around, quietly studying. The cell phone policy was laxly enforced, but students seemed to self-monitor, occasionally pulling their phone out, checking, sending a quick text, and dropping it back into their bag. Their focus was on the book in front of them. They sipped Diet Cokes from straws and shared handfuls of granola.

The other teachers from Sci and I snuck looks at each other.

Who were these alien children?

We vaguely recognized them.

We recognized ourselves.

Culturally, we knew, we could get our own scholars to be compliant, but could they be independent in this way? Could they be critical thinkers? Would we be able to cut the strings in enough time for them to walk, like Pinocchio, out into the world?

The song from this Disney movie played constantly in my head as we toured the school. "I got no strings to hold me down, to make me laugh, or make me frown. I had strings, but you can see, there are no strings on me!"

First Year...Again... A Summary

My year at Sci Academy was an absolute rollercoaster of emotions, as well as failures and triumphs. I faced a lot about my capabilities as a teacher... and a lot about myself. I realized that I was capable of a lot more than I gave myself credit for and that I deserved to be a member of the amazing place we had built.

I needed to take a deep breath, stop overreacting and taking things personally, and get to solution-oriented work. I learned to be a part of a team, to release the idea that a teacher exists on an island, and embrace being one cog in a larger machine. Moreover, I was proud of my fellow teachers' efforts, not just my own, and deeply humbled by them. I also experienced the exquisite feeling of success after a lot of hard work and sacrifice—that is a feeling unlike any other. I took deep pride in what we had done together; it had meaning and imported substantial change into a dysfunctional education system in drastic need of an overhaul.

It was painful to make so much sacrifice and work so hard only to have to switch gears completely and try something new. It was incredibly hard to never have anything be permanent, and to have to make massive changes in an instant.

There were moments in which I felt like an utter failure, and I felt this failure most poignantly because it meant failing children who needed me.

But in this year I learned it is in the hardest times that I made the most progress, and in the most disturbing moments that I found the most strength.

The reward sometimes is the struggle, and through that struggle I learned about achievement and about myself.

YEAR TWO: Work. Work Hard.
New Commitments To My Team

After the Breaux Bridge retreat, we created a "cheatsheet." This was a list of imperatives and personal statements, commitments to ourselves and each other on ways to improve.

1. I will draw on my empathy to truly listen and to share my feelings with others, without judgment.
2. I will be vulnerable and share the mistakes I have made and seek help in all things.
3. I will lead by serving, seeking always to discover new ways to support my new team.
4. I will never be too busy to listen to someone's concerns, and will not write, work, shuffle, fidget, or do anything else while I am listening.
5. I will recognize the effects that my emotions have on others and will not communicate crisis with my voice or body when there is not a crisis situation.
6. I will think about what I am about to say, especially when I am emotional.
7. I won't postpone difficult conversations, even the most uncomfortable ones.
8. I will recognize and praise the efforts of my team every chance I get.
9. I will not let my tendency to be commanding damage my relationships with my team.
10. I will not become impatient when something takes longer than I expect, and will be patient with the processes of others, even if it takes them a long time.
11. In times of darkness, I will remember when Jacob said, "You are the heart of the school. You model the dedication, commitment, and intolerance of failure and that power affects all of us. You are the gem."

In The World to Change The World

Year two would be Kaitlin's first year as a team member—a decision
which gave me a lot of strength. We had spent many evenings
debating the advantages and disadvantages of the charter school
movement in New Orleans. On one hand, the competition and
threat of closure necessitated a rigorous standard of excellence.
But veteran teachers and neighborhood input were often left out
of these changes. Charter school teachers were unable to belong to
a union, and their at-will contracts offered very little job security.

Still, Kaitlin was ready for a change. She too was ground down
from battling uphill against insurmountable odds.

When she was asked to be the Special Education coordinator
at Sci Academy, she was enthused at the opportunity for a challenge
and chance to help the most needy.

She hung her poster—*I am in the world to change the world*—
over her desk, her own banner. On it, a woman strode bravely into
the darkness.

During the first week, new staff members were asked to give a
short speech about why they'd come to Sci Academy.

Kaitlin said, "Kaycee and I argued for a long time about
whether or not charter schools were the solution to the ills of the
New Orleans public education system. I am a staunch supporter
of public schools, and it was hard for me to see charters as public
schools, themselves. Our country has no respect for teachers, and I
believe the fight to elevate the profession is an important one.

"But this shouldn't be about adult intellectual conversations
about what structure is best for us. This should be about kids, and
their crises, and what they need in order to be successful. I'm at
the point where I don't care what form the change takes. What
matters is that change happens, and Sci Academy is making the
most impact. How could I not want to be a part of that?"

Work. Work Hard.

As the Freshman Dean, I was paired with Frances, the Sophomore
Dean, and we immediately bonded over our shared love of the
scholars and our desire to make intentional changes for the good
of the school.

Frances and I became the culture's guardians. Any shift or
twinge or tweak in culture was to be made by us. Any slip or crack
in the culture had to be addressed by all members, but we were
responsible for any action plans or shifts that needed to be made.

We had no template for the culture dean positions; Frances
and I were the prototypes. The job shifted with the needs of
the teachers and school, and these duties and more presented
themselves along the way.

Frances and I scanned this unturned acreage critically and
measured out as best we could the time and effort needed to tend
to each row.

I read *Animal Farm* with a group of scholars that spring. When I'd been a teenager, I loved Napoleon with his devious greed. As an adult, I developed a fondness for Benjamin, who reminded me of Eeyore from Winnie the Pooh. This time around, I recognized my work ethic and oftentimes blinding commitment in the carthorse, Boxer. When this loyal member of the farm encountered challenge, he simply said, "I will work harder."

This cultural work was in addition to my full time class and elective load and my responsibilities to my advisees.

Add to this the knowledge that our school had doubled, but we'd never planned for a sophomore class. We'd had success with freshmen last year, but new freshmen would come with a new set of needs and obstacles—and we still had to figure out how to push our fledgling class of sophomores to independence and college-readiness.

The ocean in my head surged, and I tried hard to listen to its ebb and flow, and to embrace the fact that the work would never be done—the trick was keeping the boat from capsizing even as I bailed.

LSU

In year two, my LSU Advisory could no longer meet in my classroom. They were now tenth graders, and as a ninth grade teacher, with my hallway in the ninth grade trailer, we had to find another place for our morning and afternoon gathering.

Sci Academy had been given two extra trailers, battered leave-behinds from a defunct school site. We scrubbed the graffiti—I was becoming an indubitable expert with Goo B Gone and Magic Erasers—and chipped gum from the floor and hand-me-down desks. One of the trailers was a large room, without separate classrooms like the other two. Reagan's classroom ended up behind dividers, crammed into a space shared with Frances, Special Education, the team meeting room, and office spaces.

LSU met in the hallway in the middle of this honeycomb, determined to give them some sense of ownership, I hung the LSU banner and made a grid on a far back wall, providing each of them with a one foot by one foot square to hang pictures and completed work.

Katina hung a picture of Lil Wayne. Erica chose some anime cutout from *Sen To Chihiro Kamikakushi*. Maddie left hers blank in adolescent rebellion. Randie hung a picture of her cousins, the Sears photo curling at the edges, the two little girls adorned in green ribbons and dimpled smiles.

They reminded me daily, "We basically grown, Miss Eckhardt," and I tried to nag them less about their homework. I still walked them to the buses, and waved goodbye to them through the glass, but unlike last year, when they'd smile and wave back, they'd give me a nod and look back down at their phones.

These brushoffs didn't deter me. I need the joy before heading back to monitor a grumbling group of detention-trapped freshmen and a smattering of disgruntled sophomores.

"We're too old for that, Miss Eckhardt," Rickia said. "It's time for us to be serious, not silly."

Erica

LSU tried to tease, mock, and shun the child out of Erica, but it never quite worked. She sweetly attended her classes, drawing little hearts next to her name. She read teenage books about breakups and vampires. She made A's in all her literacy classes, B's in science and math.

Erica knew she wanted to go to college—she didn't need the coaxing and drilling that some of the others did. I spent less time with her because of this. Some of my other girls struggled with visualizing themselves studying at all, much less going on to college.

Mena *lived* in detention. She swore under her breath whenever she received a demerit, which earned her two more. Her father would yell at her and nag her about doing better, but her grades always hovered just above the danger zone.

Katina had a father who lived in another state, and was constantly devising ways to go live there instead. Her mother was firm on the subject: she'd be going nowhere, so Katina railed against me and the school daily, a litany of poisonous complaints that walked the thin line between grousing and outright disrespect. She arrived every morning and immediately started in with her exhaustive, if not repetitive, tirade about school.

"That teacher don't even know how to teach."

"How am I supposed to do all this homework?"

"You called my house last night and my mom took my phone away. You trippin, Miss Eckhardt."

"Supposed to be in tenth grade but still got all these rules around."

Maddie, who lived in Katina's shadow, would join in eagerly, followed by Nisha and Randie until I'd have a hallway of whining, petulant, venomously-negative teenage girls.

Only Erica would pull out her book and turn her back on these sessions as I corralled and eventually demanded their silence. Erica would look at me and shrug. Her only behavior problem was sleeping in class after staying up too late completing her homework to excellence each night and then reading herself to sleep by flashlight, "just because I like to read that way. It's fun."

Later on, she asked, "Some of the other LSU girls, they don't even want to be here. I do, but you spend all your time talking to them. Why, Miss Eckhardt?"

The truth—that the promises I'd made already included her—was hard to explain to a soft-spoken bookworm. Erica came from a background just as challenged as some of the other girls, yet there was never any doubt about her ability to be successful in whatever path she chose.

I looked for the magic potion in her past. What was it that kept Erica's kindhearted ways and her commitment to college intact despite a broken home, an absent mother, and a background of poverty? How was it that we instinctively knew not to worry about her? What pieces of her could we give artificially to the other scholars?

Erica never disappointed us and is fulfilling the vision we had for her and her classmates: she attends Colorado College and is majoring in computer science. When she comes home between semesters we go to lunch, and over Pho or oyster po-boys, she regales me with stories of late night dorm room escapades and skiing trips. She is designing sets and costumes for the school plays, and still titters with laughter over small, silly, light things.

It was Randie, Maddie, Mena and Katina who kept me awake at night.

How could I equip them? What had we not thought of yet?

I loved Erica, but she didn't need me in the same way and I was already stretched thread-thin.

I fear I taught her that fair is not equal, and while I attempted to be fair in my dedication to the mission for all of them, I was not always equal in the time I spent getting them there.

The Casino

In my second year at Sci, I knew a lot of eyes would be on my classroom. Our new freshman teachers would be looking for actions and techniques to emulate, and I had to be excellent not just for the scholars but for the team. Our new teachers had large deficiencies to fill and significant gains to make. Other schools would be looking to us to imitate the success we'd had in year one. NPR, *Ed Week*, and *The Times Picayune* stalked our halls, interviewing staff and scholars.

I placed a lot of pressure on myself to make sure everything was intentional and carefully planned. My room, from Day One, ran with the efficiency of a carefully measured blueprint. Summer had not caused dust to settle on all my lessons with Marc, and I was more poised and self-possessed than I had ever been. We began the year with strong Scope and Sequences, courtesy of our new DCI Megan, and my lessons were more cohesive and data-aligned.

Best of all, we had a series of benchmark assessments—real data, aligned to what scholars should be learning, that would result in a clear map of what each scholar knew and still needed to learn.

We were more prepared academically on day one and we all felt strongly that this would lead to even better gains for children—and bring us one giant step closer to the mission.

Unfortunately, my edges began fraying rather quickly. Being the Freshman Dean and supporting a hallway of new teachers was intensely time consuming, and I was very aware that I still had a lot of growing to do, even as I also began to realize my teaching ability was growing every day.

I began to seesaw back and forth, never able to come to a middle ground on how to spend my time. The To Do list for the Dean role grew with each passing day.

I was a teacher in a high needs classroom.

Scholars still needed to grow exponentially—I was first and foremost accountable to that. But I felt accountable more to the team than ever before, because it was a team with many members of a growth curve. I felt accountable to Frances as well, and her needs and priorities.

In the process of trying to build not one, but two sandcastles, I, by necessity, left some of the flourishes off. I lost lots of the elegance, trading it for utilitarian structures. My classroom was still joyful and I was still passionate about infecting scholars with a love of reading. But at the same time, I became more impatient— patience took time, and it was a luxury I could ill-afford.

Despite the snips and struggles, I was happiest when I was in my classroom, teaching. I developed a flow and rhythm that felt almost like music, catching the off-key moments and fixing them, taking time to pause and observe the movement mid-note. Scholar participation was bright and crisp, and I invested time in building a good relationship with almost every child.

In front of the classroom, I felt in control and mindful for the first time.

I felt like I was home.

It felt right to be a teacher, to live regarding every second and watch success bloom like the bicolored magnolias in early spring.

I flourished in these moments with my interactions with children. We were thriving together, and these moments propped up the difficulties throughout the rest of the day. And I gained an increased comfort in my classroom practice, began to feel less like I was scrambling and more like I was sailing a precarious but dependable ship.

Battery
Circle all that are true for you.

1. You prefer one-on-one conversations.
2. You like to talk through new ideas.
3. You feel that solitude is necessary.
4. You love large concerts.
5. You do not like interruptions when working.
6. You'd choose a cruise over a silent retreat.
7. You prefer small celebrations.
8. You tend to act first.
9. You have a constant inner monologue.
10. You've been described as outgoing or adventurous.
11. You'd rather give a speech to 500 than talk to five afterward.
12. You make new friends easily; people relate to you.
13. Friends chose you; you don't remember seeking them out.

14. Appearance means a great deal to you.
15. Networking makes you feel thin or fake.
16. You prefer stimulating, busy environments.
17. You screen your calls, even from friends and family.
18. Working on a team comes very naturally to you.
19. You feel claustrophobic around excessively chatty people.
20. You answer all your phone calls.
21. You find small talk cumbersome.
22. You'd rather be spontaneous and let the chips fall.
23. You'd rather be an expert at one thing than sample many.
24. You are a great multitasker.

If you circled more even numbers than odd ones, you're an extrovert. Your life's battery is charged by human interaction—you thrive on it. You feel more energized after collaboration. You seek out new interactions and social situations. At the end of a long week at work, you'll feel better after hanging out with several of your friends and hashing out the rollercoaster of your recent days. When you have a new idea, you imagine the team that can help you take it to reality.

If you cringed at sentences like "stimulating, busy environments" and selected mostly odds, you're like me: an introvert.

I'm guessing you may also like to work in small, clean, orderly spaces devoid of a lot of bustling, because too much activity makes you fidgety and distracted.

I bet when you go to large gatherings, you seek out people who know you well, and sometimes when you meet someone new, you forget to ask the easy return questions, like, "How was *your* holiday?" or "And what do *you* do?" Not because you're rude, but because it doesn't make sense to you to small talk, especially without purpose.

At the end of a long day, it's probably increasingly challenging for you to remain patient with group work or small conversations, and your mind wanders and talks to itself until you have to answer a question.

You hide this brain meandering well and engage often. You aren't a hermit—you are deeply involved with your close friends. You may have even gone to Mardi Gras, with its seething crowds of bead-draped drunkards, and Jazz Fest, too (but you wished that they'd capped admission at 100 people).

Fellow Introverts, fear not. This doesn't mean we hate people or hate teamwork. Extroverts feel more energized after interacting with people. Introverts feel less energized and need to recharge elsewhere after. That's the difference.

As a teacher, being an introvert was challenging, but not necessarily a bad thing. In my classroom, I was the conductor of a well-rehearsed and high-functioning orchestra, and in this way, even when surrounded, I was alone.

A teacher's life, though surrounded with children, is often by necessity a singular path. While collaboration is absolutely necessary, often the decisions about children rest in moments of deep concentration or in real-time action, singularly.

Teachers live in moments. We know the children best, all their strengths and weaknesses, their orbiting constellations of crises. We plan and act proactively; we adjust in the moment. An excellent teacher is the hub of a rapidly, efficiently spinning wheel of her own design, and this takes hours of self-sustaining effort.

Perhaps this was the reason extroverted teachers gravitate towards Sci Academy. It is a place rich with communication, support and collaboration. Where teachers once sailed solo, bravely alone on the buoyant tides, at a school like Sci no decision is made in a vacuum. Teachers and leaders talk everything through, and at no time was this more true than our first year.

Every decision had to be made, for our first year, for our first students, for the first time.

With a team whose lifeblood was communication, I sometimes struggled to be present for long conversations about scholars. *Just make a decision,* my mind screamed, as I nodded sagely and prompted for new information.

After years in Japan and then at my old school as well, I was well accustomed to being an island—to building the sandcastles on my own. Suddenly, people were stepping, critiquing, questioning, applauding, offering their own seashells for the moat walls. It was important for me to learn to pause and listen, and I did not always do this well.

As much as I thrived on all this development and involvement, sometimes I missed shoving off on my own into uncharted waters. As a teacher and member of a team founding a school, I sometimes found it hard to navigate my need for space and solitude with my passionate desire to be a great team player. It was hard to give each day so much of my battery to collaboration. I enjoyed it, and I valued it, but it made me tired.

This was never truer than Friday evenings, after four hours of team collaboration and development—PD in teacher-speak.

By 5:10, after Value Village in the hallway outside my classroom, I felt the deep and necessary desire to leave and recharge my depleted battery.

At the end of another Friday, when most of our staff went off the Sci Happy Hour at various bars around the city, I would again slink off to my car and drive straight home, for a dogwalk and a snuggle on the couch.

Several teachers spoke with me about this over the years, feeling I was distant, or aloof, hard to approach. I was told, "We want so badly to bond with you..."

I did make more efforts, even though the last place I wanted to be on Friday was a crowded, smoky bar. Sometimes I drug

Johnathan along as well, and he chatted with teachers, trying to distract them from conversations about school, steering them towards telling stories about their records or hobbies.

It was at times hard to explain to the extraordinarily extroverted that I wasn't shunning them. We refill our batteries in different ways, and it's important to respect each other's needs, especially when the hours are so long and the stakes of our work are so very treacherously high.

It was hard for me to expend so much energy on *adults*, but I also learned that it was being a part of a team. It is not just a label. It requires energy, even when the battery blinks red.

I'll Take That Charge

Randie began with me, day one of Sci Academy. Tall, and quiet, Randie made fast friends with no one; rather, she spent a lot of time observing, following my requests just a half step behind, slowly nursing her rebellion. Her mother, a graceful, albeit loud woman, kept close watch on her, and called me over any infraction.

Randie had no grey area. Either she was completely, if sullenly, amenable, or she did *exactly the opposite* of what was asked. Once, I asked Randie to hand me a stack of notebooks on my desk. I turned around to check the homework of another one of my advisees, when I heard a loud crash, and turned in time to see the stack hitting the ground and dozens of pages, let loose from their rings, fluttering to the floor. Randie stood next to the desk, the obvious culprit. Her face did not change; impassive, expressionless, she stood with her arms dangling, making direct eye contact with me.

I assigned her four demerits—an automatic detention—and she shrugged, stared down at the pile of papers, and poked them with one sneakered foot. I watched incredulous as she used her toe to unbury her own notebook. She picked it up, stepped over the rest, and walked lazily to her desk. She plunked her long frame into her chair, and began to write furiously in her journal.

I accepted another scholar into my advisory at this time, a new sophomore named Shanice. Shanice and Randie had attended the same elementary school. This was unusual—we normally separated these pairings, as we wanted scholars to be able to reinvent themselves without pressure from old friends.

Shanice's boyfriend, Shawn, was a new freshman, repeating for the second time. Shawn's behavior was often ill-tempered. He refused to serve detention, yelled at his teachers and was regularly put out of class. Once in the hallway, Shawn was sent to the desk at the end of the hall. Shawn would then pull out the teacher's chair, with its rolling wheels, out from behind the desk and whip up and down the hall on it.

Shanice, too, needed some intensive attention, I could tell immediately. She was loud, rough around the edges, and her behavior was unpredictable. Worst, she threatened to fight other scholars at a moment's notice, and Randie often found herself an unwitting partner in these hollering matches.

They both served long stints of detention. Randie's behavior began to spiral, with more outrageous incidents of disrespect, more back talk and blatant refusal of directions.

No one admitted to starting the fight, but the Biology teacher turned her back for a moment to reach for a stack of papers, and this was all the time it took for Shanice to fling herself across the computer lab desk at another scholar, baring her pencil to stab. Randie joined in, and so did three other girls—it took four teachers to pry apart the spitting, frothing, shrieking tumbleweed of nails, khaki, torn hair extensions and acrylic nails.

Randie and Shanice were brought to the front office and placed in separate rooms.

Frances went back to pick up Randie's oversized messenger bag, which had gotten shoved under a desk in the struggle. As she carried it back to the office, it felt heavy and clunky—too heavy for just binders and make-up—Sci Academy still wasn't using textbooks.

Frances brought the bag to Randie and impulsively asked permission to look in it.

Inexplicably, Randie said she could. Frances lifted the flap to find a loaded handgun stuffed between her math and English binders. She called the police.

I taught classes from eight thirty to eleven forty five without a break, so it was lunchtime when I was finally informed of what had happened. I arrived in time to watch the police handcuff Randie and place her into the back of a police car while her mother stood by, waiting.

I walked up to her, and put a hand on her shoulder. "You need to find out who put that gun in my baby's bag," she snarled. "That ain't Randie's gun. That ain't Randie's. Miss Eckhardt, go do something, that gun ain't Randie's!"

She was right. The gun, Randie informed us, belonged to either Shanice or Shawn.

Shanice denied any knowledge of the gun at all. Then she said Shawn had asked Randie to hold it for him, despite her protests, and that she'd tried everything she could to keep the gun off campus.

At this point, I was nauseous and livid. Randie was many things, but I couldn't believe she ever would have thought to bring a gun to school on her own. I wanted to know why she had it, and who else had known.

Marc and I collected Shawn from class and turned on the tape recorder.

Is the gun yours?
How did it get onto campus?
If it is yours, what were you planning to do with it?
Why would you bring a gun to school?

In response to every question he leaned over the spinning wheels of the recorder and said, "I'll take that charge."

After the third time he said this, I lost my temper, and swore at him, one of the only times I used profanity with a scholar. "Shawn, goddammit, you aren't taking any charge. My advisee has already done that for you. All we're doing now is trying to figure out the truth."

He looked confused. "What do you mean?"

The law is clear on possession. It mattered not at all where the gun came from, why Randie had it, or who it actually belonged to. The gun was in her bag and that made it Randie's.

Shawn ended up claiming that the gun was his and that Shanice didn't know anything about it.

Shanice called me that night, saying she wanted to come clean about everything.

I learned that Shanice had brought the gun to school on the bus under her baggy gray Sci Academy sweatshirt, and then asked Randie to carry it for her because her own bag wasn't big enough to hold and conceal it. She'd known a fight was going to happen and thought she'd need protection.

There was no protection for Randie.

I walked up to the window of the police car, and the cop in the driver's seat tried to wave me away. I said, "She's my advisee. She's *mine*. Gimme a minute."

I looked away, back toward the gate, where Randy's mother continued to cry inconsolably, and, Frances attempted to calm her.

I tapped on the window, where Randie's face was hidden behind her massive head of tight curls.

She looked up at me, her face a mess of tears and sniffles, and I realized she couldn't wipe her nose or eyes because of the handcuffs.

"I'm sorry," she mouthed through the glass.

Then she turned her head away, and would not look back, even though I tapped and said her name until the cop told me to get away from the car.

I had to go back and teach my last class after I watched them drive Randie away, her head hanging low against her chest.

We expelled all three of them, and I was left asking myself how I could not have somehow seen this coming. How was my attention so drawn away? Or was this just random, a terrible choice made by children playing games with toys they think they understand?

In a triple bypass irony, the then superintendent of schools enrolled his son in our school on the same afternoon.

Metal detector

Gun violence, a reality of New Orleans, had touched us and we had to adapt.

Sci Academy got a metal detector. Our scholars had a longer morning entry as security guard checked their bags, inspected the metal belt buckles and pocket change that sent the machine into high-pitched mewling.

It was something we never wanted for our school, this monstrous grey symbol of prison and punitive action, but we were naive to think that our school would be the one school in the district that didn't need one, that somehow our culture was immune to such atrocity.

Our mission would not change. But we had lost our pinhole view of it, our innocent belief that it created an island of safety.

Rebellion

Lunch ended at noon; at 11:58 I called for cleanup. Different tables gathered the trash, including the scandalous disposable styrofoam trays and threw them into bins around the room.

When I called for the first class to line up, there was a flutter of anticipation across the cafeteria. Five scholars stood and were immediately hissed and yelled at by others. They sat back down, looking guilty and complicit, forced to bet on red when they knew the odds.

I scanned the room, looking for a scholar to meet my eyes. Most shifted and turned away. I called the class again, louder and with forced cheer.

This time most of my class stood and shuffled to the door. I asked two of them to straighten the line, reinforcing the compliance and fragile beauty that it represented—order, structure, that pristine pane of glass. Jacob walked quickly to the door and called his class. Most of them lined up, but Gabe stood apart, a wild light glinting in his eyes.

"We're not going to class. We're sick of your rules. We're walking out!" He strode to the door and pushed by me. "We're leaving!"

The rest of the scholars stood up, and a wave of confusion washed over the room, a tidal wave that breached the dam. Some scholars just stood there, doe-eyed and dismayed. Others began jumping and laughing, and pushing towards the door. Others stayed on their little cafeteria stools, staring at the rapidity with which a system that had appeared so infinitely stable had been capsized.

I swallowed my panic, the flashes from Clark rolling in my gut. Four other teachers were present, one looking close to a breakdown. I skipped quickly down the steps to the cement walkway, and began to herd the scholars toward the building, directing with my hand, calling, "You are who you choose. You are scholars. It's time for class. Tower above the rest." It sounded brittle, suddenly, words against action, rain smattering along a cresting wave, dissolving.

Jacob and the other teachers followed my lead, herding scholars into groups and organizing a loose line. Most looked relieved. They'd wanted to leave chaos behind them and they'd been assured it wouldn't happen here. The desire to give in to panic was strong, but the need to restore culture for the scholars who needed it was stronger.

Gabe and about ten others were still walking in a group towards the front gate. To leave campus, they'd have to walk through the security building in which our metal detecting sentinel and security guard were housed.

The gaggle was slowing, and one by one, the band of rebels shrunk. Finally, it was Gabe and three others who made it to the security room. With a flash of inspiration they simply picked up speed and ran through.

The very definition of a Pyrrhic Victory, finding themselves outside the gates in the parking lot.

I knew our security guard, a slow moving, well-meaning man would be able to gather them up. I turned away from the gate just in time to see my advisee Tyrie slap another girl across the face.

We ended the fight quickly, and moved the molasses line of aspiring rebels towards the school.

Once in the hallway, many refused to go to class. I paused in the hallway amongst the surge of vacillating bodies, deciding whether to sit or flee or shout or comply. I held my hand up—our signal for silence—and waited fourteen heartbeats, as the shuffle and rustle quieted. A few scholars sucked their teeth, and then there was a flimsy stillness.

I raised my voice, forcing it clear and unwavering from my throat. We needed an impromptu solder, a whiteheat reconnect.

"Scholars. I am proud of you today. You have taken what you are learning to heart—you are learning to think for yourselves. We have read about nonviolent protest and the Civil Rights Movement, you are reading about the Holocaust. I am proud of you for thinking about how the lessons of the past can apply to your lives today.

"I also want you to consider. Martin Luther King protested so that you could attend a high quality public school. Many people—me, your teachers—work very, very hard for you because we know you are scholars. You choose to work harder and do more. You tower above the rest and you are headed to college. Wasn't this the dream? Wasn't this the reason so many others fought? So consider ways to make a change—talk to us, reach out, petition. Refusing to chase your education only hurts you. Your teachers are at their doors waiting for you. The future is now."

I turned, then, and grabbed the first hand, behind me, fortunately someone who was headed to my fourth period class. I said, loudly enough for the hallway to hear, "Good afternoon, Charles," and met his eyes.

He looked both ways for assistance and direction, but found no help. He suddenly was the new leader of the rebellion, with the power to either instigate or quell. It deflated quickly when he shook my hand back, mumbled "Good afternoon," and walked into my classroom.

The other teachers quickly began to do the same, gathering scholars into their rooms and getting them focused on work.

Marc came into the hallway and wrangled the remaining stragglers into classrooms.

We shuttled them through the rest of the day, quelling back talk and leveraging our strong relationships with most of them to influence the others.

At the end of the day, frazzled and threadbare, we met to discuss what had happened.

I took just a moment to feel a twinge of pride and excitement.

Were they approaching protest for the right reasons? Did they even understand what they were protesting?

Not really, but they never would have thought to stage a walkout if we hadn't taught them what one was.

The application of knowledge to action, an independence of thought and deed, was *exactly* what we wanted to see in them.

I was profoundly torn in another way. My last two years of high school, I attended Louisiana School for the Math, Science, and the Arts, a state-supported residential school for students who display exceptional potential or ability. In the last months of my senior year of high school, I was expelled from school for staging a series of protests against a new administration and a series of new rules imposed on the school and students.

I was more organized and methodical than this little protest zygote. I wrote letters, picketed, and staged performance art rebellions in the quad. The Director found cause to expel me and told my father in a meeting that "Quelling a rebellion only takes removing its head." This statement was true; without me, the demonstrations quickly ceased.

My team and I discussed who would be suspended, and for how long. There was a general consensus that we needed to calm the manifestations of unrest. Perhaps even a disciplinary hearing for Gabe, the ringleader of the insurgency.

As a Dean and school leader, I agreed, but the half-shaved blue haired, lip-ringed, picketing shadow of myself disagreed. Did I want to be the adult that discouraged nonviolent protest?

My father had pleaded with my former Dean. In a private meeting, he had begged him to excuse my behavior, so that the expulsion would not hurt my chances at a good college. My past had not been stable, my father had explained, it had been a tangle of divorce and chaos and abuse, and he, the Dean, had a chance to help me.

The Dean rolled back at my father, "Sometimes for the good of the whole, a few must be severely punished, even if that impacts their future."

Was I ready to internalize this sentiment?

Was I ready to silence my animal-eyed adolescent?

This protest began an internal struggle for me, between the good of the school and the good of the individual. This struggle rang again when I spoke to Kaitlin about power and influence, and when I made disciplinary decisions as a dean. What could be sacrificed for the good of the organization, and what was too much? Was our system of rules flexible enough to accommodate outliers, or mistakes, or lapses on judgment?

Could we justify punishing children who acted on what we had taught them?

In our quest for independence, ultimately, for our scholars, how flexible would we eventually have to be?

Letting Go

When I asked Mena why she wanted to attend Sci Academy, she said, "Because my dad thinks I should go there...and because I want a good future."

Standard answers that smacked of a reluctance that would flare, blister-like, all year.

Beyond that, Mena was unable to explain herself—she just... hated it. All the morning pep talks and hugs, and words of praise were not enough to relieve her from the constant depression and gloom that came with "being here."

I tried not to, but I took her loathing of the school personally. Sci Academy was an infant we had tended carefully, nourished with sacrifice and time for other priorities. It was a place, and a belief structure, that I held sacred; it was hard to have it so unwittingly and thoughtlessly questioned by an inarticulate child. I worked harder to make her happy, but she continued to suck her teeth, break the rules, and rack up weeks of detention.

Afterwards, I would sometimes drive her home, and she would roll her window down and put her face to the night air.

One autumn evening, dusk settling like falling leaves, we passed the abandoned Six Flags, and she'd pointed up at the abandoned wooden roller coaster, a dinosaur skeleton against the melting sky. "Ever want to make that climb up there?"

"It looks dangerous, Mena."

"But you'd be able to see so far from there. It would be like seeing straight into the future."

"But the future is now," I joked with her.

She rolled her eyes. "God, Miss Eckhardt, you really think the way you think is the only way to think."

We were silent, and I thought about what she'd said. In her convoluted way, she was asking me to let her go.

I couldn't. Letting her go would fly in the face of my belief about scholars, and that we were providing the best place for *all of them*.

Halfway through her sophomore year, I found Mena outside of the school building, curled into a tight ball on the hot metal platform at the top of the stairs. Her cellphone had gone off in class, one a little chirp and a vibration in her pocket.

Such a catalyst.

Mena had walked out of class, and gotten out the front door of the trailer. From there could go no further, locked in the misery of her choices. Return and hand over the phone, and still receive detention for walking out and refusal to follow directions? Call home to a furious father who would force her to return the cell phone?

Mena simply dissolved under the weight of these loathsome options, melted into a puddle of tears and vacillation on the stairs. I sat with her, overlooking the grassy field and abandoned school, it's crumbling walls and waist high grass swelling and dipping in the light breeze. I gave her a Kleenex, and rubbed her back until the hyperventilation stopped.

"Mena, what *is* it?"

"Miss Eckhardt," she hiccupped, "I just gotta go. I can't be here anymore. I gotta go."

When her father came, she simply kept repeating this statement, a mantra, her truth.

Her father decided to withdraw, her, though I pleaded with him to reconsider. He pulled me in for a big hug, spontaneously, and put his bear-like hands on my shoulders. I looked up at him; even at 5'7" meeting his eyes required neck-craning.

"Miss Eckhardt, I know you love Mena and you wants what's best for her. That's what I want, too. But she ain't happy here. You should see her, dragging round the house. She don't have a smile anymore and I don't understand it but she's not happy. You know I love this school, and I think it's the best place, but I can't force her anymore."

Mena hugged me goodbye. "I'll see you soon, Miss Eckhardt," she said. The salve of a soothing lie, I responded the same way.

She was gone.

Over the next several months, I called and texted several times to check on her, but she never replied.

I ran into her father a year later at Home Depot. He wrapped me in his huge arms and hugged me. Mena was doing great, he said. Straight A's and B's. She loved her new school, and never got into any trouble. He gave me her new cellphone number and promised to send my love.

It was a hard thing to accept the reality that love was not enough. I loved Mena, and I loved the school, but I could not cultivate a love between the two of them.

Do The Right Thing

My only pieces of classroom technology were my Mac laptop, a projector, and a document camera called an Elmo. I was able to switch back and forth between my computer screen to a PowerPoint or video and then back to the Elmo, which projected whatever I placed beneath it.

Sci Academy did not have bells, and we used email and text for nearly everything, so keeping the computer handy was a necessary part of the job. I set the system up each morning, testing the ability switch back and forth, and then went into the hallway to lead the morning meeting with the scholars, which included announcements, a rallying speech, Value Village, and the credo.

On this particular morning, a film crew for *EdWeek* was in my classroom, and they set up their camera and mics as I made final adjustments to the technology and agenda on the board.

The crew joined me in the hallway to film the scholars participating in Value Village. They were learning to give each other shoutouts now, rather than just receiving them from teachers. The experiment was gaining momentum, even if it sometimes dissolved into silliness. I was in the hall for no more than five minutes before greeting my class at the door and guiding them in.

Usually they began work immediately, taking out their notebooks and answering the questions on the board. Instead, I heard shuffling, and throat clearing, and turned to see that the board was black, the projector shining a white square rather than the questions from my prepped computer...

...Which was missing.

Where it stood, only a snarled tangle of cords remained.

In the short amount of time that I'd turned my back, the computer had disappeared, which means it had occurred in the middle of morning meeting, which also meant that several scholars would have seen who went into my classroom.

We always encouraged scholars to "do the right thing without being told," and inform us when they are aware of actions that could harm their team or community. But I also knew that the rules of their lives away from us were very different. "Snitches get stitches;" nobody could afford the reputation of being a "rat."

In the meantime, I had about twenty seconds to solve the problem of my lesson, which involved a video I would no longer be able to show, and the more immediate need for work to be done while my scholars waited for me, increasingly impatient.

And the cameras were rolling.

I shifted to a shorter lesson and a "book checkout day." Academically, the day remained productive.

But it feels like a kick to the gut to be stolen from, by the same kids I loved beyond understanding, and for who I sacrificed so much. It rings in the body like a teenager's broken heart, a shimmer ache of betrayal in the stomach. It flickers, surprises, the temporary suspicion of everyone, until enough time passes for the heart and will to stabilize.

By lunch, the news had spread throughout the school. Some scholars ambled up to me, said they were sorry my computer was gone. But no one was saying who did it, though everybody knew. And that "snitches get stitches" knowledge makes sense, but it's painful, and the pain dulls very slowly.

What's Worth It

Anne asking, "What's this word, Miss Eckhardt? Oh, wait, let me try to sound it out."

Scholars snapping enthusiastically over someone's answer, smiling patiently when someone struggled with reading a passage aloud.

Joy in success, in struggle, in progress.

Treyvon wearing lipstick and asking we refer to him as her and other scholars just shrugging and smiling instead of calling him the names that must have come to their minds.

Three scholars mock-arguing that they'd throw the V first.

Tyrone saying, "Are we gonna read another story like the last one? That was *fire!*"

The magic of a room of children, learning, with rapt attention and internal motivation.

The bath of smiles pouring off the bus each morning.

Love and hard work, made into a reality worth living.

Realizing that I had started as a mediocre teacher, and could now say confidently that I was working towards greatness.

Proving everyone who said it couldn't be done wrong.

An Awkward Pause

"Hello, may I speak to Mrs. Thomas?"

"This is she."

"Mrs. Thomas, this is Kaycee Eckhardt, Freshman Dean of Sci Academy. I am calling because we have suspicions that your scholar may have come to school under the influence of marijuana."

"What suspicions?"

"Mrs. Thomas, his eyes are red, and his speech is slightly slurred."

"So? He's got allergies. He probably took some medicine this morning."

"Mrs. Thomas, his clothing, hair, and bookbag smell strongly of marijuana. He is in the office right now, and I can smell the marijuana from several feet away."

"Well, how do you know what it smells like anyway?"

"..."

"Well?"

Sigh.

"Mrs. Thomas, can you please come and get your son?"

Resignation

I resigned from the role of Dean because I could no longer ignore the tide within that pulled me only one way.

I did not want to lead adults if it meant feeling like I was short-changing my scholars.

The third of our four reading benchmark tests showed the scholars with an average growth of two and a half years. I knew I could push them to three years of growth, but not the three and a half of the year before. I could explain this data several ways, but if I was deeply honest with myself I knew this was because of the corners I had snipped in order to spend time on the logistics and workload of the Dean role.

I no longer wanted to feel conflicted. I wanted to be free to be a *teacher* and to become the teacher I knew I could be.

I was also feeling incredibly frayed, and began a stomach-pit worry that the long hours and constant stress were causing me the fabled "burnout" that so many teachers before me had cautioned about.

I spoke to Marc about these concerns several times. He'd given me tips on organizing my inbox and responding to mail, and asked me to complete an experiment in which I tracked how I spent my time, and then intentionally tried to cut ten percent of the time off of each.

Yet despite my efforts, I couldn't see a way to keep the boat from capsizing, besides bailing constantly. I'd cut everything I could—exercise, time with family, dinner. I worked every day except Saturday, a sacred day of rest—except to answer the phone calls from teachers and scholars about their concerns and crises, which I did every day.

I felt like Mena; I had nothing to say except, "I don't know what else to cut. I'm so tired."

When I'd first brought up the idea of resigning from the Dean role, Marc had asked me to think about it. When I returned to say I still thought it was the right decision, he asked me to consider the mission, and whether my resignation was in alignment with my commitment to it.

I left feeling even more conflicted. Would resigning be damaging for scholars and their progress? Would, somehow, my not being a Dean really have that kind of impact?

My answer to this—finally—was yes, but perhaps not in the way I believe Marc intended. I believe he intended to sway me to the realization that service to the scholars and mission was, as always, paramount, and serving as Dean doubled my impact.

I did decide that being a Dean was having an impact, but not always the right one. I was good at it, and I was good at being a teacher, but I was less of a teacher while doing it, and scholars needed to learn to read, well and often, most of all.

So I resigned.

I felt awash in Marc's disappointment, but chose not to internalize it. Instead, I stored it into a quiet place to dissolve in its own time.

Power and Influence Revisited

Five minutes into the conversation, I realized what was happening.

We had returned from our retreat and Dave, the teacher who would become the Freshman Dean in my stead, had asked to speak to me. He hadn't gotten to specifically what he wanted, though he'd been speaking for a few minutes. I forgot my cheat sheet, and became rapidly impatient.

"So Kaycee, I think that, if you make this change, it will have a lasting impact on our scholars. It's important to make changes for the better, I know that's really important to you. Also as the new Dean, I'm going to need your help in the beginning. I think you do a great job with scholar management and ...:"

"Dave," I said, interrupting. "I appreciate that you thought about this conversation, and I also appreciate that you're attempting to use reward and legitimate power, combined with my power motivation, to achieve your goal. But can you just tell me what you need, and I'll let you know whether I can handle it or not? I don't have time for practice right now."

He paused, and looked surprised, and then burst into laughter. I laughed with him.

"Sometimes it's ok to set the bullshit aside and just ask for what you want."

He snickered.

Agreed.

Growth

The average reading level improvement this year was 3.2 grades.

Less than last year.

I had a myriad of reasons, but ultimately no excuses.

Next year would have to be different.

YEAR THREE: NO SHORTCUTS. NO EXCUSES
Cheatsheet: Year Three

While my cheatsheet this year still encompassed some of the goals about emotional regulation and emotional intelligence development as last year, it took a decidedly different tone. My desire to become, not just a teacher, but the best teacher I could be, began to infuse my every thought.

Without the Dean job, I felt freed to finally focus on what I wanted to do, not what I had to do.

1. I will be aware of the impact my emotions have on others.
2. I will not assume that private exchanges or conversations are about me.
3. I will remember that other people have different styles of getting things done.
4. I will teach people by having them generate their own solutions rather than offering one, even if I know it will work.
5. I will do the thing I want to do least, first.
6. I won't spend more time organizing a task than actually following through on that task.
7. I will not assume that, just because I said it, it was heard— accountability for teachers is as important as it is with scholars.

8. I won't let my tendency to micromanage get in the way—I will delegate effectively!
9. I will think about a conversation before I have one.
10. I will take feedback from all members of my team equally, without bias to who they are or how long they have been on the team.
11. I will remember that I am an emotional sender—my emotions have a huge impact on those around me, and that I *cannot* send negative energy out!
12. I will *listen*.

Phoenix

In the middle of summer training, I was on my way to the office when I saw a group of boys from the school we shared a campus with staring down at something they had encircled. One boy was nudging it with his toe, and they laughed when it appeared to twitch.

I strode over and elbowed them out of the way, to find the most emaciated dog I'd ever seen. It was lying in the gravel, panting weakly; its eyes were glazed grey and unseeing, it's tongue lolled on the gravel.

I called one of our scholars over and asked him to get me some water. Samuel cringed back.

"Uh uh, Miss Eckhardt, that's a pitbull. You don't wanna mess around with that. That thing's gonna bite you."

It was, indeed, a pitbull. It's clunky head was as conspicuous as its ribs. It had a frayed tangle of rope around its neck, cuts and bites all over its body. I leaned over it, and the other boys stepped back, and slowly scattered.

"I'm aware of that, Samuel. I have one at home. Please get me some water."

I crouched next to the dog's head, and it didn't move. Its paws were rash red and sunburnt, and a wound on its stomach was bulbous and festering. It gasped like a fish on the pavement, ribs hitching up and down unevenly. It didn't recoil when I lifted its head, past apathy.

The water revived it a little. Samuel and I poured a little into its mouth and got it onto its feet, but the animal was only able to stand on its carpels, crawling forward in a disturbing hunch. We fed it some hamburger buns from the teacher's lounge, and he swallowed them without chewing, unexpectedly rolling pink-rimmed eyes at us.

Hurricane Katrina killed or stranded more than 600,000 animals, and years later, the problem had only been exacerbated by blight, neglect, rampant breeding, an opposition to spaying and neutering, and dog fighting.

This pitbull appeared to have been a bait dog in a "sport" in which one dog is tethered and other dogs are allowed to attack and maim it. The raw, chapped ring around its neck under the matted ropes suggested it had tried often to escape its confinement, while the bites and claw marks along with the emaciation, indicated that whoever had kept it had not intended for it to live very long.

Dog fighting was an issue in New Orleans. Backyard breeding was common, and the weakest of puppies discarded, left to wander the streets until starvation, dehydration, or sickness swallowed them, a car ran them over, or the SPCA picked them up and carried them to almost certain annihilation.

More than 80% of the dogs in the shelters are considered pitbulls.

Fewer than 20% are adopted out.

I sat there with it for a moment, picking fleas off its hide, trying to make a decision. My lunch break would be over soon. When I picked it up and flocked it into the crook of my arm, I first saw how young it was, barely past adolescence but already so close to death. It stared at me, making eye contact in that way pitbulls do, a discerning stare filled with portent.

We already had one pitbull, a rescue from the Treme. Johnathan had found that one on Craigslist—a post from a woman who had cared for a female dog when she'd been thrown, pregnant, into her yard over the fence. Kuro had grown into a massive hulk of an animal, with brown-bear eyes and a friendly, unassuming intensity.

Some pitbulls, young and filled with potential as rare as a pearl, already with futures emaciated, untended by their experiences, attended with scorn and caution by strangers.

When I walked down the street with my scholars, I watched tourists clutch their bags, judging their youth and race as quickly as they might scan a window filled with shoes.

Employees followed them surreptitiously around the gift shops on college campuses, assuming they would steal something, eyeing the cheap lanyards and stickers in their hands protectively, even as the scholars walked to the register to purchase the school's paraphernalia.

A certain private school in Memphis had even managed to deny us admission, dodging our requests for a tour until they finally sent an email expressing "regretfully" that their school probably wasn't a "good fit" for "our population."

In its quivering body I saw the possibility of a symbol carried to fruition, if someone bothered to take the proper time and care. This puppy, our scholars—both were quivering potential, ready to thrive if someone would just take the time.

Marc was off campus for the day, so I snuck the dog into his office, throwing a Sci Academy sweatshirt over its body and hustling past the administration offices for the other school. Indoors for the first time, it was terrified and shaking, and immediately urinated all over the floor.

I called Johnathan, and he reluctantly interrupted his workday to pick the dog up.

"That's still a puppy," he said, frowning. "What happens when it gets bigger? And, Jesus, what's that growth on its stomach?"

We found out.

Over the next week we spent nearly $2,000, learning about umbilical hernias, collapsed tracheas, heartworms, and trigeminal neuritis. Empathy can be expensive. Love takes more than romantic, intangible sacrifice.

For several weeks John kept asking, "Have you found a home for the dog yet?" and I would reply, "No. Not yet, but I'm trying," while not really trying very hard at all. He needed us.

We named him Basil, though I thought Phoenix would have been a more suitable name.

He rapidly shook off the scarring, though it would be months before he walked properly and his collapsed trachea would give him a permanent gasp and wheeze.

Basil grew into a 70 pound pitbull with a gigantic head and snout like a horse's muzzle, but for all his rippling muscles and toothy grin, he's gentle, sits in laps, and is all the more loving because of the origins I am sure that he remembers.

From my scholars, I never wanted gratitude. I wanted them to have the ability to have the self-awareness and imagination to envision a series of fates, and select carefully.

I wanted them to rise from their own ashes.

Orchestra

In Sarah Carr's book, *Hope Against Hope*, she writes, "Kaycee, who grew up in Louisiana, has an infectious passion: watching her preach the virtues of the school at a student ceremony or event feels akin to attending a religious revival."

Sounding the rallying call came with the territory of motivating freshman who had never worked hard in school to push themselves past the point of fatigue.

In my fourth year as a post-Katrina teacher I hung a sign next to my clock that said, "Be the hub, not the wheel."

My intention this year with scholars was to have them do the heavy lifting—I wanted to orchestrate, listening and adjusting tone and volume, as they created the magic of learning on their own.

I wanted to remove myself from the spotlight, so I pushed them more quickly towards independence. We did more group work; I held debates and allowed myself to take some risks with chaos and structure in order to allow them some room to breathe.

This class thrummed like hummingbirds. They internalized the rules more quickly than last year's scrappers and seemed to shrug them off more easily. I spent the summer examining the Common Core, and began experimenting with close reading and deep examinations of more rigorous excerpts than I'd attempted before.

It worked. No matter what the reading level, they responded well to the challenges I presented them.

I believe this was due to the fact that I had nothing else to focus on—just them, and the ebb and flow of a classroom loving the written word. Where year two had felt like drowning, year three felt like floating weightless on the open sea, still with the occasional wave, but with control and air to breathe.

Stature

Gerome: small in stature, large in smiles.

The kind of child who would put his foot in the aisle to pretend he was going to trip me, but laugh because it was too obvious and he didn't want to in the first place. Too mischievous to be malicious, too quick to laugh to be deceitful.

One morning, he came to school speechless, vacantly staring—not the Gerome I knew. He shuffled into my room, a uniformed ghost, curled up on a beanbag, and shut his mouth and mind. Not knowing what to do for him, first period came and went. His advisor tried to speak to him, as did I, but he turned his face further into the blue vinyl of the chair and refused to speak. My students cast bemused glances at his small frame, curled into a tight ball, backpack still looped over one shoulder. I conducted my class around him, redirecting any stares at him back to me.

Lunch arrived before he was able to sit up and announce to me, as I herded third period out of the room, that his uncle had been shot on the street in front of their house. Gerome got onto the school bus that morning, not knowing whether his uncle would live or die.

Glancing back at my line of twenty impatient ninth graders waiting to be herded to lunch, wanting badly to be able to send them unescorted so I could give Gerome my full attention, I said, "Gerome, you could have stayed home today. I'm so sorry."

"The Biology End of Course Test is in two days, Miss Eckhardt," he said. "I can't miss a day of school."

The logic of this confused me. "I have to ask, Gerome. Why come to school and then refuse to attend class? Why sit in the back of the room in which you are most successful, when it is biology that gives you hives?"

Gerome shrugged and went back to his beanbag. I tried to bring him lunch from the cafeteria, but the workers informed me that the child had to receive the lunch in person—they couldn't hand it over to "just anyone." So I slipped an apple into my pocket and gave him my sandwich. When he discovered that what he thought was peanut butter was made of almonds, he looked at me incredulously. But he ate.

He sat in the back of my classroom all afternoon. I found small jobs for him—staple this, file that—I had other students to attend to but tried to pass by him, put a hand on his shoulder, make eye contact. His voice sounded hollow, coming from the bottom of a well. I had no way to reach him, and no time. Our single social worker, for 300 children, struggled to meet the needs of the most needy. Gerome's advisor came by again to check on him. In this instance, like so many, he and I used our love like a poultice. We said the magic words, pressed our love against his wounds, tried to allow our lack of understanding to disguise itself in bravery.

Why would he come to school, with the knowledge that his uncle was dying? Why would he choose school over the net of his family?

The answer, very simply, was that the school was the safest place he knew. Being at school felt more secure, more comforting, than being nearer to the tragedy. Helping me put a sticker on the top of "A" homework was a greater balm than anything the outside world could offer him.

The next day, Gerome arrived at school, reunited with his jovial and carefree self. Gone were the hollow well-voice and the limp despair. Surprised and pleased, I gave him a quick hug and asked about his uncle.

He said, "Oh, everything's cool. He didn't even much die or nothing!" Nonchalant and relieved, he headed off to Biology.

As I stood in the breezeway and watched him go, I thought of the things Gerome had probably seen and experienced in order to believe survival of a gunshot made everything OK.

Again, I pinched myself to keep from crying, pressing my finger into the permanent yellowish pinch-bruise on my inner arm. I envied and pitied the sheer resilience of a child accustomed to disaster.

Bird Of Paradise

In the third year after Katrina, the RSD had an idea to turn all of its remaining high schools into "career-ready" schools. Students could select the high school they wanted to attend based on their career interests.

One of these schools was to be a "culinary arts academy," which seemed, from the boardrooms of the district office, rather logical. New Orleans thrived on tourism, and a career as a chef or baker would be a respectable, profitable profession, which might lead to better career pathways. Management, perhaps a future ownership.

White men in Dillard's suits shook hands and smiled at their ingenuity and passed down the mandates.

"The way we structure this is important. Not for a lifetime of servitude, but for bringing them from employee to employer," said the then-principal of the historically black school. "This is an opportunity for an RSD high school to take on a life of its own, to draw from all over the city."

Unfortunately, besides shoddy plumbing and being unequipped with any kitchen areas, the school hired no culinary experts. Teachers taught the same classes, in much the same lackluster way I'd seen at Clark, and their electives consisted of courses on dining room preparation, plate garnishing, and sanitation.

Sanitation?

Students were learning to prepare food by helping the cafeteria workers heat the school lunch. They were washing dishes and wiping the tabletops after lunch service.

In "Dining Room Preparation," they were learning the different ways a napkin could be folded. Pyramid, bird of paradise, standing fan, crown.

What did all this dishwashing and napkin folding tell these students about the expectations the adults in their lives had for them?

In the wake of this failure, Charter Management from Los Angeles took over the school and, despite protests from the community, opened it up to filming for a reality TV show called *BlackBoard Wars*.

The show featured violent fights and kids being slammed into the tops of police cars and handcuffed and shots of sobbing Teach For America teachers saying, "This is trial by fire." A school leader began speeches for the children with such sentimental intros like, "a member of the community was shot in the face" and such compassionate statements as "the next time you disrespect me, do not come back."

His advice for his teachers: "This is a tough ass job."

The takeover was an utter failure, and now the school sits empty, its Trojans finally silenced, the first slashes of graffiti quickly appearing on its vacant walls.

The hulking reminder of where expectations can, and do not, lead.

Turkey Day

Over Thanksgiving break, I hit an emotional wall. I was exhausted, frustrated, and overwhelmed. I had a week to spend with Johnathan at home, and I had big plans on catching up on all of the crafty activities I enjoy so much. The list included making seitan, packing garlic pickles, making soap, homemade cards and candles for Christmas presents, painting, and possibly setting up a chicken coop in the backyard. I was really looking forward to a long, quiet, selfish holiday.

The holiday began. I slept for the first day, relaxed for the second, graded papers, wrote lesson plans, and caught up on school work for the next three days, ran errands and cleaned the house, cooked Thanksgiving dinner.

On Friday before we returned to school, I realized that none of my art or cooking projects would be getting done. I would not be making canned goods. There would be no chickens. I simply did not have the time to do these things. It was a humorless, painful moment, and I again felt the paperthin dryness in my chest, expanding.

I had to ask myself, "What am I willing to give up for this job? How much will I sacrifice before I can't anymore?" The lack of an answer scared me.

The Smart Race

In year three we stopped saying the word "smart."

Kids come in with stereotypes and assumptions about what it means to be "smart."

They say, some kids are just "smarter" than others.

Smart kids are nerds.

I'm good at English, but I'm just not "smart" at math.

Smart is a word that implies a fixed status.

Smart suggests that some people are "just better" at things than others.

Kim can do that because she's "smart."

I can't do things as well as Kim because I'm not smart.

As teachers, if we referred to actions or knowledge bytes as "smart," we indicated a state of being rather than an action or thought worth imitating, worth attempting. We were inadvertently feeding these beliefs about what it took to be "smart." For kids who are several years behind, beliefs about the fixed nature of "smart" can be extremely poisonous. Kids can believe in their own stagnancy, as much as they believe that smarts are hereditary rather than earned; the terrible belief that our destinies are not determined by our own actions, but rather inflicted upon us.

Hasn't that been a disturbing truth for generations of the children of New Orleans? Destiny too often determined by a hurtling trajectory of poverty, socioeconomic status, race, perjorative schooling, and segregation? Education failed these children, up to the point they arrived on our proverbial doorstep. They developed defense mechanisms to explain the reasons why they "just can't do" certain things.

How else can they explain it? They can't call themselves dumb—they at least know better than that. But it's easy, sometimes to be so fearfully behind in academics to say, "That's just not what I'm smart at."

We have to start by rewriting this identity.

We found a new word instead: "yet" began to act like punctuation at the end of many of our sentences.

Your answer's not quite there...yet.

Your essay is decent, but it's not excellent... yet.

Your thought is interesting, but you haven't provided any evidence...yet.

To be "smart" became taboo. To be working hard became the new cool.

When students are in a classroom where a reputation for being smart became less important than being focused, working hard, trying again, staying engaged, they suddenly feel a new ownership.

No matter where they are at in the race, they feel like they are in the running. No more forgone conclusions, no more assumptions from their teacher.

They can no longer just look at their neighbor and wish they were "smarter." Instead, they get to decide—how quickly am I going to move towards my own improvement?

How far will you go today? Will you own the attempt?

Gullible

"I can't stay for detention. I have a *baby*."

Our newest scholar, William, was filled with excuses for why he could never serve detention, but this one was a new one, and surprising.

His advisor, Kaitlin, perked up.

"How have I not heard about this before?"

"It's *private*. I don't want drama with my girlfriend. But I can't stay, and I gotta use my phone, in case his momma calls. What if I gotta pick up diapers? Or she needs something?"

A baby. *An involved father figure.*

Kaitlin and I were elated, and made exceptions, allowing him to call the child's mother—not, incidentally, his girlfriend—at lunch time, giving him privacy out of the walkway.

When he had detention, he was also allowed to serve at lunch, so that he could go home to spend time with his son.

Months later, I was talking to one of my advisees, a distant cousin of William's.

"I think it's wonderful that William is so attentive to his son and its mother," I said wistfully.

She snorted through her nose. "You for real Miss Eckhardt? That boy don't have no kinda son. He just sayin that so he don't have to go to detention. He plays all ya'll. He sells drugs at the park 'cross the street. He using those phone calls to place orders."

She studied my face incredulously.

"Miss Eckhardt, *everybody* knows that."

Oh.

Grasshoppers

On the boardwalk today, a grasshopper child with pants bagging and legs flapping hops away from Kaitlin, screeching and spitting grasshopper green violence. Kaitlin turns to me and says, "I can't do this anymore. Let them sue."

I scuttle on. My moments are oozing away and I must press forward, to crisis and deficit and need, class in five minutes, "I'm sorry" I say, and leave her snatching for his escaping sail-shirttail.

Later, a quiet moment. I see her curl her lovely slender arm around this same young man. She tells him he will be fine. She whispers, soothing tones into the wild. And as he shrugs and hitches at his pants and sneers and scoffs with his chapped lips and scars, scars everywhere, she curls her beauty into his like an exaggeration, she cuddles the dead child in him, hoping she and Lazarus can briefly talk.

A tear sneaks in. I have no time for it, but I ache for her unbridled passion, as much as for the loathing she feels, the way her fingers tip up at the end—she withdraws the pressure at the last centimeter of skin, a minor reservation of herself and her sanity. She loves him, a confusing love, she bends herself into his necessities, she fights for him and this reluctant war eats away at her, a sacrifice gone astray.

She looks through him and then away, over the battered tin trailer rooftops and one scraggly tree, half strangled in sewage at its feet. She sweats through the bend of her polyester collar and the fabric of her entrapment, taking deep humid breaths.

Here, I too embrace the insane dichotomy of love with sometimes loathing. This toxic tug-of-war tracks exhaustion-tinted age into the flesh beneath my eyes. This bounding Acrididae fight can feel hopeless, but we all fight to make it translate into something akin to a future full of a freedom we adults have clearly defined. Freedom to understand taxes and student loans, social graces and balancing checkbooks, college quads and gluten-free options. To wear pants that fit and confident toothy smiles. To evolve.

The child wriggles, spits on the floor, again a grasshopper hacking tobacco stains.

I wondered, just for a second: How much more free is he than she and I to spit and dance, touch and love, and fly away and die so soon?

Perhaps our hitching flailing child has had it right, all along...?

Is his grasshopper dance more appropriate here than our slogans and civilization and rules?

Is his spitting and posturing meant as a Morse code message to us, to forego the trappings of society and try a different freedom than the one we bleed ourselves to offer?

Maybe our little grasshopper realizes that the ugliness and violence of his life is nothing but the broken symbols of a space he cannot control, and, a fleeting arthropod, he chooses rebellious deconstructed circles, selects the chaos rather than trying to make sense of our world: a society that longs to squash him into oblivion, if it could.

We pity him. We pity his ridiculous, benighted ways.

But is he closer to nature than any of us?

What else is it that he understands that we, in our supposed civilized ignorance, cannot grasp?

Grasshopper is not his name, but Kevon came to our school itching and chawing and smirking, a living parody of himself, larger than life and wilder than the grass growing between the cracks on the boardwalk. Kevon was one of the living horror stories of our city, an attestation to what happens when children from inequitable backgrounds do not receive the individual help they need.

Kevon's obstacles were stacked so high against him that he was hardly visible from underneath—perhaps this was the reason he was so abrasive. Life had quickly taught him that attention and help would only come through chaos and violence.

Kevon had been passed from a family member's home to an evacuation to Georgia and finally returned to New Orleans after the storm only to be shot in the back while attending a basketball game—his rebel-hitch was not one of posturing, but necessity. He'd been fourteen at the time, and had spent several months recovering in the hospital, which put him even further behind in school than he'd been before.

His great uncle was raising him, an imposing but loving man who wanted the best for Kevon. In just two years, Kevon had been enrolled in half a dozen RSD schools, suspended from all of them and expelled from some, before washing up on the shores of Sci Academy.

Kevon's behavior, both before and after the shooting that left him with scars and a permanent limp, was erratic and violent. Within the first two weeks of being enrolled at Sci Academy, he punched another scholar in the back of the head for "being a white wanna-be-nigger bitch." When the scholar fell over, blindsided, Kevon stood over him, yelling, "See? I told you I was gonna fucking sneak you, bitch!"

His hair trigger responses were as unpredictable as they were unnerving. The episodes pushed beyond the boundaries of anything we'd ever seen at Sci, and even what I'd experienced at Clark. His attacks could be racial, or worse, sexually aggressive, and were extraordinarily brutal.

In another altercation, Kevon broke a window, then attempted to pick up the glass with his bare hands in order to slash at the other scholar. Once removed from the situation, he pummeled huge holes in the back of a door, holes we gingerly covered with posters from Goucher and Xavier University. Other scholars avoided him, out of respect and fear.

His great uncle worked tirelessly for Kevon. He responded to phone calls day or night, and was at the school any day he was not working, watching Kevon in class and participating in his tutoring. His involvement with Kevon was one of love and blazing hope, and he infected us with it even as we struggled to meet his nephew's needs.

Kevon came with a dizzying array of needs, and Sci Academy was the first school in his long stint of transfers to realistically attempt to address them. Kaitlin, in particular, worked daily with him. She established a tutoring program with his teachers, and spent hours tutoring him herself. She demanded that he attend class, which was where, she insisted, he would learn the skills he needed to acclimate.

Kaitlin reminded us that he was a *scholar*, one of the children we had made a promise to, when we committed to the mission of "all scholars."

She reminded me that it wasn't the Ericas that we had to fight for—it was the Kevons, most of all, who needed the specific commitment and love that Sci Academy brought to its children.

She held the flashlight in the darkness, filtered high to the words we'd etched there together: All scholars. Equipped. Success.

11:10 am: Kevon approached my advisee's lunch table. He leaned over to (name removed)'s face and said to her, "I'm gonna bat you in the fucking mouth, bitch." I asked him to return to his table. He said to me, pointing in my face, "You really gonna make me fucking hit you, I hate you white teachers, just wait, you gonna get yours." Then he passed by me, "bodychecking" me by bumping hard into my left side.

11:50 am: I found Kevon sketching a gun on the wall of the hall near the restrooms. I asked him where he needed to be, and if I could help him get back to class. Kevon said "Why you always fucking with me? You really gonna make me tell you something! I'm really gonna do you something soon." He took his hands, pointed into gun shapes, and pointed them at my face. "Blam, blam, bitch," he said, laughing. He then grabbed his crotch area and shook it at me. "Suck it bitch," he said. Then he left the hall.

We hired a mentor from a group called the Circle of Courage who aimed to support and teach children like Kevon. His mentor walked with him throughout the day, talked him out of his violence, and was able to intervene with him.

After Kevon threatened to fight his bus driver, growling into his face and throwing rocks at him, the driver refused to pick him up anymore; we couldn't ask him to monitor Kevon's behavior while also driving the bus. The school paid for a taxi to pick him up and return him home, so that he would meet the requirements of his homebound status and be at school on time if his great uncle could not bring him.

Because of a series of incidents with the law, Kevon wore an ankle bracelet, which kept constant track of his whereabouts. The bracelet would occasionally run out of batteries, and then it would beep...beep...beep...until we plugged it, with him attached, into the wall.

Over the months he spent with us, there were also moments of great progress. He occasionally raised his hand to ask a question. Our tutoring sessions happened in the afternoons, and sometimes his great uncle would join us, smiling benevolently as Kevon worked through a couple of paragraphs. I looked forward to working with him individually. On his own, he was smiling and almost gentle, offering small glimpses at the child he may have been, once. Praising him for a well-written sentence or piece of insight would illuminate his face from the inside. He would smirk crookedly, and say, "I can do it. Just don't want to most of the time."

I was deeply conflicted about Kevon. His violence frightened the other scholars and impacted the learning environment; scholars simply learned less during his outbursts, which could be prolonged and nightmarish.

In him, I also saw the worst of what I had left behind at Clark, but also potential for greatness, and change.

We made great efforts to help Kevon, but we also made mistakes, and tensions rose exponentially when Kevon became one of ten children involved in a lawsuit against the Louisiana Department of Education. The lawsuit alleged that the city's fragmented education system had resulted in "systemic failures to ensure that students with disabilities have equal access to educational services and are protected from discrimination."

His lawyers accused us of discriminating against Kevon, specifically around an incident that had occurred earlier in the year.

Marc had been invited on the *Oprah Winfrey Show*, where we and a handful of other charter schools were given $1,000,000 each. Still in modular trailers, Sci Academy did not have an auditorium large enough to hold our ninth to eleventh grade classes, but the church next door allowed us to bring our entire population over, to sit and watch the taping as a community. When the announcement was made, the camera zoomed in on Marc's stunned face. The montage of film that aired on the show gave many of the scholars glimpses of themselves on national television, working in class or saying the credo. The mayor came to speak to us, and we celebrated. We invited parents and had a brass band play.

We had not invited Kevon. We'd decided to leave him behind in the office to wait for his great uncle to pick him up. We'd been worried about his behavior especially in the church, an environment not our own. And we'd been selfish. We'd wanted to celebrate without having to keep him under surveillance, as well.

This must have hurt him, and communicated to him what half a dozen other schools had before.

Kevon told his uncle, "They left me. They left me out."

We had. It was the wrong decision, and it was unfair.

But we were all on a steep learning curve, everyone scrambling, and the involvement with the lawsuit and lawyers complicated matters further. We had meetings that lasted all day, tense, emotionally-charged meetings where everyone wanted the best for Kevon, and everyone had a different opinion of what that was.

The truths were complicated too.

We were an open-enrollment public charter school. Kevon had a right to a wonderful school, with teachers who loved him and met his needs. We wanted to be that school for him.

We were required by law to provide Kevon with an education. Kevon deserved a high-quality, free education that would prepare him for his future.

We were doing our best to do this for him, but did not always have the resources or ability available.

Kevon challenged all of our ideas on what "all scholars" meant. We were working to include him, but we did not always know how, and we were afraid that in the process of figuring it out we could do more damage than good.

We had the best of intentions, but no roadmap for the situation, and everyone involved struggled.

Kaitlin's life became a ticker tape of meetings with lawyers, phone calls, paperwork, heated conversations with teachers, incident reports, interventions, more meetings, conferences with Kevon's uncle and lawyers, and, increasingly, attendance at his many court dates and hearings.

She told me later, "I realized that I was truly lost as a teacher when I found myself on the treadmill at five AM, with my phone propped in front of me and my headphones in, dictating a letter to a lawyer." She walked forward on the running wheel but made no progress, a kinetic symbol of her life. She told herself, "This is not who I am."

Kevon, with his hitching grasshopper walk and baggy pants, is currently serving an impossibly long sentence. He has been knifed; his jaw has been broken.

He deserved to be more than a cautionary tale.

We failed him. Not just Sci Academy, or New Orleans, or his neighborhood, or Katrina, or the bullets that he took.

All of us.

Open-Enrollment

The lawsuit brought to the public arena what communities had been discussing for years. While the charter schools of New Orleans were intended to be open enrollment, many of them were not equipped to meet the needs of students with disabilities. In a public school system, schools would share a specialist who would visit different schools to work with students over the course of a week. A speech therapist, for example, might visit as many as four schools each week. But charters were self-governing, with no central office to schedule these visits. When children with severe needs showed up, some charter schools would be forced to admit that they did not have the staff or resources to serve the child.

For this reason, public schools not run by charters suddenly found themselves serving nearly double the numbers of special-needs children. They overflowed with specific needs. Vision impairment. Autism. Speech impediments. Emotional disturbances. Dyslexia. Physical impairment. Down's Syndrome. Unspecified learning disabilities.

The process of charter schools counseling families out of enrolling their children was illegal, immoral, and wrong. That it occurred was a travesty.

Sci Academy did indeed struggle to meet the needs of the scholars who walked through our doors. We had children who met every common disability, children with seizure disorders and Asperger's. When the average charter school's percentage of Special Needs population was around seven percent, ours was nearly three times higher.

We never counseled children out of attending, and we made every possible effort to include and accommodate our scholars.

All of them.

Messy Freedom

I loved Kiana. Her passion for books immediately inserted her into my heart, but her social antics and lack of work earned her poor grades, and she was constantly in danger of failing. She attended summer school every year because of her consistent failures in math. Her math teachers tutored her for long hours that they could scarcely afford to spend. I kept her after school in my room as I prepped for the next day, trying to force her to do her math homework before driving her home or to her mother's nail shop.

Kiana would be obediently present for these sessions, but her work was shoddy and excessively lazy. More than once, I would leave the room to make copies or speak to another teacher, returning to find her shifting guiltily in the desk, trying to hide the paperback she'd been reading under her binder.

Infuriating, but hilarious and infinitely lovable. She was the only child who actually frustrated me by reading and being too damn clever for her own good.

But then report cards came in and I had to call her mother in for a meeting. We walked to my room silently, foregoing the usual small talk that usually came easily. Jada's mouth was set in a wide scarlet line, and her boot heels clicked angrily on the cheap hallway tile. Her Louis Vuitton purse hung over one long arm. Kiana trailed behind her mother, shuffling her sneakered feet, staring at the floor.

I sat across from them at one of the island clusters of desks in my room and said, bluntly, "Kiana is in danger of failing, and I'm out of ideas. She simply isn't doing her work, and I can honestly say that I've done just about everything I know how to do. Kiana has a choice to make about whether or not she wants to graduate with her class, and whether she wants to remain in my advisory."

I slid the report card across the desktops. A's in English. F's in all the rest. Jada's livid mouth tightened even further. "I don't have time for this, Kiana!"

She turned to me. "She tells me she does all her homework at school!"

"She does," I replied. "Her English homework."

Jada turned on Kiana, imparting a sharp pinch. "How do you explain this, huh?"

Kiana sat silently, pulling at the sleeves of her Mickey Mouse sweatshirt. She picked some lint off her pant leg. She sighed deeply. She could not reply. She had no angles except the sharp ones signaling the lines of failure next to Geometry, History, and Biology.

Jada snatched the paper up, and sailed out of the room. I asked Kiana to look at me. She turned her round face up, tears dolloped on the thick fringe of her lower eyelashes.

"This is on you, lady. You know I'll bend over backwards for you. I'll do whatever you need me to do, you know that, but you've got to decide that you can do this. You've got to do the work. You're a junior—you'll be graduating soon. This is on you now."

Kiana nodded, and the tears escaped her lashes and tumbled down her cheeks.

Kiana stayed after for tutoring the next day, math open in front of her, erasing more than writing, but after a week her commitment again became inconsistent. She would slip by me at the school gates, hunching behind gaggles of other scholars, and run to escape for her bus. I would call after her and she would pretend not to hear. Later she would say she forgot, or that she had to babysit.

I was mad with frustration at her, but she could soften me with a single benign smile. She knew that I loved her, and she used that love against me, slipping through my frustration with cherubic deviousness. Her ability to be so stunningly sweet made her impossible to stay angry with for long.

Kiana, Jada, and I had two more déjà vu meetings, two more cycles of slight improvement and renewed commitment, followed by a rapid avalanching of her grades in every subject except English, in which Kiana continued to be an absolute joy.

Jada came in for a final conference with me in April and for the first time had trouble meeting my eyes. She stared down at the bag in her lap, already knowing what news I had to deliver.

Kiana knew as well. She wept and pleaded with me, begging me not to let her fail, asking me what she could do.

Some of the most painful words I have ever said. I, too, was openly weeping.

"It's too late."

Freedom is earned. Perhaps I could have done more for Kiana. I loved her enough. What is the line between natural consequences and remaining a constant support? Was failure the right lesson for Kiana?

In some ways, apparently. She is now happily in college, majoring in Literature. Though she started with a remedial class, she hasn't failed a math course yet.

Drawback

Over the past two years I had become accustomed to being intimately involved with the decisions made about the school. Not being on the leadership team caused me to feel isolated. I spoke to Marc about this and he suggested I attend the weekly leadership meetings, in order to feel like I still had a finger on the pulse of the school.

The next week, I squeezed into the tiny office and joined the circle. Everyone welcomed me, and I felt a sense of relief that I still belonged, even if I had shed my title as dean.

Everyone went around in a circle, listing off their main tasks for the week, the cultural or academic projects they'd be working on in addition to their teaching. Dave explained his new push for answers with evidence in freshman classes. Frances, to my right, described a new program for sexual health that she was instituting. I was next, and there was a pause.

"I'm teaching my class," I quipped, smiling. A pause.

"We're all *teaching*," the silence whispered; I stared at my Converse and knew it was true. All these leaders were also teachers, and I knew well what that burden weighed. After three uncomfortable heartbeats, the meeting continued.

I never went back.

Superdome Kid

Carver signed up with Sci Academy, the same Carver who, a lifetime ago, had asked me about what the Superdome looked like. He sauntered up to me and tapped me on the shoulder. "You recognize me, Miss E?"

"It's Miss Eckhardt," I corrected automatically, then pulled him in for a hug. My nose barely reached his shoulder.

Carver was deeply involved in a gang, and we found his tag everywhere. Along the bannisters, in the bathrooms, his little gun insignias blossomed like evil Sharpie dandelions. He was rowdy and talkative, often stoned, and he refused to tuck his shirt in. He just didn't go to detention, and was suspended several times for this refusal.

On one of these days, Carver was at home when a rival gang member crept up to his window and tapped on it. When Carver lifted the blinds back, the assailant shot him. Point blank, in the face.

The bullet grazed him, missing his eye by a fraction of an inch. Carver was left with a bone-scraping groove in his cheek, a war wound scar that would forever mark him.

While he was out of school, his teachers gathered work for him, and his advisor Dave delivered it, coaching him through math and checking his reading log.

Carver worked diligently while he healed. His mother kept him in the house, away from the streets and situations that might finish the job the rival gang member had started. The shooter had not been caught, and fires blazed between contending gangs.

He arrived back at school with a deep but healing canyon in his cheek. He immediately returned to his old antics, refusing directions and sneaking off, somehow, for the occasional cigarette. Only a couple of weeks passed before he was arrested for breaking and entering and was sent to Juvenile Hall.

We all wondered, but did not say, what lesson would it take if a bullet to the face was not it?

Benchmark

By March, our average reading scores had already grown by three years, and for the first time in my teaching career I was able to designate six PM on Friday nights until eleven AM Sunday mornings as personal time.

I felt exhaustedly, presumptuously *sustainable*.

Artifacts

Leave me, little monsters, little demons, little dragon flies, little moments, I do not want to bear you so well.

What are you concocting beneath the surface of my experience? What lesson is here that I will not learn for a long, long time?

Tonight, we hold a dance to pay for a funeral.

What vivid, uncivil, violent connections were here.

Tall, silent Anthony had been skipping school, was shot attempting to leave a house he'd broken into to rob.

The paramedics arrived to find his body, prone and bleeding in the backyard.

On the boardwalk, children swapped stories about Anthony, all swearing they knew him well, mourned him most grievously.

A riotous, twerking celebration of a death mourned by everyone present.

Finally, small sacrifices to the unavailing loss of a sixteen-year-old child.

A vicious fistfight between his mourners—the offering of a tooth, a smatter of blood, a swollen cheek.

Do these artifacts prove life, or do they prove trajectory?

How do I shield? Who do I shield?

How do I, and do I, re-enter the fray?

New Castles

Marc spent more and more time away from the school. At a retreat in the spring he revealed to his founding team the reason why—he'd been asked to expand and open more schools.

We met this news with a mixture of enthusiasm and concern. When would we find the time? Who would be the leaders? A takeover of a historic school, or new ones altogether?

Marc asked us to back up, and focus on why we'd open new schools in the first place.

Why did we do what we do?

Letting go of the idea of being "Sci Academy" and becoming something bigger meant letting go of emotions we had carried for a long time. Marc brought his founders on a final retreat together to allow us the space and time together to process these emotions and say goodbye.

We would never be together in a room like that again, our intrepid little team bracing our sandcastles against the torrential rains. Marc would no longer be a school leader—he would lead the entire organization, and no longer play an integral role at the school level. This, I think, was terrifying for all of us. We had been coached and led by him so long. Replacing his leadership with another person would be very hard.

Change is hard. Letting go is hard, and growth is harder.

Marc labeled the next year, year four, the "Neutral Zone."

Reagan would transition into a position of new leadership— vice principal—in order to prepare to become the school leader the following year.

Marc could anticipate that he would be largely absent from campus, though he still intended to play as large a role as possible, preparing the seniors for their final year of high school before they went to college.

He asked us to write what we felt we would be letting go of, to express what made us feel afraid about expanding.

I think I am letting go of the idea that I work at a small school that I own, and yes, I am letting go of ownership and my identity as a founder. I am letting go of the small team that I have had, I am letting go of my relationship with Marc, because next year will be the last year that he guides me as a leader. I mourn that loss deeply. I am letting go of the closeness that only a small school can have, and I will have to learn better, and quickly to fully trust others to lead me.

We are all going to have to let go of the idea of our founding team. We will go to different places within the organization. We will have new founders, and the loss of this identity will not be an easy one.

I spent some time with Reagan on the retreat, anticipating that there might be some difficulty once she became my school's new leader. She and I had continued to maintain a careful kindness, avoiding confrontation with each other. We'd just never learned to do it well. My intimidation caused me to bristle too quickly, and the dislike that she sometimes felt for me was made worse because she tried to hide it.

The founding team of Sci Academy again stayed up late, told secrets, drank whiskey from the bottle, and listened to Bob Dylan late into the night. Frances and I sat with our shoulders leaned into one another and talked as the moon tracked across the dark Louisiana sky.

Adieu

The goodbyes of year three were not over.

Kaitlin left teaching and New Orleans at the end of this year. She applied to graduate school in creative writing and took off for New York in a glittery whirl of burlesque and with her formidable talent for fiction.

I walked a tightrope of fierce pride and jealousy. She was a cornerstone of my experience in New Orleans, and had brought out the optimist in me when there had been cause for none. We had survived the University of New Orleans graduate school, with its atrociously poor programming. We'd studied for the Praxis exams together, giggling when the proctors made us sit all the way in the back after checking our IDs twice. We'd persisted through the master cleanse together and had taken long runs along the levee to escape the stress and pressure of our daily lives.

Kaitlin had struggled at Sci Academy. Her job as the Special Education Coordinator had left her in an impossible position, attempting to negotiate the mission with scholars with severe needs. She'd come to be a better teacher, to change and be changed for the better. But the situation with our grasshopper and his myriad of needs had taken so much of her time she'd had to neglect other scholars who desperately needed her. She bore this neglect deeply and personally, a constant shroud of guilt and quicksand.

She'd felt increasingly ineffective, even more than she had before coming to Sci, a radical difference between my experience and her own.

Kaitlin's farewell burlesque performance, a parting gift to the city, was characteristically marvelous.

She pranced on the stage in a gigantic hoop dress shaped like a house, twirling and tapping to "She's A Brick House." She sashayed across the brightly lit space, calling her cheers and waving her arms seductively.

Until the storm hit.

Lights went blue, and sirens raged. She flung away her aprons, and from her arms fell tassels, shimmering like rain. Her bright eyes shifted fearfully, and her hoop house fell apart with a tug of velcro. Tossed by the unseen winds and torrential rains of our imaginations, she spun and twisted and finally collapsed as the music changed suddenly into a weeping melody, an inconsolable voice mourning.

When she stood, she held her hoop dress house inside out, its clever underpinnings a tarp that she slowly stripped away. The contrast was both queasy and fascinating—a beautiful woman performing a striptease of a house destroyed by Katrina. We wanted to cheer for her exquisite beauty, for the lithe turn of her neck and flashing thighs, but we also wanted to turn away, the shock of it too brutal: Katrina, and my best friend, peeling herself away.

Then the costume came apart entirely, leaving her wrapped in the almost biblical "Katrina X"—the X that had been painted by search teams on the doors of homes after the Storm. She stood before us, chin caught haughtily in the light, a representation of rebirth of our city and herself.

We whooped with encouragement and love and pride through hiccupped sobs, we were torn between prostration and a renaissance. She was not just describing the collapse of a house and of our city, but the collapse of herself.

She had given everything she could to the system of reform, to the grasshopper and the other children she met. What she had received in return only she could decide, a future fraught with friction and decadent possibility. And now, cicada-like, she would shed herself once more to become something new.

A rare creature, destined for flight.

The end of her performance had her tearing away the X to stand, bathed in blue light, firmly on two strong feet, naked and blown away and ready to rebuild again.

She was a fighter, and she would rebuild, and I envied her empowered phoenix flight.

Unlike Icarus, she'd melted in the sun, and emerged scathed and scalded but still aflight.

YEAR FOUR: CUT THE STRINGS
Cheat Sheet, Year Four:
Retreat, February 25

1. I will avoid being an island and make myself available.
2. I will be proud and excited about the choice I have made to stay in this place.
3. I will *not* regret this choice and will engage in a positive, productive manner
4. I will *not* be threatened by those who are moving into powerful positions.
5. I will not prioritize simple tasks over a teammate. I will *make time*.
6. I will lead by example and be aware of that influence at all times.
7. I will not allow the media attention I get to convince me that I am the best teacher ever.
8. I will go to someone as soon as I need help.
9. I will be vulnerable.
10. I will not send an email when I can have a conversation.

Teacher: A Speech to Rally The Troops
I entered year four at Sci Academy with ambivalence. Saying goodbye to Kaitlin was hard, and not seeing her face each day at morning meeting impacted me more than I wanted to admit. I was worried about the transition from one tiny school to becoming a network of schools, and was afraid of the changes to come. I continued to

feel dry and thin, and claimed this thinness was caused by a lack of sleep, rather than a symptom requiring grave attention.

Summer was scarcely three weeks long before it was time to begin work again, planning my summer school course and beginning the development of my units for the upcoming year.

At summer orientation, Marc asked me to give a speech to the new teachers. It was a new addition to the summer programming—story time—a name that made me smile and recall *The Giving Tree*. Our new team members circled around, and I read them a story of the past three years.

I told them:

"I wake up every day and know exactly what I can do. In the course of a single day, I am a doctor, a lawyer, a therapist, a bodyguard, a general manager, and the CEO of the most important corporation around—my classroom. Geoffrey Canada says that when "you see a great teacher, you are seeing a work of art."

There is nothing more impactful, or powerful, or more awe-inspiring than being a great teacher. I am not there yet, but I am on my way. For me, this is about love for the children in my school and for the team I am on, and a desire to improve every day. It is about making a commitment to growth and excellence that will take several years to accomplish, and about loving that journey.

Bob Marley

Joseph and Janice looked so much alike that they could have been twins. Both had long, arched necks, small, flat, almost rabbit-like noses. Joseph's skin was the color of sand at high noon, the wet lick right along the surf, and his wide eyes gave him an innocent stare. Rail thin, he sauntered with his smile hung like a crooked picture frame underneath those eyes, adoptable.

Janice was the color of that lick at midnight, her eyes inscrutable. Some of my toughest freshman students, both siblings had a penchant for outright defiance. When asked to do something, more often than not they would simply shake their heads, smile their identical off-center picture frame smiles, and turn their backs.

Despite a rough start, Janice worked hard. Entering her junior year, she was clearly envisioning her future as a college student, even as she and Joseph's amateur tattooing hobby left both their arms covered with permanent foolishness—a peace sign, a smiley face.

Entering a year later, Joseph gave me trouble for the very beginning. He glared with open mistrust at all the teachers. He tried to pull his Bob Marley necklace out from underneath his shirt, despite the fact that it was wildly beyond the boundaries of our strict dress code. His mother was the first call I made that year—

and she knew it was me when she picked up, having already become very familiar with my number from when Janice was a freshman.

"Miss Eckhardt, I ain't got time for it today."

"Ms. Martin," I began, and paused, choosing my words.

"Ms. Martin, I meant to call you earlier, but I've been busy, I just wanted to say that it was wonderful to see Joseph today—I met him a week before school started and he seems like a sincere young man. I'm looking forward to teaching him this year."

Long pause. Caught off guard.

"Alright Miss Eckhardt, You let me know if he act up now. I always got the time for you."

"Yes ma'am," I said. "Goodnight."

There would be time enough. And yet, there wouldn't be.

In the spring, we took a field trip to New Orleans City Park. I volunteered the class to mulch a new trail through an undeveloped part of the park. Twenty-five scholars, sweating in their polos and khakis, learned to shovel, rake, and drag piles of mulch through scratching trees and brush, and then scrape and coax the trail into existence.

Initially, they regaled me with complaints, moaning and sucking their teeth over having to work, but soon they were racing up and down the hills. Girls squealed and ran from the spiders that would scamper from under the wood chips. Teenagers devolved into giggling boys, slipping earthworms into friend's short collars and tossing leaves into each other's hair.

Joseph discovered the wheelbarrow and, long after most of the others wilted in the heat, he pushed it back and forth importantly, directing others. "Nah, man, it ain't full yet! I can push more than that!"

His eagerness to finish the job made us late getting back to school, but he refused to leave until the final pile of mulch was placed along the new walking path. Then he and a friend raked it all into place, patted it down, and turned around grinning brilliantly all the way back to the bus.

This is my favorite image of Joseph: smiling broadly, the rusted wheelbarrow thrust before him, sunlight filtering on his face through the trees. He was a beautiful promise, in that moment. He was the change I wanted to see.

Joseph was not able to survive detention, his energy spark plug too bright. Instead, I adopted him as my classroom helper. He straightened desks, alphabetized papers, and redid bulletin boards. When work was over, we'd collapse into the beanbags in the back of the room, and read together. He was insightful about character's motivations in a way I didn't often see in readers a few years behind, who tended to take actions at face value. He was intuitive, always questioning, making inferences long before their truths were obvious.

Joseph made a slow, meandering academic progress, hindered by a deep-seated sadness. But like his poetry interpretations, he had a deliberate and introspective quality. Even when he was wildly disrespectful, he chose his words rather than flinging random obscenity. I hoped for the day that he would begin to put his own words down on paper consistently, smiled at the talent rumbling just beneath his disgruntled surface.

He saw the end of "The Lottery" coming and nearly ruined it for everyone. "Something bad about to happen, you watch."

He picked apart "The Jabberwocky" as delicately as picking bones from a fish, identifying the speaker at the end as an old and powerful king. The girls sighed and hummed over "Oranges" by Gary Soto, but Joseph informed us, condescendingly, that it was trite and tacky, except for the last lines.

Someone might have thought
I was making a fire in my hands.

But he found "The Truth the Dead Know" by Anne Sexton fascinating. We argued it on the beanbags one evening. I found it profoundly sad, while he thought it to be empowering.

Gone, I say and walk from church,
refusing the stiff procession to the grave,
letting the dead ride alone in the hearse.
It is June. I am tired of being brave.

Just a few days later, in a flash of heartrending impulsiveness, Joseph put a gun in his mouth and took his own life.

I did not know him to be an impulsive young man, which is why this decision, just a few weeks after our adventure, stunned us all into an appalled silence.

His mother took hers a few short weeks later, and Janice found herself alone.

And what of the dead? They lie without shoes
in the stone boats. They are more like stone
than the sea would be if it stopped. They refuse
to be blessed, throat, eye and knucklebone.

The choices of children, ripples that spread beyond the length of all our experience, carving a hollow place where love once lived.

Joseph reminded me that I, too, was growing worn of being brave, and I missed him with a raw and exposed ache that would not heal.

Wounded By Ingratitude

One of my advisees, Angele, halfway through her applications to college, found herself homeless after her mother was evicted from their Bywater home. Rather than taking her to a shelter for homeless children, Johnathan and I installed her in the guest bedroom upstairs.

She slept until one o'clock on weekends, and stayed up late watching Netflix. We had dinner at the table every night. Her mother was concerned for her, and protective, but I convinced her to allow Angele to escort her to prom.

She was accepted to a prestigious East Coast school, and on the ride to school one morning expressed concern that she'd be able to find a way there in the fall. I spoke to the college counselor about it, who was aware of her situation; she'd been storing her belongings in large Tupperware boxes in his office for months.

He approached her casually—his family lived near her college, perhaps they could drive up together?

She came after me later, eyes flashing warning signs. I'd betrayed her trust, she said, spreading her personal business to others.

Confused, I defended myself. My job was to figure out solutions for her. Why would she be so upset?

There was no consoling her. She flared peacock strutting, offended and threatened.

I learned that she dropped out of college after only one year, debt and a few possessions under her arm.

I saw her just this past year at Mardi Gras, sporting waist-long braid extensions and a sarcastic smile. She came up to me, pretended like she was going to give me a hug, and then turned her back, tossing her braids over the shoulder, disappearing into the crowd.

I had no right to ask for gratitude, but the lack of it carved a slice from my heart, exposing a willing bitterness beneath.

Maelstrom

Sci Academy became a full-fledged high school for the first time, even as it prepared to open two founding schools.

More critically, the district had invited Sci to become a "takeover" model, meaning that it would move into a historic New Orleans high school and phase out the current infrastructure, implanting its own culture grade by grade.

These takeovers were met with strong resistance from communities who wanted to protect the integrity of their school's history. They began picketing outside the school, with banners and signs reading "Hands *off* our school!" A bleak way to start the day, slowing the car to a crawl to prevent gravel from spitting at the picketers, biting in accusations, "Don't you know how much we love these kids? Don't you know how much we *do*?" A cultural divide, a swath of miscommunication and good intentions, value systems unintentionally misaligned.

So many new staff members at Sci Academy meant that attention needed to be paid to their rapid development. Veteran teachers at the school were selected to become leaders at the Charter Management Organization (CMO) level and at the new school sites, and their attentions was drawn away, as well.

In previous years, every teacher had a development meeting every two weeks with a Dean or DCI, going over goals and making plans for the next two weeks. This year, I had one development meeting, rushed, with no outcomes. I knew the threadbare look well, and didn't press.

Even as I became an increasingly effective teacher, I began to feel drawn to other movements and interests. I joined several Fellowships and traveled to Denver and New York to speak about teacher sustainability, the importance of evaluations and the potential in the Common Core. I was interviewed by Brian Williams at the first Education Nation in New York. When he asked me what we could do for American students, I said, "teach them to read."

In year three, I had been the model for sustainability. I assured struggling teachers that things got easier, that tasks shrunk to the time allotted to them, and that systems would stabilize. I was working 65 hours a week, down from 80-85, and was lauded as "sustainable."

I was also a few years older than many of our early-twenties staff. I didn't want children—which was good, considering I would never have time for one—but I was feeling the weight of so much time spent away from home, of other parts of my life grown cobwebbed with disuse.

The six-day workweeks were wearing on me. Marc would tell us that rejuvenation was about quality, not quantity, and I earnestly tried to put "quality" into practice. I returned to yoga and took morning jogs through my drowsy neighborhood. I wrote more in my journal and learned to cook progressively elaborate meals.

But I still felt a little see-through, cellphone on uncracked glass, and I feared the sudden clatter of pebbles. Self-sanctuary pushed a stem and two small leaves through the dry ground of my heart, and I began to tend it carefully.

Meanwhile, we were facing the harsh realities of our seniors, whose Pre-ACT tests had come back woefully low, too low even to be admitted to the least selective four year schools in Louisiana.

We juxtaposed these scores against the reading assessments, and sure enough they aligned almost perfectly.

Scholars who can't read on or above level cannot do well on the ACT. It's just impossible.

We organized a reading push, similar to the nine reading groups of their freshman year. We planned advisory lessons around balancing checkbooks and dealing with the stresses of college life.

We dared not ask the question.

All scholars? Was college right for every one of this beloved but motley crew?

My doubts surged even as I swallowed them, shielding this sandcastle most protectively of all. To begin to question this destiny would be to question five years of my life, and I refused to do that.

"Little Wish"

Thi joined my classroom after only a year in the United States. She struggled with reading in her own language, which made reading in a second one even more challenging. She was afraid to speak up in class and even though I modified her homework she refused to do it.

I tried to speak to her, but she would tear up and turn away, or ask another student to translate.

Finally I wrote her a little note, and stapled it to her homework assignment that night. It read, "Thi, I am so happy to have you here in my classroom. I know you are shy and English is hard for you. But we have no excuses for not reading. You must try. I will help you, but you have to do the hard work. I believe in you."

The note was a pinpoint on the map of her progress. She began to work hard, attend study sessions, and plan for one moment of participation in class. I gave her our reading assignments recorded on a flash drive ahead of time, so she could listen to my voice reading the words as she followed along. I prepared her for a question I might ask in class, and for the first time she began raising her hand high to participate.

At the end of our year together, I invited her to participate in our annual poetry slam. She practiced with her advisory for a week, but was still terrified to stand in front of 100 people and recite her poem, "The Little Wish."

Halfway through her recitation, her quiet voice gathered strength and volume. She gestured, in carefully practiced hand motions, though the paper shook in her trembling fingers.

> ....*They don't know the taste of the honey cake*
> *The sweet taste of the honey cake....*

The room was dead silent, most of us leaning forward to catch her halting words. A judge lifted her glasses to swipe at an eye. When she finished, she looked up and across the room with a fatalistic frown. We all stared back at her, and a long pause held, before one clap turned into thunderous applause.

Thi turned to me confused, and when I gave her a huge thumbs up, her smile broke like the sun.

She won third place, and when the awards were announced, her advisory wrapped her in a hug that swallowed her thin shoulders.

Thi is now in AP English. It's extremely difficult for her, but she has learned to be proud of progress rather than disappointed by a constant quest for perfection.

At the end of the year, she wrote me a note back. It said, "You gave me a key to open the bright door for my future. You helped me with poetry and now it help me to express my feeling whenever I feel sad. You let me know that nothing was hard unless you not try. I want to be happy, my past wasn't nice so I want my future to be better. Thank you for making a part of life better."

Saliva

Yesterday, Rebecca threatened to spit on me, walked all over the room and had to be distracted by four teachers as I shuttled my other scholars out of the room at dismissal.

Today she actually spit on me, in the hallway, during the transition between classes.

"You'll have to let this go."

I said this aloud to myself, looking into the mirror at my disheveled face, after several washings with hand soap. Despite the vigorous cleanliness, I could still feel the slippery trail of spit on my eye, bridge of my nose and across my mouth, a phantom snail, thick and perversely dense I as it rolled across my skin.

You'll have to let this go.

I wanted to, but I was itching and trembling all over, and I had class in a few short minutes and imagined the line outside of my room already forming. They would be waiting, binders under their left arms, to shake my hand at the door with their right. They would wait to say, "Good afternoon" and shake my hand, they would track my eyes with theirs, and we would smile and greet each other and begin our quest for knowledge anew.

FTS. Firm. Track. Smile.

Though I tried, I could not make my body stay firm, it tracked with rage, not commitment, even as I loved Rebecca. I was so angry, violated, I could not smile.

You'll have to let this go.

Fresh tears, a waterfall of them, salty on the corners of my mouth. I had a job to do and I said aloud, voice shivering but more firm.

"You'll have to let this go."

I straightened my collar, redid my ponytail, and emerged from the bathroom scrubbed pink, eyes red and flashing, but smiling a fierce and toothy smile, forced but fixed to my exfoliated face.

Children needed me, so I would make it through the day.

Though I tried, in every way I knew, this was the one instance, one moment of cruelty, that I could not entirely release.

I hacked away at it, dug at its roots, eventually refused to acknowledge it, and the offense remained.

Invasive, bamboo rooted, bamboo strong, bamboo runners across my heart, it spread.

Different Tears

Slamming the door too hard, I realized that I'd left my coffee on the kitchen table but there was no time to go back for it—I was already five minutes behind schedule and I'd never get my classroom prepped before morning meeting if I didn't leave right then. Muttering cliché curses, I peeled out of the driveway and turned sharply onto Magazine Street, up to Louisiana to Claiborne to jump on the Interstate.

I'd been waking up at the same time every day and after clicking my alarm clock off, lay there staring at the ceiling, blanket pulled up to my chin, Johnathan's slumbering frame breathing rhythmically beside me.

I lay there in the dark, feeling rather than hearing the seconds pass. My mind skimmed over the state my classroom had been left in: clean white boards waiting for the day's objectives to be posted. Desks needing to be straightened. I had copies to make—and a wait in the inevitable line of teachers anxious to use the overworked machine.

Urgency caused my toes to twitch and yet I could not move. This alone was not enough to spur me to action, and this concerned me. Without urgency as fuel, what would cause me to put my feet onto the cold wood floor, pad down the hallway, put on water to boil, throw fruit into the blender, let the dogs out and feed them, search for a clean polo, tie my shoes...without urgency, why not roll over and fall back asleep?

Finally, it was love, not urgency, that forced my arm to throw back the covers, taking a moment to tuck a pillow in next to Johnathan so he would not roll over into an empty space. Love turned the shower on and pressed start on the blender. Love wrote the note that said, "Good morning! Your smoothie is in the fridge. Don't forget Basil's vet appointment at two o'clock. I'll be home around seven thirty. Have a lovely day! xoxo." Love checked the email on my phone as I juggled bag and computer, lunch and graded papers in a crate out to the car. Love, for school and scholar, turned on the engine in my car.

But I cried on the way to school. I cried because it was still dark, and the city of New Orleans can be cold and foreboding in the moments before dawn. I cried because I remembered crying for a different reason in my car, years ago, when a cop pulled me over. I wasn't crying out of the mission or compassion for my students, but for reasons I could not verbalize to myself expect in childish words.

I'm tired. I'm cold. I can't. I don't want to.

The Interstate is still a slipstream at six thirty, and I hurtled through the air towards another day. I sniffled into the sleeves of my sweater and thought for the first time: Maybe I need some time.

This thought caught the breath in my throat, but I let it sit at the surface of my thoughts for a moment before sinking like a weighted buoy. The pond was shallow, and I could see it below the still surface, bobbing almost playful, fish nibbling at the string.

I thought of Kaitlin's Katrina house, crumbling and turned inside out, shuddering and rebuilding.

Maybe I need some time.

Ambivalence

Though all of my advisees came to school looking as attractive and winsome as the dress code allowed, Nisha was always the most polished. She had beautiful light brown eyes and high cheekbones and applied makeup with a professional flair. Her nails were painted extravagantly; she even managed to make her uniform look sharp, popping up the collar or sneaking by little star-shaped grommets on her belt.

It could never be said of Nisha that she did not work hard. Her binder overflowed with notes and outlines; she stayed for tutoring and extra credit. She had a difficult time turning in her work by the deadline, so we met daily to look over her assignment calendar and talk through prioritization.

In her senior year, Nisha was reluctant to apply to colleges. She wanted to go to beauty school, she said, and learn how to do hair and nails. When I asked about college, she said she wanted to attend Delgado, the local community college, and take some business classes.

I pushed on her commandingly, the mission statement of the school resounding like a Buddhist singing bowl. College success. My task was to get Nisha to and through college. Over the next few months I wheedled and cajoled, and even guilted. I quoted her statistics and reminded her of the extra million on average that a college graduate made in today's society.

Nisha went through the motions of applying to colleges. She took the ACT and scored below the minimum score to apply to the state public colleges. I pushed her to try again and again. She finally scraped into a bracket to apply to the schools with the lowest GAP and ACT requirements, but it still wasn't enough for a scholarship.

The college counselor and I had a candid conversation at this time, about Nisha's future. I was torn. On one hand, I wanted her in college. My alignment to the mission of the school and my belief that college was the best place for our scholars forced me to see a four-year school as the only option. Her dream of beauty school and community college classes didn't fit within the definition of "all scholars" and "college success."

On the other hand, even if I helped place Nisha into a four-year college, her reality would be remedial classes. And while she would receive financial aid, her grades would not yield her any scholarships. She would struggle; she did already, even with her mother's guidance and my ever-present advice and nagging. On her own, I feared greatly that she would fail to complete even her first year, much less all four. It wasn't a matter of effort on her part—Nisha would commit herself—but was she *prepared?*

This vision of the future for Nisha was unacceptable. Saddled with loans for an incomplete college education, she would be unable to take out any new ones, for beauty school or otherwise, until she had paid them off. So she would enter the workforce with only a high school education and attempt to pay these loans. Meanwhile the interest would accrue, there would be bills to pay, car insurance and rent. Nisha might never be able to pay off her loans, and if she did, how old would she be?

Would she still dream of her own beauty salon, of business classes?

Would she dream at all?

The vision of Sci Academy is to prepare all scholars for college success, equipped with the passion and tools to begin innovative and world-changing pursuits.

To admit that Nisha was not prepared would be to turn a spotlight on our failure to achieve the mission with her. She had joined Sci Academy as a sophomore, and had not gone through the ninth grade reading and math classes we had designed to fill deficiencies and assess and treat individual needs. Her reading level had not skyrocketed, and she struggled to do math without a calculator.

A four-year college was not the right place for Nisha. Was this because we had not prepared her? Had we failed? Was the only issue that she had not been *equipped with the passion and tools to begin innovative and world-changing pursuits?*

Was this true?

Nisha struck me as particularly equipped to begin an innovative pursuit. Of all my advisees, she was the one with a clearly defined dream and a course of action. Moreover, this was a dream she had cultivated while with us. She had gained confidence and a sense of self, and learned valuable and permanent habits of study. Of all my Ladies, she seemed to know best who she was and what she wanted.

So perhaps it was hubris to refuse to accept this as a reasonable and satisfactory dream, simply because it didn't fit our school's definition of success.

My tunnel vision prevented me from visualizing a future for Nisha outside of this definition of achievement. Although the facts and her wishes were right in front of me, I continued to push at her.

Fortunately, Nisha was headstrong and stubbornly committed to her aspirations. She said to me, "Miss Eckhardt, you're always telling us to visualize our future, and then make a plan to get to what we want. So why are you down on me for doing that, just because you don't agree with my dreams?"

After graduating, Nisha applied and was accepted to beauty school and attends Delgado part-time, studying business. Just like she envisioned.

Once in a while she texts me, little notes like "Happy Easter Miss Eckhardt! I got a B on my midterms. I'll be done with beauty school, I can do your dreads! Hah hah! I miss you."

Unplanned Lesson

Nisha taught me one of the most powerful lessons I learned as a teacher.

Sometimes, in service of the mission, I was blinded to the needs of the scholars.

Sometimes, it's not only appropriate, but necessary, to make accommodations and exceptions.

The part of me that believed, beyond all else, in the school's mission asked: what right do I have to make exceptions?

But also, what right did I have *not* to?

My doubts, my questions, would be misinterpreted.

So let me set the record straight: I never questioned whether all scholars *could*. And my belief that education was deserved, a right, was never shaken.

My first question was whether or not we, the adults of Sci Academy, were actually equipped with the tools to meet the myriad of needs. The needs of our grasshopper, or Rebecca, or Ashley, or Terrence.

My second question was, simply: are we *listening?* When scholars say, "That mission might not be mine..." or when their actions declare it as eloquently as words ever could, how far and how long do we push before we take a moment to be mindful of what they are saying, and why?

The answers were not easy.

First of all, if not Sci Academy, then where? We may not have been equipped to meet every single need every child came with, though we tried with every breath. But if scholars who were truly struggling could not make it with us, where could they go where their needs could be met?

The unfortunate answer was *nowhere*. No schools were able to do the work we were doing with scholars at such an accelerated rate.

There simply was no place else to send them. And Sci Academy is a truly *great* school.

Secondly, not every child was Nisha, with clear goals and the ability, with hard work, to reach them. Without the goal of placement in college, many scholars would never prioritize an education, or a life outside of their neighborhoods, or perhaps even a life at all past their teens.

Then again, maybe there were other scholars who envisioned good lives for themselves that didn't include college, but weren't bold enough to tell us. What future did they plan, and could we help them achieve it, if we broadened our lens to include other choices—choices we made for ourselves at this age, because of education and privilege.

These questions cycloned in my mind.. Without a vision, we might as well be throwing rocks at windows—or admitting that we were building, once in awhile, with sand.

Sand is a fine medium, if we can accept it for what it is, but to call it always and forever a brick is an action in futility: the clothing of a hubristic Emperor.

Graduation

Eight of my ladies walked across the stage today and received their diplomas.

The founders of Sci Academy sat in the front row. Rickia pinned a rose to my chest, next to my beating heart, and said "Don't start crying now, Miss Eckhardt. You do that and we all gonna cry."

Outside the stadium, in the brilliant sunshine, I gave them each a gift. I'd bought them each journals, writing a letter in the front to each of them, and pasting a picture of our advisory in the inside cover. I held each of them close to me, feeling them flutter and shuffle, I touched each of them for the last time as my scholars.

Then they were gone, towards the brilliant futures I dreamed for them, and towards the futures they would dream up, now, on their own.

My heart sang like a cicada, and soared like Icarus on his final, fated flight.

On this day, each moment was made worthwhile.

Today, the sandcastles did not fall.

PART

The Bucket Brigade

Maybe I Quit Teaching

Just when I was becoming great at it.

I quit 30 years too soon.

This knowledge leads me to tell little, hot true-lies to my mentors, to my friends, to myself.

True because I believe them, lies sometimes when I look very close.

I just needed a break.

I felt myself losing control.

I needed more time to myself.

I'll go back someday.

Sometimes I don't know why I am not, at this very moment, preparing for another day in my classroom.

My time teaching was often the happiest, most motivated, most centered, I have ever been.

I feel my center cracking, ballast lost on one side in a storm.

I came to New Orleans to have an impact.

I came to Sci Academy to learn how to be the best at making that impact.

I stayed with Sci Academy to change the world.

I left because I asked questions that could not be answered, and had experiences that forced my hand.

What happens when the telescope slides back, after years?

What dizziness, the unexpected panorama!

From a visionary azul pinprick to the open sea, uncharted but frothing with possibility?

Decisions

It took me more than a year to decide to leave. I voiced the decision for the first time to a small group of America Achieves Fellows. I didn't even realize my mind had been made up until I said it aloud, voice wavering, tears threatening the banks of my downturned eyes.

The Fellows met twice a year to discuss policy and education reform. We met with the likes of David Coleman, the ninth president of organization that designed the SAT and AP tests, and Arne Duncan, U.S. Secretary of Education. We attended large, high visibility gatherings like NBC's Education Nation. In the spring of 2012, we met in Denver and attended the state legislature with Mike Johnston, a Colorado state legislator and policy adviser to New Leaders for New Schools.

Mike is an enigmatic figure with an unwavering belief in the value of education and the necessity for equitable rights. He began his career deep in the Mississippi Delta and charted a blessed trajectory across the educational hemisphere. He wrote a book about teaching, started a school, cofounded New Leaders for New Schools, and then moved into politics. Despite years of intense work, he still remembers people's first names, wears cowboy boots to formal functions, and hugs like he means it.

I blurted it out as we were discussing sustainability for teachers. The words, "I am not going back to the classroom next year" fell out of my mouth like stones and each hit the tile, sounding off and echoing loudly, rolling two or three times before settling with a dull thud.

I anticipated disappointment and disdain. I expected, and felt that I deserved, to be looked down upon and treated as if I was abandoning the children.

A long silence did follow.

Yet there was no judgment, no backlash. The honesty opened the floodgates for a larger conversation. Why do the best teachers leave? Why does talent bleed out of this profession? Why do the best schools ignore sustainability as a real problem, while still saying that teachers are their number one assets? Rather than the conversation revolving around my experience and my personal reasons for stepping away, it revolved around these reasons as being both symbolic and exemplary of what thousands of others experience.

At the end of the conference, Mike Johnston pulled us all into a tight circle and told us the story of the bucket brigade.

He said that education was like a house on fire, and all the people working in education reform were like the bucket brigade, passing their bucket of water down the line. The hard part, he said, about being in this line is that when someone doesn't pass their bucket, or they drop it, the water doesn't get to the fire. The hardest part about being teachers is that we are the ones closest to the fire, and when someone doesn't pass their bucket we can all hear the screams. Sometimes, more than sometimes, all the breaks farther down the lane are blamed on teachers.

I thought of Joseph and Terrence and Kiana and Rickia. I thought of Robyn and Kennedy and Joeniqua. I thought of Isaiah and Darius and even of Kevon and Steven and Rebecca. All those I have listened to as they screamed, and for whom I gave everything I had to pour water on these fires. I hadn't failed to pass my bucket—but someone along the line of their past definitely did, and no matter how close I was standing to that fire, I never had enough water. I just felt so dry.

What matters, Mike told us, is that we put out this fire. It doesn't matter where we are standing in the line. He looked at me and I began to cry as I felt the eyes of the group on me.

He said, "Sometimes if we don't step away from that fire for awhile, it will burn us up, and, burned, we will never be able to return to the work. We remove ourselves so that we do not become so scarred we cannot continue. We step away for a time because if we don't the heat will consume us and, in the end, what matters is that the buckets keep moving on. Sometimes we just have to take a different place in the line."

Mike again turned to me and said, "Kaycee, you are smart and charismatic, you are good with people, you're a hard worker and well-respected in this field. Finding a job is not the problem. Finding what you want to do, for the sake of yourself and for the sake of this movement, is what you absolutely must do. But stay in the brigade, no matter where you place yourself in the line. Be one of the people passing the bucket."

Goodbye

My affair with Sci Academy began and ended in a bar with Marc.

I was deeply distraught on the drive towards the Lower Garden District, and arrived more than fifteen minutes early.

I had learned more from Marc than anyone else in my life. Under his guidance and constant support I had gone from floundering around, barely able to manage a classroom, to "Teacher of the Year" and interviews with Brian Williams. I had no illusions; without him, I would have strayed from the path of teaching. In teaching I had found a home.

I still had no real words to explain how difficult leaving the classroom would be for me.

As I made the decision, I focused on the activities I would undertake once I left: reading for hours, renovating our ramshackle house, long walks, reconnecting with all the people and activities I had missed for so long. I would seek work in education policy and thrive for a while without the daily demands of the classroom.

When I thought about doing these things I felt excited, a deep anticipation in my stomach and throat, the feeling of being moments away from embracing a distant friend. When my thoughts lingered too long on what I would be giving up—my classroom, Sci Academy, the scholars—I grew weightless and panicky, my hands would fidget, and I felt a little... *less*.

Being a teacher at Sci Academy, was a huge part of my identity. Being a teacher meant to battle inequity, to acknowledge the issues of poverty and racism in our society. It was to be an agent of change for children and their families. It meant valuing sacrifice for a greater cause. It meant work I could be proud of, a mission-aligned day-to-day reality.

My fear, lurking just below the surface, was that I was unequipped to do anything else, that I would never be as good at anything else, and that I would never be able to enact real change or impact education outside of the classroom. I called to mind, again and again, the words of the bucket brigade, and also of my own heart:

The truth is I am tired.

Marc came in smiling and gave me a huge embrace, showed me pictures of his gorgeous baby, updated me on his life, which for the past year had included a lot of travel. Then he asked me if I had seen *Goodwill Hunting.*

I had not.

Marc said that on the way over to meet me, he'd been thinking of all the things he wanted to say to me, and one the last scenes of the movie kept playing through his head.

In it, he explained, a math savant decides he'd rather be a construction worker, and his friend says something like, "Every day I just hope you'll wake up and realize you want to fulfill your calling."

Marc said this character was me.

He said I would never find anything I was as good at as being a teacher.

He said that the decision not to cultivate a great talent should not be taken lightly.

He urged me to consider not only the scholars, but the teachers that came to observe my classroom, whom I supported and shared resources with and encouraged through hard moments. The thousands I had the potential to impact. He asked me what I would say to them about my departure from the profession, after speaking so loudly, sometimes on a national stage, about the grave importance of staying in the classroom.

He said, "Every day I'll hope that you'll come back to your calling."

He also told me that my greatest area of growth was still my weakness: I still allowed passion and emotions to interfere with my ability to teach and overcome obstacles. He said he feared that I was letting emotions interfere with a clarity of thought about ways to make teaching sustainable, and allowing a few instances with scholars like Kevon and Rebecca to cloud my judgment.

As always with Marc, I listened closely, absorbed, kept his words as possible, invaluable truths.

I hugged Marc goodbye on St. Charles Avenue, and said thank you, streetlight spilling onto the damp pavement. I watched him walk briskly into the darkness. I turned and walked quickly the opposite way, barely made it to my car and slamming the door before breaking into sobs that wrung shakes from my body. I wailed and pounded the steering wheel and hiccupped for half an hour.

I wept mostly, for myself. The goodbye had been extremely painful. After four years, the separation from Sci Academy, my team, my scholars, my work, and all it had meant would be agonizing. I wept for the loss of Marc's love and mentorship, the end of Sci

Academy as a small school, the loss my team and commitment and friendships, of myself as the gem of a place that I deeply loved.

I wept because I didn't fully understand why I had to leave, I feared the regret and the absence of all I had built and known.

These were the most painful tears of my adult life but they rained upon the dry place in my chest as well. I felt a loosening in my breath, a timid relief.

Change is never easy, for me, for anyone.

It was the right time for me to leave, and while I knew I would miss it terribly, I never felt the regret I feared that night.

Also, I'll never, ever see that movie.

A Reccurring Dream

I am in my Sci Academy polo shirt and running for my car, throwing open the door and driving at hurricane speed.

I circle the skyline of New Orleans, cross the Mississippi Bridge and trace the stringline interstate around the Superdome, and then a straight arrow east, the Treme on my left below me, past the Quarter, and out until the larger buildings disappear and the terrain changes. The houses grow sallow and the factories that line the canal like soldiers spew smoke, almost gallantly. Over the high rise, where the interstate bumps far into the air and then further out, to Read Boulevard. I speed, trying not to do so.

Once in the parking lot, I jerk to a stop, run doubletime up the stairs, down the open breezeway to my classroom, yanking my dreads into a bun and smoothing my khakis. Politely but firmly I say, "You are excused," to the teacher in the room and I simply take my place again, pulling my strings into place and orchestrating my comeback. Awash with the sense of things again in place, the turn of the right key in the right lock, an appropriate and almost righteous motion.

I feel a deep ache clenching in my heart, as I awake again, in the same sheets, in a different time.

I do not want pleasantries.

I want to roll my sleeves up again and stick my hands into the good work of making every child's life better. It is hard for me, even when I love the work I do now, know that this work has impact, and meaning, too, even if it is not the teeth grinding rush of teaching.

Teaching may have been my greatest talent.

Teaching may have been calling, a sparrow flying by, aiming east.

Perhaps the final lesson, the one I never stayed for, was the one in which I learned how to be a teacher and love myself at the same time.

PART

5

Conclusions

Breaking Ground

I visited Sci Academy today.

The freshmen I taught have grown up.

Two classes have graduated, and the others I taught are now juniors and seniors.

Of our first graduating class, only a tragic scant few remain in college. Of my advisory, only two. The school, and its new sister schools, have a long way to go before they can claim that they are truly meeting the mission of college success, not just admittance. But even in this failure there is brilliant hope. Without Sci Academy, perhaps these children never would have dreamt a dream like college in the first place. They may not have had the time to dream at all.

The old trailers are lined up like sentinels, connected with slightly warping boardwalks. My classroom window is dark and curtainless. Last year the campus moved for the third time, a block up the street, into nicer trailers abandoned by a dysfunctional school the RSD closed down, and the old campus houses only boardrooms and the administrative offices.

In front of these silent sentinels, a large bulldozer is tearing out the scrabbling pine trees that stand crookedly around the property. As I drive by, I hear a crack, and one battered trunk cave and crashes. The RSD is finally making good on a promise several years old: Sci Academy is finally being constructed.

While the felling of the trees feels tragic and a little symbolic, I smile. The scholars of Sci Academy deserve a building. Hallways that are not breezeways between one trailer and another. A real school. One that isn't a daily reminder of Hurricane Katrina, of trailers and inconstancy. A building with a football field and proud goalposts. A basketball court. A science lab. Classrooms with real walls, and no mold blowing through the air vents or seeping through the walls.

A place of exquisite permanence.

The seniors, class of 2014, are at lunch, though only a smattering are indoors. It is late February, and the weather is warming, just in time for Mardi Gras. They stand around in the moist sunlight, unsupervised. They don't need constant supervision anymore, and as they chat about ACT scores and their final projects, I realize they look like regular high school students. They don't look "high needs." They don't look bedraggled or full of angst. Their uniforms are neat and tidy, they exude an air of collective maturity that reflects nothing of their wilder former freshmen selves.

They are reading *Native Son*; one of them asks if I've read it and when I say, "Of course," she giggles and jokes, "So what's it about then? You can give me the summary. I wanna be reading my 'TV book.'"

"TV Book" is a phrase from freshman year. I encouraged them to read both books that improved their minds and also books that may not make the world a better place, but are just fun to read. Stephen King writes my favorite "TV Books," I explained. Reading makes us more knowledgeable, but it's also *fun*. When I read Stephen King. I feel like I am watching TV. He just writes a good story—it's hard to put down.

I laugh. "*Native Son* is not really a 'TV book,' you're right. But it'll change you, and that's even better, right? What 'TV Book' could be better than *Native Son* anyway?" She turns a light shade of maroon and rummages around in her bag to show me her "TV Book," a trashy romance novel with a muscular black man adorning the cover: *Recipe for Temptation*. The "o" in "Temptation" is an apple, and the rippling young man on the cover is seductively eating one. I fake a gag and tell her to stop rotting her brain and she laughs a third time, hugs me lightly, meanders off.

This jovial familiarity about two very different books, and the fact that she's reading them, reminds me why I became a teacher, and my heart aches a little, missing her and missing this place.

They are three months from graduating, and have the beatific, faintly tired looks of runners at the end of the finish line. They are cool, collected in little groups, nibbling on goldfish and the everpresent cheesy puffs. They are throwing their litter into wastebaskets; two of them trade notes. Rachel is pregnant, a surprise, but she is still applying to colleges, hoping to manage her newborn while attending at least part time. They have almost shed their babyfat antics and are trying hard to appear grown up, especially for me. Several of them move quickly to run and embrace me, then check themselves and stroll over more deliberately instead. Nick throws a casual arm around me, asks about my dogs, brags lightly about his job at McDonald's. Many faces are missing, but not nearly as many as were missing from the classes of 2012 and 2013. More and more scholars are staying all four years and this, alone, is reason to celebrate.

The juniors, my last ninth grade class, are childishly delighted to see me, and this immaturity touches me deeply. When they see me, their faces burst into thrilled grins, and they run at me, hug me tightly, jump on me, pat me, pull lightly at my hair.

"Miss Eckhardt, I missed you!"

"Are you back?"

"Can you come teach us next year?"

"We miss you a lot! How come you ain't been out here in awhile?"

"Here, read my new poem!"

"You like my hair?"

"Did you see my name on the wall? Scholar of the week?"

"I made honor roll!"

Tuan races down the hallway, tossing his velvety black hair. He's wearing bright red lipstick, impeccably applied, and a jean jacket studded with hearts, and I remember to tell him that he— *she*—is looking beautiful as ever. *She* tosses her hair with one loose hand, manicured nails flashing brightly. "Thanks!"

This incredible brilliant lightness of safety. A place where being nerdy about books and test scores is made both acceptable and cool. A place where success is celebrated, and obstacles are removed. The safety to explore sexuality, knowing that bullying will not be tolerated, and the liberty to change and be changed. A place to yield and a time to push back.

This feeling of safety allows them to be children for awhile longer, and this playfulness makes them lighthearted and vulnerable. A place where values live, and freedom has been earned.

Tyler says, "You know Miss Eckhardt, you abandoned us, just when I was getting famished for learning. I been distraught ever since."

Jada and Kayla "throw the V" jubilantly and giggle. "Famished! Distraught!"

They dismiss, backpacks clunking, arms around each other. They are especially dear to me because they are my last class of scholars. I do not love them more, but their faces are closest to the crescent surface of my heart. I have not yet forgotten any of their names, though some come more quickly to my lips than others. Being with them is like coming home, and I feel disoriented as I watch them walk towards their busses. A wave of belonging, and yet not, comes over me. When they graduate, there will no longer be any New Orleans students still in school who know me.

They are my final anchors here, my final sandcastles.

Were I to come back, it would be without status with the children here; it would be starting again. The thought is both thrilling and terrifying.

The potential energy of starting again is always the hardest part.

Personal Conclusion

A singing panic scurrying behind my rib cage. Sunlight pouring pink and fierce behind my eyelids.

The sun's rays means the worst had happened: I am late for school.

A jolt out of sleep, bathed in cold fear, and it takes a brief flash of orientation, a few rapid blinks, to unshutter my mind and realize that the sun is up and, for the first time in years, that it's OK.

I do not have school today, though it is a Wednesday and I am very busy.

In my final year at Sci Academy, after meeting David Coleman in New York, I learned about the Common Core state standards from one of its primary authors. They read to me as clear, concise, rigorous benchmarks for what children should be able to do at each grade, and I began using them to develop the curriculum for my classroom. I saw wild amounts of growth in my scholars, and I continue to believe in them as a great lever to student achievement in this country, To that end, much of my continued work supports effective implementation of the Common Core in diverse classrooms. I have a trip next week, training teachers on conducting close reading with high needs children. I also work with a nonprofit on a literacy platform for children of poverty, train teachers in Doug Lemov's Taxonomy, a teacher-training working group, and write open source curriculum for several non-profits.

My days are filled with work aligned to reforming our education system, providing equity for teachers, and ensuring every child has a high-quality, well-equipped teacher. I am learning every day, working to improve education nationally, using what I learned at Sci Academy to make classrooms better everywhere. I am proud of this work. It has significance.

Though my place in the bucket brigade has shifted, I am still, as Kaitlin's poster proclaimed years ago, "in the world to change the world."

I am still reconciling the fact that in the midst of this schedule, I will have time for coffee on my back porch. Later this afternoon, I will take a run along the top of the levee, accompanied by the New Orleans skyline.

And I will try not to miss it, the hectic urgent scuttle of a day in a school.

I will try to appreciate each moment I spend in the sunshine, and not believe it is at the cost of children who need me.

I still work for children and I will also have the capacity to make dinner tonight, set the table, and delight in the placement of the forks. I will even enjoy doing the dishes, wiping each one clean, relishing that there is time, finally, for the mundane.

But I will miss it, in this stillness.

My phone will not ring—a parent's call, a child needing homework help. I will watch a movie, dogs piled up on either side of me instead of reading a series of student essays, stamps and stickers.

I miss the burning rush of need and being needed. I miss their voices challenging each other, laughing. I will even miss their misbehaviors, their subtle gum chewing and petty arguments. I miss my team, miss shout outs and conversations, data collection and joking in the hallways about scholar antic at the end of the day.

But I have not grown weary of missing these things, in ways I grew weary of missing myself. Missing teaching is still bitter sweet and fragrant. Like standing too close to a funeral bouquet, it both draws and repulses me.

And I will stay in this moment of repel-attraction, because I sacrificed much, and there are many lessons here.

And in the end, I am thankful that I have so much to notice.

I am thankful I have so much that I love.

I am thankful that I have so much to do.

And finally, I am thankful that I have so much to miss and also so many new ways to grow. This missing is justifiable, and poignant, and also appropriate and OK.

Things fall apart and longing and regret is a part of that. But it's OK. We make decisions, out of love and longing, all the time. And nostalgia can be brittle and sharp, but this too, is OK.

What matters is that we continue to love and work hard, and change the world for the better in the most meaningful way we can muster, and still live in each moment with ownership and compassion for others and equally for ourslelves.

It's OK.

**Final Truths for
New Teachers**

SHIFT One: To Panic is Human. To Laugh is Divine.

Getting locked in bathrooms, having the power going out in the middle of a lesson completely dependent on a projector, chocolate milk rotting in a classroom trash can for two weeks over Christmas break.

Sunflower seeds everywhere.

There's a lot to get stressed out about, and I got stressed about all of it. Schedule changes, parent phone calls, meetings with teachers... sometimes, you just have to let it go. These things are all a part of the world-changing you have tasked yourself with.

I wish more than anything that I had laughed more.

So when the copier explodes, your computer freezes, the music doesn't cue up, or when you sit in gum, and then a potato chip and don't know about it for a few hours, remember that laughter isn't medicine—it is a bridge, and a moment of release. You can teach kids a valuable lesson about how to handle stress—and they'll need these lessons outside of your classroom walls.

Students need to see that you, too, can fail—and more importantly, how you react to it.

SHIFT Two: The Best-Laid Plans...Aren't.

You will never plan for every contingency.

You will never be prepared.

You will never predict every oddball question, intense moment, or eliminate every crisis.

That shouldn't stop you from trying, but you should absolutely expect that it is all going to go to hell on you.

And on a regular basis.

Being the insanely structured person that I am, this part of teaching was really hard for me.

Breathe.

SHIFT Three: You Won't Always Like Them.

I spent four grueling years trying to meet every need that each member of my advisory had. I drove them home, bought them food, tracked their grades, paid for their ACT tests, taught them to email, edited their essays, talked to their parents constantly, took them to movies and sushi. And sometimes they would say thank you, and sometimes they would be so cruel that I would have to turn my back on them, teeth clenched on words I couldn't dare to say.

Now most of them are off at college, or chasing other dreams, and I don't hear from them very much.

I miss them, but definitely not every moment.

You won't always like them and it feels taboo to say it, but no one can like everyone all the time.

This goes both ways, too—though your students will be more intentional about it.

In fact, the more they grow to love you, the less they are going to like you because if you're doing something right, your nagging, pushing, coercing, challenging, and demanding will begin to have an impact.

Don't let up—it is in these moments of frustration that everyone is going to learn something.

You won't always like them, *but you'll always love them.*

If you ever find you don't anymore, it's time for you to leave. Immediately.

SHIFT Four: It Won't Be Like You Imagine.

When I began teaching, I had grandiose visions of myself, waxing poetic about e.e. cummings before a captive and enraptured audience.

There's where I can feel you smirking—but admit that there's some truth to this image in each new teacher. All of us want to become, in some way, that teacher who illuminated in us that quest for knowledge, that one teacher who stood out from the rest.

I am going to challenge you to set this image of yourself on fire. The longer you hold on to it, the more painful it will be to realize that you'll have to become the teacher your students need...

They aren't going to adapt to the image you have of yourself.

Please be willing to shift the image of yourself. Be willing to be changed from the inside out.

SHIFT Five: Do Not Sacrifice What Keeps You Sane.

Of all the mistakes I made, deciding to quit running so I would "have more time to focus on teaching" may have been the worst. What I thought was a good sacrifice for my students actually made me more tired and less patient—a dangerous combination when dealing with the likes of Jason or Charles.

Giving up your balance leads to extracurriculars like "complain to anyone who will listen for hours" time, or "getting drunk because you're stressed" time.

You must add yourself to your to-do list—time to exercise, read trashy paperbacks, make candles, paint, bike, listen to records, stare at the wall, make cupcakes, stand on your head, do breath of fire, meander down Frenchman, get eaten by mosquitos at Lafite Park, paint your toes, kick a soccer ball, read the trashiest of romance novels, slurp some oysters, drive in circles...whatever it is that makes you feel *like yourself again.*

I promise you, this is just as important as the lesson plans that need to be written and the phone calls that need to be made.

To de-prioritize them does more harm than you may realize.

You are a teacher—but that means prioritizing what gives you the strength to be a teacher, too. Love your support system as much as you can—and say thank you. They are going through this with you.

SHIFT Six: Help! is Not a Four-Letter Word.

Ask for it. Ask the right people. Ask often. Keep asking.

Rather than being a sign of weakness, it is the best sign of strength and endurance.

If you ask for help, you process towards becoming a better teacher will move much more quickly.

SHIFT Seven: We are Never Done. We are Never Finished.

Being a teacher is an elegant balancing act. You'll discover quickly that you simply will never be finished. Time management isn't breaking things into little pieces on a to-do list, and feeling overwhelmed by its length, as I used to do. It is knowing that a there is no end to the list, and that it will only feel more, or less, complete.

SHIFT Eight: Believe. You are the Change You Wish To See.

Believe that you will really suck at this.

And you will hate this.

And you won't be very good at it for a long time.

And you will want to quit.

There's no shame in fearing these admissions.

Know that you may never see the impact that you are having on those you touch. Seeds take a long time to cultivate, and you may never have the chance to see what the seeds you plant will become. That's the hardest part about teaching—it is a labor that does not bear immediate fruit, and the ground you are digging can be dry and hot and hard.

SHIFT Nine: Never Give Up. Ever.

You just can't.

No matter what you need to ask for, whatever support you need, whatever you need to do to care for yourself, you cannot leave your kids today.

The chance may be very good that the person who replaces you will not love the way you do, care the way you do, work as hard as you do, have the passion and strength that you do, or see the future for those children that you can see, right now, so clearly.

SHIFT Ten: Here is the Hardest Truth.

You may truly and actually be the only thing standing between a child and an uncertain future.

I am so, so sorry to put that on you, but my apology doesn't make it any less true.

Do not give up—on your growth, on yourself, or on the kids that depend on you. No trial will last forever, and all that is bitter in the moment can become a chance to shift and grow—for you, and for your students.

Whether you have come to this path because of civil rights, love for children, an interest in political science, a passion for your content, a love for this great city or a melting pot of all of them, thank you.

You have not chosen the path of least resistance.

You have chosen a long, but stunning road.

The landscape and light will shift around you.

The rules will break and change.

It is imperative that you grow quickly and with grace.

You must bend, but not break.

The kids need this from you. And they are what this is all about.

Be willing to be changed, and be willing to allow others to see you changing, and you will be the change you wish to see.

Finally, Thank You.

Thank you for your commitment, bravery, and selflessness. Because you aren't here for money. You aren't here because you have to be. You are here because you believe in something larger than yourself. You believe in a better future, and you believe this begins with the seeds that we plant. Perhaps you don't see yourself as a farmer, but you are here to plant the right seeds, check acidity, nurture, and scour for gnawing predators.

You are a watchful gardener. You will plant carefully.

Be ready to shift your thinking, to challenge your own expectations, and help you to be ready to evolve.

The work you are about to do is the most important work you will ever embark upon. You have a right to be excited, and proud.

But I need you to stabilize your heart against the onslaught that is coming.

Because make no mistake: it will be an onslaught.

Be brave. To shift will be to survive, and to do this work you must be a survivor.

Lives are counting on you.

And that is not an exaggeration.

SUGGESTED READING FOR EDUCATORS OF ALL KINDS.

I have shelves of books on teaching, curriculum development, interventions for language learners, and classroom support. The following books are my favorites.

Alexander, Michelle. *The New Jim Crow: Mass Incarceration in the Age of Colorblindness.* New Press, 2010.

Beck, Isabel, Margaret G. McKeown, and Linda Kucan. *Bringing Words To Life: Robust Vocabulary Instruction.* Guilford Press, 2002.

Beers, Kylene and Robert E. Probst. *Notice and Note: Strategies for Close Reading.* Heinemann, 2012.

Beers, Kylene. *When Kids Can't Read, What Teachers Can Do.* Heinemann, 2002.

Carr, Sarah, *Hope Against Hope: Three Schools, One City, and the Struggle to Educate America's Children.* Bloomsbury, 2013.

Chodron, Pema. *When Things Fall Apart: Heart Advice for Difficult Times.* Shambhala Press, 2000.

Coyle, Daniel. *The Talent Code: Greatness Isn't Born. It's Grown. Here's How.* Bantam, 2009.

Cunningham, Daniel T. *Why Don't Kids Like School?: A Cognitive Scientist Answers Questions About How the Mind Works and What It Means for the Classroom.* Jossey Bass, 2010.

Dweck, Carol. *Mindset: The New Psychology of Success.* Ballantine, 2007.

Fischer, Douglas and Nancy Frey. *Teaching Students to Read Like Detectives: Comprehending, Analyzing, and Discussing Text.* Solution Tree, 2010.

Greene, Ross W. *Lost At School: Why Our Kids with Behavioral Challenges are Falling Through the Cracks and How We Can Help Them.* Scribner, 2009.

Johnston, Michael and Robert Coles. *In the Deep Heart's Core.* Grover Press, 2003.

Jones, Fredric. *Tools For Teaching.* Fredric Jones and Associates, 2000.

Kagan, Spencer. *Kagan Cooperative Learning.* Kagan Cooperative Learning, 2009.

Kotiowitz, Alex. *There Are No Children Here.* Doubleday, 1992.

Kozol, Jonathan. *Savage Inequalities.* Harper Perennial, 1991.

Lemov, Doug. *Teach Like A Champion: 49 Techniques That Put Kids On The Path To College.* Jossey-Bass, 2012.

Lemov, Doug, Erica Woolway, Katie Yezzi, and Dan Heath. *Practice Perfect: 42 Rules For Getting Better At Getting Better.* Jossey-Bass, 2012.

Moorish, Ronald G. *With All Due Respect: Keys For Building Effective School Discipline.* Purposeful Design Publication, 2003.

Rose, Chris. *1 Dead In Attic: After Katrina.* Simon and Schuster, 2007.

Rose, Mike. *Back To School.* New Press, 2012.

Rose, Mike. *Lives on the Boundary.* Penguin, 2005.

Stone, Douglas, Bruce Patton, and Roger Fisher. *Difficult Conversations: How To Discuss What Matters Most.* Penguin Books, 2000.

Tough, Paul. *How Children Succeed: Grit, Curiosity, and the Hidden Power of Character.* Mariner Books, 2012.

Tovani, Cris. *I Read It, But I Don't Get It.* Stenhouse Publishers, 2000.

Wong, Harry. *The First Days of School: How to Be an Effective Teacher.* Harry Wong Publishing, 2004.

WITH ALL MY LOVE AND GRATITUDE

To Joe Biel, the staff of Microcosm, and Elly Blue:
You were a veritable cornucopia of patience, support, encouragement, sweetness, while insistently firmly nudging me to get this done. Thank you for believing this was, and I am, worth it, especially in times when I had convinced myself otherwise, and in the darkest of 11th hours!

To Sarah Zuckerman:
Your critical and loving eyes first wrangled this into something readable, and then corralled it several more times. This book would simply, absolutely not exist without you.

To Breckany Eckhardt:
For walking the beach with me when my personal sandcastle came crashing down, and reminding me that the seashells, the sun, the salt, and my breath matters more than all the soggy sand. All hail solace and logistics!

To Ben Marcovitz:
Your belief and vision have become a vital and tangible movement for thousands, and your belief in me made me more than I thought possible.

To the Founders of Sci Academy: Laying the first bricks with you was an unspeakable honor and I am deeply grateful.

To all the teachers of Collegiate Academies: you are the change you wish to see. Know in the hardest moments, you are the change.

To my Ladies of LSU: You taught me that love and belief is always worth it. I love all of you, always.

To my grandparents: For teaching me that valuable, meaningful work comes at a high and worthwhile price.

To my mentors: David and Meredith Liben, Hugh Ishikawa, and Mary Beth Plauche.

To America Achieves: A huge part of the reason I will never leave the bucket brigade, no matter where I am in line.

And especially to my father:
The first person to teach me that reading is knowledge and knowledge is freedom, and for being my first and forever hero.

Gratitude also to those who continue to put up with me: my parents, Simone "Lobo" Eckhardt for the fountain of youth, Erin Corbino for listening, Deanna Gaharan for swimming the open stretches, Kelley Hubbell for an excess of heart, Caitlin Corrigan for urging me towards a better self, Moxie Sazarac for the glitter, Evan Kilgore for wisdom and bikes, Lelia Gowland for her cookies, Katie Witry for being a rockstar, Vicky Ravin for 6 AM yoga and 10 PM cider, Allie Levey for truth and seitan, Daniela Marx for art and broken dinner dates, Kim Frusciante for football, Tim Kershenstine for patience and lotus flowers, and Steve, who first sent me the application to teachNOLA.

Finally, to the professionals and organizations who do meaningful work for children and the reform of education, and who made me more knowledgeable than I thought possible: Motoyuki-sensei and Haragughi-sensei, the Ogawa family, Doug Lemov and The Taxonomy, Mike Rose, Sibyll Carnochan Catalan, Mike Johnston, Jon Schnur and everyone at America Achieves, Wendy Uptain and Hope Street Group, Ana Menezes, The New Teacher Project, teachNOLA, Julie Louse and Kate Mehok of Crescent City, New Schools for New Orleans, Student Achievement Partners, Judson and Odell Education, ISKME, and, obviously, everyone at Collegiate Academies.

SUBSCRIBE TO EVERYTHING WE PUBLISH!

Do you love what Microcosm publishes?

Do you want us to publish more great stuff?

Would you like to receive each new title as it's published?

Subscribe as a BFF to our new titles and we'll mail them all to you as they are released!

$10-30/mo, pay what you can afford. Include your t-shirt size and month/date of birthday for a possible surprise! Subscription begins the month after it is purchased.

microcosmpublishing.com/bff

...AND HELP US GROW YOUR SMALL WORLD!